Tuck Pat

"We are all in this together,"

says JOSEPH WOOD KRUTCH, and from the treasure house of nature writings that have won him acclaim as another Thoreau, he selects thirty-four essays to represent his view of man's relationship to the natural world. From his ponderings on the personalities of frogs to his preoccupation with conservation, Mr. Krutch's humanist philosophy prevails—that just as one man is involved with all other men, so he is bound to all nature, and the fate of the natural world is his fate.

JOSEPH WOOD KRUTCH was a man of many careers: drama critic, teacher, naturalist, philosopher and man of letters. From his first book in 1924, his writings have ranged in subject matter from Restoration comedy to American wildlife to the Cinema's New Wave.

**THE BEST NATURE WRITING
OF JOSEPH WOOD KRUTCH**
was originally published by
William Morrow & Company, Inc.

Other books by Joseph Wood Krutch

American Drama Since 1918: **An Informal History**
And Even If You Do
The Best of Two Worlds
The Desert Year
Edgar Allan Poe: **A Study In Genius**
Experience and Art: **Some Aspects of the Esthetics of Literature**
Five Masters: **A Study in the Mutation of the Novel**
Grand Canyon
The Great Chain of Life
Henry David Thoreau
Human Nature and the Human Condition
If You Don't Mind My Saying So
Measure of Man
Modern Temper: **A Study and a Confession**
Modernism In Modern Drama: **A Definition and an Estimate**
More Lives Than One
Samuel Johnson
The Twelve Seasons
The Voice of the Desert
Was Europe a Success?
The World of Animals

THE BEST
NATURE WRITING
OF
JOSEPH WOOD
KRUTCH

THE BEST
NATURE WRITING
OF
JOSEPH WOOD
KRUTCH

Illustrations by Lydia Rosier

PUBLISHED BY POCKET BOOKS NEW YORK

Grateful acknowledgment is made to Houghton Mifflin Company for permission to include the Prologue, Epilogue, and two chapters from **The Great Chain of Life** (copyright, ©, 1956, by Joseph Wood Krutch) in this volume.

THE BEST NATURE WRITING OF JOSEPH WOOD KRUTCH

William Morrow edition published March, 1970

Pocket Book edition published April, 1971

Excerpts from this book appeared in the June 1970 issue of **Travel and Camera** Magazine.

This *Pocket Book* edition includes every word contained in the original, higher-priced edition. It is printed from brand-new plates made from completely reset, clear, easy-to-read type. *Pocket Book* editions are published by Pocket Books, a division of Simon & Schuster, Inc., 630 Fifth Avenue, New York, N.Y. 10020. Trademarks registered in the United States and other countries.

Standard Book Number: 671-77260-0.
Library of Congress Catalog Card Number: 70-92837.
Printed in the U.S.A.

For Ann Woodin, an ever-present help in time of trouble.

Contents

IV. NATURE AND HUMAN NATURE

V. THE MEANING OF CONSERVATION

To him who in the love of Nature holds
Communion with her visible forms, she speaks
A various language.

WILLIAM CULLEN BRYANT

Introduction

To some members of the scientific community the "nature writer" is an abomination. He trespasses upon a field where he has at best insufficient competence and he assumes emotional attitudes which they feel bound to expose as dangerously unscientific. He not only admits—he actually boasts—of "loving nature," while science sometimes insists that love is a dangerous enemy of the objectivity indispensable to it.

The distinction is one which the nature writer readily acknowledges though he can hardly be expected to accept all of its implications. Science is *knowledge about* natural phenomena while the proper subject of nature writing is an account of the writer's *experience with* the natural world. He is concerned with "knowledge about" only insofar as it helps define or color that experience.

The modern nature writer differs from the nature poets of the eighteenth and nineteenth centuries because he seeks as much knowledge as will enrich or justify his love of nature. Instead of echoing Keats's rhetorical question, "Do not all charms fly at the mere touch of cold philosophy?" he believes that reality is quite as likely as fantasy to provide powerful aesthetic and emotional experiences. He agrees that pure science must be unemotional and objective, but he doubts that even the scientist, much less the nonprofessional, can realize full human potentials if he is without wonder, or love, or a sense of beauty; if he never looks at the nature of which he is a part except with the cold eye of an outsider.

Natural history is the ancestor of nature writing. In fact, the two are today often indistinguishable as both separate themselves from those biological sciences which have come more and more to concern themselves with controlled experiment in the laboratory rather than with observation in the field. Thus the nature writer tends to take over the function once performed by those who were called "naturalists" and especially that of the naturalists who belong to literature as much as to even the most informal sort of science. In English, the tradition begins with Gilbert White, includes Thoreau as perhaps the most perfect example of the type, and continues through W. H. Hudson, John Muir, John Burroughs, and others down to our own contemporaries.

One of the most striking aspects of the human condition is the simple fact that we share the earth with a vast number and a vast variety of other living things. We are enormously different in many respects from any of them—much more different from some than from others—but we are like them all in that they too are endowed with that mysterious thing called life.

This fact may seem so obvious as to be hardly worth mentioning. But suppose that it were, as I suppose it might be, otherwise. Suppose instead that we were the only living creatures, that we nourished ourselves as plants do on dead minerals, or perhaps that we were pure lonely spirits, the only sentient creatures in the universe. If that were true, then the whole experience of being human, of being alive, would be vastly different from what it is—more different, I suppose, for some of us than for others—but different for everyone. And the real subject of the nature writer is just the difference which sharing the earth with others does make.

Because our situation is what it is, the question of what our relation is, or ought to be, toward other living things is one which has concerned man ever since he became capable of thought. It includes, of course, the question: How much like or how different are we from these other living things? It includes also a somewhat different question: How ought we to think about and how ought we behave toward these other living things?

Consciously or unconsciously we always do and we always have given some answer to both of these questions. Sometimes the first question is answered by saying that man is utterly different from anything else except in superficialities. Sometimes, as some modern biologists tend to say, man is simply one of the animals. The answer to the second question is similarly varied. Sometimes it is assumed that only man has rights and that how he treats other living creatures is of no importance whatsoever. At the other extreme, animals are granted almost the same rights and importance as we ourselves.

From the anthropologists we learn that primitive man was much concerned with these questions and, on the whole, tended to emphasize his closeness to rather than his remoteness from other creatures. He often attributed to the animals a consciousness much like his own; he made of them ancestors, fellow creatures, or gods. Though he might live by hunting them, he often found it desirable to placate even his victims, and he sometimes offered them formal apology for having killed and eaten them. In many cultures, of course, the clan system depended upon which animal the individual was most closely identified with.

The Hebraic tradition, on the other hand, tended to go to the other extreme. The reason was, I suspect, not any impulse toward cruelty but simply that the new monotheism was aware how easily deep concern with animals leads to animal gods and polytheism. Consequently, it tended to insist upon the absolute uniqueness of man, and from that it encouraged the notion that all other living creatures exist only to serve man's needs.

In Genesis, God instructs Adam to this effect, and after the Flood He is even more explicit to Noah:

"And the fear of you and the dread of you shall be upon every beast of the earth, and upon every fowl of the air, upon all that moveth upon the earth, and upon all the fishes of the sea; into your hand are they delivered."

God, in other words, is absolutely distinct from man; man is absolutely distinct from all other living creatures. Man is at God's mercy; everything else is at man's.

Though it was not perhaps the intention, that verse seems to predict the whole history of man's cruelty to what are, from a different point of view, his fellow creatures. Most animals who have had any contact with man throughout most history have had good reason to go in the fear of him and in the dread of him.

According to the Catholic Encyclopedia, the doctrine of St. Thomas of Aquinas was that since man alone has a soul or a *persona* and since God is concerned with the soul only, animals have no rights. Hence cruelty to them is not per se sinful. This seemingly harsh doctrine St. Thomas neutralized to some extent by pointing out that though cruelty to animals is not evil per se it easily leads to cruelty to man and is therefore the cause of evil if not evil in itself. But even this corollary is not always taken into consideration, and theology, as distinguished from the feelings of the Christian spirit, is antihumanitarian in its attitude toward other living things. Christian feeling, on the other hand, has certainly produced a civilization in which the rights of animals are much more likely to be recognized than they were before.

Despite all the ambiguities in contemporary attitudes toward man and toward the rest of animal creation, despite all the differences between individual feeling and behavior, there is no doubt about the fact that society, as it expresses itself in laws and customs, has become increasingly what we call humane. Nominally, at least, cruelty to animals is today a crime—either because animals have rights, because we are fellow creatures, or perhaps, as Catholic doctrine has it, because it encourages cruelty to men. In other words, the law conforms to our sentiment rather than to any specific doctrine. Historically, it can easily be shown that sentiment preceded law.

It would probably surprise most people to learn how recent in Anglo-American history are the first laws regulating in any way the treatment of animals. Gardens for bull baiting and other blood sports were not legally abolished in England until 1835. It was only thirteen years earlier that the very first English law made the inhumane treatment of animals an offense per se. Up until that time, such treatment was an offense only if it could be shown that it depreciated the value of another's property. You could, in other words, torture your dog, if it amused you to do so, but were forbidden to beat another man's horse severely enough to damage him. As late as 1794 a judge in England ruled that "in order to convict a man of barbarous treatment of a beast, it should appear that he had malice toward the possessor"; that is to say, malice toward the owner of the beast, rather than toward the beast itself.

What was the cause of the change in law and the public attitude? It was not, I think, theological doctrine, and I suspect that the broadest and truest answer would be that it was not a doctrine or theory at all but rather an increased intensity of imagination, the power of sympathy, the power of feeling into, which a certain stage of civilization exhibits and which is encouraged by literature, philosophy, and the other arts. But, so far as I am familiar with the history of man's explicit ideas concerning his relations with nonhuman beings, it appears that the first great change was announced, not by professional humanists, but by the early students of what we have now learned to call biology.

The classical expression of the new attitude is first given in English by the first great student of natural history, John Ray, who, besides many technical contributions to the beginning science, published in 1691 a book widely read for almost a hundred years thereafter and called *The Wisdom of God Manifest in the Works of His Creation*. It is, first of all, a defense of, and a plea for, the study of nature as well as the study of books. But in the course of that plea he reverses the previous formal conviction concerning the all-importance of man to God. Reduced to barest outlines, Ray's fundamental propositions are:

(1) Animals other than man are not created merely to serve him but for their own sakes as well as for his.

"For if a good man be merciful to his beast [thus the Old Testament, of course] then surely a good God takes pleasure that all His creatures enjoy themselves that have life and sense and are capable of enjoying it."

(2) The second proposition is "God can be known chiefly through His works, and animate nature is the most wonderful of His works. It is therefore man's duty as well as pleasure, to examine them, to study them, and to admire them.

"Let us then consider the works of God and observe the operations of His hands. Let us take note of and admire His infinite goodness and wisdom in the formation of them. No creature in the sublunary world is capable of doing this except man, and yet we have been deficient therein."

Note the last sentence: man is unique, not because he alone is worth God's concern, but because he alone is capable of observing, understanding, and admiring the infinitely complex world of nature which God created. Notice also that Ray is the humanistic scientist, in contrast to his recent predecessor, Francis Bacon, to whom science seemed to mean chiefly utilitarian technology.

A generation after Ray's book was published, Alexander Pope put the new attitude into epigrammatic form in his

"Essay on Man," one of the most widely read poems ever written. Here is the crucial passage:

> Has God, thou fool! work'd solely for thy good,
> Thy joy, thy pastime, thy attire, thy food?. . .
> Is it for thee the lark ascends and sings?
> Joy tunes his voice, joy elevates his wings.
> Is it for thee the linnet pours his throat?
> Loves of his own and raptures swell the note.
> The bounding steed you pompously bestride,
> Shares with his lord the pleasure and the pride. . . .
>   Know, Nature's children all divide her care;
> The fur that warms a monarch, warm'd a bear.
> While Man exclaims, "See all things for my use!"
> "See man for mine!" replies a pamper'd goose:
> And just as short of reason he must fall
> Who thinks all made for one, not one for all.

A hundred years before that, John Donne had warned that no man is an island, meaning not joined to other men. Pope adds that mankind itself is not an island, but that as man is involved with all other men, so is mankind involved with all living things. And that, I think, is the first premise upon which nature writing exists and upon which conservation can be based. Hence what may be called the humanistic attitude toward the living universe was first clearly stated by a biological scientist who happened to be, as is not always the case, a humanist also. And there is no problem with which civilization is faced today more important than the general problem of keeping science humanistic; or, perhaps we should say, human. This problem faces us today in many different forms. We are threatened not only by physicists and technicians but also by psychologists and sociologists who put physics or technology and the manipulation of human beings ahead of the human beings themselves.

In history, the conflict between humanistic and antihumanistic biology begins almost as soon as the humanistic attitude is clearly defined. The major villain, curiously enough, was that great man, the mathematician and philosopher, Descartes, who happened to possess one of the most astonishing minds in all history. But he had one great and fatal aberration. He had convinced himself that—all appearances to the contrary—man and all other living creatures were totally and absolutely different. Animals, he insisted, were only machines. Because they had no souls, they could not be conscious, and hence, though they might seem to enjoy or suffer, that seeming was an illusion. As many of his disciples believed and as one of them phrased it: "Animals eat without pleasure; they cry without pain; grow without knowing it; they feel nothing; they know nothing." Hundreds of people not only believed this absurdity but acted accordingly.

One might offer a dreadful anthology of pieces in which are described the experiments of men who captured, abused, and tortured animals while they marveled that such convincing imitations of agony could be given by mere unconscious machines. But fortunately, not all seventeenth-century scientists were Cartesians. Some protested against the ruling doctrine. Even more important, perhaps, were the pure humanists, poets and essayists, who protested directly or indirectly: Pope himself and Dr. Johnson, for example, as well as, of course, Blake, Cowper, and Burns. In fact, the reaction against Cartesianism may be in part responsible for the phenomenal growth of what we call humanitarianism in the eighteenth century. As a result of it, there is an indescribable difference between, say, even Shakespeare and most eighteenth-century writing in the implied attitude toward living things other than man.

Nevertheless, new excuses for cruelty seem always ready to emerge. In an earlier age, Christianity justified the Inquisition, and in our own, science and technology are the occasion of new outrages. If we no longer put whole cities to the sword, we nevertheless obliterate them from a distance so that we cannot see what we are doing. And if we no longer torture animals either for fun or because we think they are incapable of feeling pain, we may torture as many animals in our laboratories as were ever tortured during the Middle Ages or the heyday of Cartesianism. Science, like religion and military necessity, is beyond criticism.

No one would, I suppose, call himself a Cartesian today, but the tendency to move in that direction is always present. In its mildest form it is the tendency to regard animals as so nearly machines that any attempt to consider their mental or emotional life is dismissed as mere sentimentality or anthropomorphism. In its technical aspect, it is the father of behaviorism, the attempt to reduce all animal behavior to instinct and the conditioned reflex. Even if you happen to be one of those to whom this seems at least a useful method, remember that the usual corollary today is that man also is an animal and therefore also a machine. Hence he is to be studied as such by biologist and psychologist, to be manipulated as such by propagandists and advertisers; never to be considered a sentient and independent, self-directive human creature.

Psychology, sociology, and even biology tend more and more to think of man as a machine—something which merely obeys laws, responds to conditions, can be manipulated in one way or another. And it sometimes seems that the reason for this increasing tendency to regard man as mechanical is simply that more and more of his own experience has tended to be with machines. He compares himself with what he knows best, and what he knows best are machines. Therefore, he also is a machine and can be treated, manipulated and repaired like a machine.

It is through contact with living nature that we are reminded of the nonmechanical aspects of all living organisms, including ourselves, and can sense the independence, the unpredictableness, and the mystery of the living as opposed to the mechanical. Only by recognizing in man those characteristics which he shares with all living creatures can we base a recognition of his dignity. If we continue to act as though men were machines, they may in the end come to be more and more like them.

When I first began to read the nature writers, old and new, it was simply because they enabled me to participate in experiences of which I was deprived by my own profession as urban journalist. In other words, they afforded me what is now commonly called "escape," though it is a sad commentary on our world that it tends to reprehend as escapism any pursuit of beauty or, for that matter, of truth, simply for its own sake—as though to experience delight or joy were a crime.

When I began to do some nature writing of my own it was first of all—and I think still is—simply because I hoped to achieve for myself, and perhaps to pass on to others, delight and joy. But there is no escaping the fact that we are today very much "problem oriented," and I have come increasingly to feel that nature writing may influence the possible solution of two problems. It resists the tendency to think of man as a machine and the determination to manipulate him as such. It is also an indispensable ally of the effort to conserve some of the earth's natural beauties. That effort cannot succeed unless sustained by the very "love of nature" which the scientist sometimes distrusts.

Thoreau was still at Harvard when he unconsciously echoed (and characteristically exaggerated) the attitude which Ray had defined. "This curious world which we inhabit," wrote Thoreau, "is more wonderful than it is convenient; more beautiful than it is useful; it is more to be admired than it is to be used." Today most people are more likely to talk about "healthful recreation" than about admiration for the achievements of God or nature. Others (among whom I would include myself) believe that some familiarity with the natural world is important not only for physical health and in order to avoid the psychological effects of overcrowding but also for deeper reasons. We are inclined to insist that there is such a thing as a permanent human nature and that it needs some contact with the natural world of which it is a part; that (to use two current clichés) modern man will always be "alienated" and always "in search of an identity" until he comes to understand that the thing he belongs to and must not alienate himself from is the whole of the enterprise called living.

Perhaps the late William Morton Wheeler, an impeccable technical scientist, put the whole thing most succinctly when he wrote this about our fellow creatures: ". . . that, apart from the members of our own species, they are our only companions in an infinite and unsympathetic waste of electrons, planets, nebulae and stars, is a perennial joy and consolation."

I hope it will not be irrelevant to add to this introduction an autobiographical fragment from my *More Lives Than One:*

One winter night shortly after I had finished *Thoreau* I was reading a "nature essay" which pleased me greatly and it suddenly occurred to me for the first time to wonder if I could do something of the sort. I cast about for a subject and decided upon the most conventional of all, namely Spring.

It couldn't be far behind, as both Shelley and the calendar assured me. Those little frogs known to all New Englanders as the spring peepers would soon be making their premature announcement and it was something for which I had long been accustomed to wait. This "Day of the Peepers" I considered as my spring festival and rather more meaningful than Easter—which moves back and forth too widely to have great meteorological significance—while the voice of the frogs has a definite meaning: the temperature has been above freezing often enough and for long enough periods to bring them to life. As a subject it would do.

Style and tone was another problem. All of my books had been both serious and rather more solemn than I would have liked them to be. I wanted something lighter and more definitely in the manner of the now generally despised "familiar essay." I wrote half a dozen first paragraphs before I hit upon one which seemed to me reasonably satisfactory and I then went on to finish the first essay without thinking beyond it. It concluded:

> Surely one day a year might be set aside on which to celebrate our ancient loyalties and to remember our ancient origins. And I know of none more suitable for that purpose than the Day of the Peepers. "Spring is come!" I say when I hear them, and: "The most ancient of Christs has risen!" But I also add something which, for me at least, is even more important. "Don't forget," I whisper to the peepers, "we are all in this together."

This last sentence was important to me because it stated for the first time a conviction and an attitude which had come to mean more to me than I realized and, indeed, summed up a kind of pantheism which was gradually coming to be an essential part of the faith—if you can call it that—which would form the basis of an escape from the pessimism of *The Modern Temper*, upon which I had turned my back without ever having conquered it. From another standpoint this paragraph was unfortunate because when the publisher of the book to which my experiment soon led sent the first chapter to a leading literary monthly the editor replied that his magazine "could not possibly publish an essay which spoke disrespectfully of Easter."

Having finished that essay I started another called "A Question for Meloe," the lady referred to being a blister beetle which has one of the most extraordinary of life histories, even among the insects which are remarkable for the strange complications of their lives. The survival of Meloe depends upon a series of accidents so improbable that the vast majority of her offspring inevitably perish somewhere along the line before they reach maturity and it is a wonder that any ever survive. Pressure of college work led me to abandon this essay after only a few paragraphs had been written and it lay neglected until summer when I decided to try to finish it.

Then something happened very much like what had happened in the case of *The Modern Temper* but never, since then, has happened again. By the time I had finished this essay I knew what the next would be and I completed the short book of twelve chapters in about thirty days. Since each chapter was assigned to a month Mark Van Doren suggested that I call it *The Twelve Seasons* and I submitted it very hesitantly to Bill Sloane. He and his assistant editor, Helen Stewart, were enthusiastic and the book was published in 1949, when it had a good reception and modestly good sales.

Charles Poore wrote in the *New York Times* daily book column an amiably flippant review in which (thinking also no doubt of his colleague Brooks Atkinson) he called me "another Broadwayite doubling as Connecticut Yankee." But he had the thing the wrong way around. I had found a new subject and for the next few years I was to be a literary naturalist doubling as Broadwayite.

Doubling (or tripling) as Broadwayite, college teacher, and Connecticut Yankee had not become as much easier as I had hoped it might with the ending of the war. Transportation was simpler and so was finding a night's lodging in town. But the huge influx of students into the

University placed an unprecedented burden even upon those who did not attempt to lead more than one professional life. My graduate courses swelled to such proportions that I had to give one of them in the Mac-Millan Theater auditorium. Candidates for the Doctorate multiplied to such unheard-of numbers that theses piled high on our desks and oral examinations were scheduled twice a week (sometimes oftener) throughout the year. Margery Nicolson, by now chairman of the department and the victim of a Scotch conscience, was the wonder of us all even though we also were more harassed than we would have believed it possible to be and survive. There was no longer time for the chats I had so much valued with my special friends like Clifford, Harbage, or even, for that matter, with Mark.

One day there appeared at my office an unusually pretty girl. When she asked rather timidly if she might see me for a moment, I invited her in with more than usual cordiality. *"What,"* I asked hopefully, "can I do for you?" "Well," she replied, "I am writing a paper in American literature at —— university. And I have been told that . . . well, that *you* were *alive* during the F. Scott Fitzgerald period." Perhaps that had something to do with my growing conviction that it was time for me to retire from the world.

By the late forties various influences had begun to converge upon me, all tending in the same direction. A time had come to make the most drastic change in my life since the day, some thirty-five years past, when I had said good-by to Knoxville.

The fact that I was beginning to feel that my interest in the theater had passed its crest had something to do with it. So, too, did my increasing interest in the country, not merely as an escape from the city, but also for what positive pleasures it had to offer. But health was the decisive factor without which mere inertia would probably have persuaded me to continue in the way I had been going.

Drastic as I knew the break with my past life would be, I had no intention of merely—in Professor Campbell's phrase —"presiding over a vacuum." I was running away from something, of course, but I firmly intended to run into something else, and as it turned out I found more than I had hoped for to say about what I did and saw, learned and thought, in the unfamiliar country I was trying to make my own.

Nevertheless this was not all I had come for. I hoped also, in Thoreau's incomparable phrase, "to meet myself face to face," to be compelled, indeed, to do so. In the busy life I had been leading it was too easy to think only of immediate tasks and to solve only immediate intellectual problems. I knew that *The Modern Temper* no longer summed up, as it once had, what I thought about the universe and man's place in it. But I did not know precisely what I did think. Perhaps I would now be able, not necessarily to reach final conclusions, but at least to bring up to date my hitherto somewhat unfocused ideas. One result was the book called *The Measure of Man.*

THE BEST
NATURE WRITING
OF
JOSEPH WOOD
KRUTCH

I. NEW ENGLAND AND THE DESERT

The man of science studies nature as a dead language. I pray for such inward experience as will make nature significant.

HENRY DAVID THOREAU

The Day of the Peepers

Hyla crucifer is what the biologists call him, but to most of us he is simply the Spring Peeper. The popularizers of natural history have by no means neglected him but even without their aid he has made himself known to many whose only wild flower is the daisy and whose only bird is the robin. Everyone who has ever visited the country in the spring has heard him trilling from the marsh at twilight, and though few have ever caught sight of him most know that he is a little, inch-long frog who has just awaked from his winter sleep. In southern Connecticut he usually begins to pipe on some day between the middle of March and the middle of April, and I, like most country dwellers, listen for the first of his shrill cold notes.

Throughout the winter, neighbors who met in the village street have been greeting one another with the conventional question: "Is it cold enough for you?" Or, perhaps, if they are of the type which watches a bit more carefully than most the phenomenon of the seasons, they have been comparing thermometers in the hope that someone will admit to a minimum at least one degree higher than what was recorded "over my way." Now, however, one announces triumphantly: "Heard the peepers last night," and the other goes home to tell his wife. Few are High Church enough to risk a "Christ is risen" on Easter morning, but the peepers are mentioned without undue self-consciousness.

Even this, however, is not enough for me and I have often wondered that a world which pretends to mark so many days and to celebrate so many occasions should accept quite so casually the day when *Hyla crucifer* announces that winter is over. One swallow does not make a spring, and the robin arrives with all the philistine unconcern of a worldling back from his winter at Aiken or Palm Beach. But the peeper seems to realize, rather better than we, the significance of his resurrection, and I wonder if there is any other phenomenon in the heavens above or in the earth beneath which so simply and so definitely announces that life is resurgent again.

We who have kept artificially warm and active through the winter act as though we were really independent of the seasons, but we forget how brief our immunity is and are less anxious than we might be if habit had not dulled our awareness. One summer which failed to arrive and we should realize well enough before we perished of hunger that we are only a little less at the mercy of the seasons than the weed that dies in October. One winter which lasted not six months but twelve and we should recognize our affinity with the insects who give up the ghost after laying the eggs that would never hatch if they did not lie chill and dead through the cold of a winter as necessary to them as warmth was to the males who fertilized and the females who laid them. We waited through the long period during which our accumulated supplies of food grew smaller and we waited calmly in a blind assurance that warmth would return and that nature would reawaken. Now, the voice of the peeper from the marsh announces the tremendous fact that our faith has been justified. A sigh of relief should go up and men should look at one another with a wild surprise. "It" has happened again, though there was nothing during the long months that passed to support our conviction that it could and would.

We had, to be sure, the waiting pages of our calendars marked "June," "July," and even, of all things, "August." The sun, so the astronomers had assured us, had turned northward on a certain date and theoretically had been growing stronger day by day. But there was, often enough, little in the mercury of our thermometers or the feel of our fingers to confirm the fact. Many a March day had felt colder than the milder days of February. And merely astronomical seasons have, after all, very little relation to any actual human experience either as visible phenomena or as events bringing with them concomitant earthly effects.

Not one man out of a hundred thousand would be aware of the solstices or the equinoxes if he did not see their dates set down in the almanac or did not read about them in the newspaper. They cannot be determined without accurate instruments and they correspond to no phenomena he is aware of. But the year as we live it does have its procession of recurring events, and it is a curious commentary on the extent to which we live by mere symbols that ten men know that the spring equinox occurs near the twenty-first of March to one who could give you even the approximate date when the peepers begin in his community; and that remains true even if he happens to be a countryman and even if he usually remarks, year after year, when they do begin.

It is true that the Day of the Peepers is a movable feast. But so is Easter, which—as a matter of fact—can come earlier or later by just about the same number of days that, on the calendar I have kept, separates the earliest from the latest date upon which *Hyla crucifer* begins to call. Moreover, the earliness or the lateness of the peepers means something, as the earliness or lateness of Easter does not.

Whatever the stars may say or whatever the sun's altitude may be, spring has not begun until the ice has melted and life begun to stir again. Your peeper makes a calculation which would baffle a meteorologist. He takes into consideration the maximum to which the temperature has risen, the minimum to which it has fallen during the night, the relative length of the warmer and the colder periods, besides, no doubt, other factors hard to get down in tables or charts. But at last he knows that the moment has come. It has been just warm enough just long enough, and without too much cold in between. He inflates the little bubble in his throat and sends out the clear note audible for half a mile. On that day something older than any Christian God has risen. The earth is alive again.

The human tendency to prefer abstractions to phenomena is, I know, a very ancient one. Some anthropologists, noting that abstract design seems usually to come before the pictorial representation of anything in primitive man's environment, have said that the first picture drawn by any beginning culture is a picture of God. Certainly in the European world astronomy was the first of the sciences, and it is curious to remember that men knew a great deal about the intricate dance of the heavenly bodies before they had so much as noticed the phenomena of life about them. The constellations were named before any except the most obvious animals or plants and were studied before a science of botany or physiology had begun. The Greeks, who thought that bees were generated in the carcasses of dead animals and that swallows hibernated under the water, could predict eclipses, and the very Druids were concerned to mark the day on which the sun turned northward again. But the earliest of the sciences is also the most remote and the most abstract. The objects with which it deals are not living things and its crucial events do not correspond directly or immediately to any phenomena which are crucial in the procession of events as they affect animal or vegetable life.

Easter is an anniversary, and the conception of an anniversary is not only abstract but so difficult to define that the attempt to fix Easter used up an appalling proportion of the mental energy of learned men for many hundreds of years— ultimately to result in nothing except a cumbersome complexity that is absolutely meaningless in the end. Why should we celebrate the first Sunday after the first full moon on or after the twenty-first of March? What possible meaning can the result of such a calculation have? Yet even that meaningless definition of Easter is not really accurate. For the purpose of determining the festival, the date of the full moon is assumed to be, not that of the actual full moon, but that on which the full moon would have fallen if the table worked out by Pope Gregory's learned men had been—as it is not— really accurate. Even the relatively few men who remember the commonly given formula will occasionally find that they have missed their attempt to determine when Easter will be because they consulted a lay calendar to find the full moon instead of concerning themselves with the Epact and considering the theoretical ecclesiastical full moon rather than the actual one. How much easier it is to celebrate the Day of the Peepers instead, and how much more meaningful too! On that day something miraculous and full of promise has actually happened, and that something announces itself in no uncertain terms.

Over any astronomically determined festival, the Day of the Peepers has, moreover, another advantage even greater than the simplicity with which it defines itself or the actuality of its relation to the season it announces, for *Hyla crucifer* is a sentient creature who shares with us the drama and the exultation; who, indeed, sings our hosannahs for us. The music of the spheres is a myth; to say that the heavens rejoice is a pathetic fallacy; but there is no missing the rejoicings from the marsh and no denying that they are something shared. Under the stars we feel alone, but by the pond side we have company.

To most, to be sure, Hyla is a *vox et praeterea nihil*. Out of a thousand who have heard him, hardly one has ever seen him at the time of his singing or recognized him if perchance he has happened by pure accident to see squatting on the branch of some shrub the tiny inch-long creature, gray or green according to his mood, and with a dark cross over his back. But it was this tiny creature who, some months before, had congregated with his fellows in the cold winter to sing and make love. No one could possibly humanize him as one humanizes a pet and so come to feel that he belongs to us rather than—what is infinitely more important—that we both, equally, belong to something more inclusive than ourselves.

Like all the reptiles and the amphibians he has an aspect which is inscrutable and antediluvian. His thoughts must be inconceivably different from ours and his joy hardly less so. But the fact is comforting rather than the reverse, for if we are nevertheless somehow united with him in that vast category of living things which is so sharply cut off from everything that does not live at all, then we realize how broad the base of the category is, how much besides ourselves is, as it were, on our side. Over against the atoms and the stars are set both men and frogs. Life is not something entrenched in man alone, in a creature who has not been here so very long and may not continue to be here so very much longer. We are not its sole guardians, not alone in enjoying or enduring it. It is not something that will fail if we should.

Strangely enough, however, man's development takes him farther and farther away from association with his fellows, seems to condemn him more and more to live with what is dead rather than with what is alive. It is not merely that he dwells in cities and associates with machines rather than with plants and with animals. That, indeed, is but a small and a relatively unimportant part of his growing isolation. Far more important is the fact that more and more he thinks in terms of abstractions, generalizations, and laws; less and less participates in the experience of living in a world of sights, and sounds, and natural urges.

Electricity, the most powerful of his servants, flows silently and invisibly. It isn't really there except in its effects. We plan our greatest works on paper and in adding machines. Push the button, turn the switch! Things happen. But they are things we know about only in terms of symbols and formulae. Do we inevitably, in the process, come ourselves to be more and more like the inanimate forces with which we deal, less and less like the animals among whom we arose? Yet it is of protoplasm that we are made. We cannot possibly become like atoms or like suns. Do we dare to forget as completely as we threaten to forget that we belong rejoicing by the marsh more anciently and more fundamentally than we belong by the machine or over the drawing board?

No doubt astronomy especially fascinated the first men who began to think because the world in which they lived was predominantly so immediate and so confused a thing, was composed so largely of phenomena which they could see and hear but could not understand or predict and to which they so easily fell victim. The night sky spread out above them defined itself clearly and exhibited a relatively simple pattern of surely recurring events. They could perceive an order and impose a scheme, thus satisfying an intellectual need to which the natural phenomena close about them refused to cater.

But the situation of modern man is exactly the reverse. He "understands" more and more as he sees and hears less and less. By the time he has reached high-school age he has been introduced to the paradox that the chair on which he sits is not the hard object it seems to be but a collection of dancing molecules. He learns to deal, not with objects but with statistics, and before long he is introduced to the idea that God is a mathematician, not the creator of things seen, and heard, and felt. As he is taught to trust less and less the evidence of the five senses with which he was born, he lives less and less in the world which they seem to reveal, more and more with the concepts of physics and biology. Even his body is no longer most importantly the organs and muscles of which he is aware but the hormones of which he is told.

The very works of art that he looks at when he seeks delight through the senses are no longer representations of what the eye has seen but constructions and designs—or, in other words, another order of abstractions. It is no wonder that for such a one spring should come, not when the peepers begin, but when the sun crosses the equator or rather—since that is only a human interpretation of the phenomenon—when the inclined axis of the earth is for an instant pointed neither toward nor away from the sun but out into space in such a way that it permits the sun's rays to fall upon all parts of the earth's surface for an equal length of time. For him astronomy does not, as it did for primitive man, represent the one successful attempt to intellectualize and render abstract a series of natural phenomena. It is, instead, merely one more of the many systems by which understanding is substituted for experience.

Surely one day a year might be set aside on which to celebrate our ancient loyalties and to remember our ancient origins. And I know of none more suitable for that purpose than the Day of the Peepers. "Spring is come!" I say when I hear them, and: "The most ancient of Christs has risen!" But I also add something which, for me at least, is even more important. "Don't forget," I whisper to the peepers, "we are all in this together."

1949

May

At some moment when my back was turned the Connecticut spring slipped up on me again. As usual I had noted the grosser, more publicized phenomena as they appeared in their expected order. The first sound of the peepers and the first appearance of a fox sparrow were duly noted in my diary. So too was the blooming of the hepatica and, in the little wood pools, the appearance of feathery-gilled tadpoles hatched from eggs laid by a salamander a few weeks before.

But it is not these things that really change the landscape and give the whole world a new look. We await them eagerly because we know that they are the points of reference; that by them we can gauge the advance of the season. But there are a thousand other phenomena no less important and far more elusive—the slow greening of the grass and the slow appearance from the ground of the thousands upon thousands of weeds and flowers.

Your peeper is either singing or he isn't; your fox sparrow is either there or not there. But who can say that he ever saw a blade of grass come up out of the ground, much less that he ever saw one of the spears which survived the winter turn green? These things do nevertheless happen, and suddenly one is aware that they have happened.

Again and again I have resolved that I would catch them at it, or at least be able to say: "Yesterday the grass looked as it has looked ever since the snow left; today it is different." But, as usual, I missed this as I missed all the other important things. Suddenly I realized that the world no longer looked as it had looked ten days ago. But when did the thing happen? Was it during yesterday, or during last night? Or was it perhaps three days or three nights ago? I cannot, alas, answer that question, though no one, I am sure, would like better than I to be able to do so.

So many different things have responded almost simultaneously to warmth and moisture that it is difficult not to think of them as to some extent cooperating, one with another; of putting on some sort of coordinated show for the benefit of the spectator. The image that comes most immediately to mind is the image of a magician waving his wand or, perhaps, a conductor his baton. Each performer seems to know his part and eagerly to make his contribution.

But so pretty a picture is purely fanciful. Every tree, every bird, every blade of grass, is fiercely individualistic. It springs to life, not in order to make its contribution to a pageant, but in order not to be left behind in the struggle for water, and sun, and the few cubic centimeters of soil which this year it will contest not only with the roots of the neighboring plantlet—which last summer it fought to a draw—but also with the new seeds dropped perhaps as autumn drew to a close. Murder will be done this spring in the woods, on my lawn, and even in the crannies of my garden wall.

A great many people have been impressed by the orderliness of nature, but if by nature is meant the aggregate of living things, then I must confess that her untidiness is what has most often struck me. As a countryman who just barely escapes the shame of suburbanity, I have struggled almost as much as the suburbanite does against summer's disorderly profusion and against autumn's messy habit of scattering leaves where they least ought to be. However, I am willing to admit that all this is significant only when seen from the standpoint of a very late comer into the universe whose fussy little preferences are of no great importance; and it is not what I really mean when I say that nature does not seem to operate in accordance with any well-thought-out scheme of her own; that hers is not, so to say, a planned economy.

I can understand how an astronomer may conclude that God is a mathematician. The planets seem to know where they are going and what they are about. Theirs is a formal, unvarying dance which moves in accord with an abstract scheme of delightful regularity; and the mathematical physicist seems to have discovered that the microcosm is, despite the disturbing presence of certain principles suggesting indeterminacy, a good deal like its big brother the system of heavenly bodies. But the world of living things exhibits no such cooperation of part with part, no such subordination of the unit to the whole. The God who planned the well-working machines which function as atom and solar system seems to have had no part in arranging the curiously inefficient society of plants and animals in which everything works against everything else.

No one, it seems to me, who has ever watched the contest between two weeds for a few square inches of soil; no one who has seen all the intricate history of the one, from seed to leaf, come to nothing—can possibly suppose that so wasteful a game of cross-purposes was deliberately devised by the astronomer's mathematical God, or indeed by any intelligence which knew what it wanted. If a God made the world of atoms and suns, then perhaps life intruded itself unexpectedly to impose, through some will of its own, multiplicity upon unity, disorder upon order, conflict upon balance. The individual plant or animal is no doubt marvelously contrived to achieve its purposes, but the society of living things is an anarchy in which events may work themselves out to this conclusion or that—but over which no unity of purpose seems to preside.

1949

August

This is the very dead of summer. I am not sure that I ever heard just that phrase before, but I don't see why not. Surely, it describes at least the impression that August creates as she slumbers, replete and satisfied. Spring was a fever and autumn will be a regret, but this is the month too aware of its own successful achievement to be more than barely sentient. The growth which continues seems without effort, like the accumulation of fat. If nature is ever purely *vegetative,* it is now. She is but barely conscious.

The season of seed and fruit lies just ahead, but it is already assured and inevitable. The epoch of competition and doubt is past, the weeks when the individual did not know whether or not he was one of those who would get along in the world. The survivors are complacent; the coming months of retrenchment and death are too far away to cast a shadow, and it is at this time if ever that nature is bourgeois. At least, August is the month when the solid and the domestic triumph, when the prudent come into their own. The very birds, whose springtime was devoted to love and music, are now responsible parents who have forgotten how to sing. The early flowers of the woods waved their brief blossoms and are forgotten, but the roadsides and the fields are taken over now by the strong, coarse, and confident weeds.

If the bold premature piping of the frog symbolizes spring, and the plaintive, never-say-die stridulation of the cricket symbolizes autumn, then, to me, the woodchuck embodies the spirit of summer. I see him, fat and sleek, pushing his way through the tall grass down the bank which leads to my old apple tree. From time to time he rears to peer about for danger, but by now this is hardly more than a habit—he is not really afraid. He picks up an apple or pretends that one

13

weed is more succulent than another. Presently he will waddle away again, confident that he has been laying up, in his very belly, treasures that moths will not corrupt and no thief break through to steal.

So far as the plant kingdom is concerned, this is the epoch of the Compositae, those efficient producers of seed which represent nature's latest, most improved model. Their teeming cooperative flower heads have reduced the wasteful display of petal to the minimum and some of them have learned to dispense with it entirely, like a society which has got rid of the frills. Unmistakably they are inheriting the earth. "Give us a few more million years," they seem to be saying, "and we will show you how the world ought really to be run. Produce, distribute, and consume. It is only a problem of technology, of chemistry, and of mechanism."

Perhaps it is unfortunate that this is the time which your ordinary city dweller is most likely to choose for his brief annual visit to the country. No doubt it is the season when the town is most uncomfortable, and he thinks more of what he is getting away from than of what he is coming to. But there is no other period when nature is so little dramatic. Even the countryman himself will tend to fall, if he does not watch himself, into nature's own mood of somnolent content. He loses something of his alertness now that he is neither startled by newness, nor reminded (as soon he will be) that summer, which seems so motionlessly established, will not last forever. He can hardly believe that there was a spring or that there will ever be a winter.

Moreover, and what is even worse, he may find himself becoming a bit bourgeois, a little inclined to take too complacently for granted the warmth and flourishing abundance, to ask fewer questions, to be aware of fewer ecstasies as well as fewer doubts. He is less a pilgrim and more of a landowner. He looks about at "my house" and "my woods" and "my fields." He thinks of owning things and covets his neighbor's land. He wonders if the proprietor of that strip across the road might be persuaded to sell.

This question of ownership, of property, is a thorny one. Thoreau thought he had solved it when he concluded that he had taken possession of whatever he had enjoyed and that, recorded deeds notwithstanding, the fields he wandered over belonged more truly to him than to the nominal proprietor who had no idea what was going on in them. But for most people, at least, it is not quite so simple. "Mine" is a warm and colorful word which it is possible to utter with many intonations and with many intentions. It may mean "keep off." It may also mean what it means when we say "my home" or "my brother." August is the month to ponder it without too much disfavor. It is the time when the plant has established its right to a few square inches of soil, the bird to its nesting site and the woodchuck to his burrow.

There are some to whom the neighbor's fields always look greener; that is acquisitiveness and envy. There are others to whom it is their own things that seem the best—even though only their own catbird or their own tall spire of purple wild lettuce. And that is something not objectionable in August or in any other month. There is, for example, a certain tree-frog which I own; who is "mine." He is a *Hyla versicolor*—a larger first cousin of the spring peeper—and he has spent many hours of five successive summers sitting on the edge of a decayed knothole in an apple tree a few feet from the front door. Obviously that knothole is "his." I have taken a great deal of pleasure in having this tree-frog for mine and I am sorry to have to say that apparently he does not reciprocate.

Several times, out of a sheer selfish desire to make him acknowledge that, from a frog's point of view, I am good for something, I have elevated some tidbit, on the end of a straw, under his very nose. Twice he has snatched it casually; twice, when I became very insistent, he impatiently brushed it away with his foreleg. But usually he simply stares motionless and straight ahead after the fashion of the Buddha he so much resembles. Frogs, he tells me, do not need men. They can get along very well without them, would rather not acknowledge their existence. The sense of independence is worth more than an occasional supererogatory worm. Mankind, so far as frogs are concerned, serves no useful purpose. There is no teleological explanation for the human race's existence.

I have also done something else which he would never do for me or for anyone. I wrote to a great expert on the Amphibia to ask a question that none of my books ever even raised. Do tree-frogs commonly return, year after year, to the same station? They are said to make an annual journey to the pond for love and reproduction. Has "my" frog forgotten this call of pleasure and duty? Is he old, or is he prematurely philosophical? Or does the fact that I have noticed his absence during a period between his first appearance and early summer mean that he woke from a winter sleep in the hole, made his pilgrimage in the water, and then, on five successive occasions, returned across the woods and fields to "his" home?

The great authority took the trouble to answer me courteously and at considerable length. He offered a number of facts about frogs in general and tree-frogs in particular. But, so far as my specific questions were concerned, it all boiled down to "I don't know." "I don't know what your own particular frog has done and I don't know what the species in general does." He suggested, of course, what had already occurred to me—namely, the possibility (at least) that it wasn't actually the same individual year after year. But the appearance is too regular, the particular hole too like many others which are not inhabited and never to my knowledge have been. He even suggested that there was a rather awkward way of banding frogs for identification, as birds are banded. But I do not think I shall try the experiment. I think I know my frog. Besides, if one had two friends who could be told apart only by banding, would one really care which one of them one was talking to?

I shall not try to pretend that I own nothing except in the sense that I own my frog and that Thoreau thought he owned the best part of his neighbors' fields. I am not so pure as all that. But I should like to think that most of my feeling of proprietorship is at least tinged and softened by some admixture of this more admirable kind of possessiveness. For certainly there are two kinds of owning. One of them has to do with the power complex. Its very essence is the ability and the right to control, to change, and to destroy; most of all, perhaps, to destroy. "Gee up, all my fine horses," said Little Klaus to the mixed team of his own and his neighbor's beasts. Then Big Klaus, because his sense of one kind of ownership was outraged, killed those which were not legally his just to prove that, in actual fact, he owned them all.

That story from Hans Christian Andersen is the very first

story I remember having heard, and perhaps it made an impression so deep because it so perfectly typifies—better even than the story of the dog in the manger—the meaning of one kind of ownership. Also, perhaps, because it suggests by contrast the other kind; the kind whose essence is intimacy and responsibility, the privilege of communication and understanding. Both kinds are in nature. The bird has "his" territory and also "his" fledglings. No wonder, then, that both kinds are in human nature too. But human beings differ more from one another than do the individuals composing any other species of animal. And you can observe that difference in their attitudes toward what they own, especially in the cases where the thing owned is capable of inspiring either of the two emotions.

I do not suppose that there is more than one way of owning a bond, a block of stock, or a trust fund held in perpetuity—comforting though the last must be. But decidedly there are at least two ways of owning a house, a farm, a dog, or even a child. Everyone has observed the difference among his own acquaintances in their attitudes toward the house where they live, and, if they are lucky, the land which may be theirs to go with it. Probably most of us know some father or mother who "has" a son or daughter almost in the fashion that Big Klaus "had" his horses. But it is in the ownership of animals that the difference most clearly appears. It is not a question of how much they are valued, or how large a part they play in the thoughts of their owners, but entirely a question of *why* they are valued and *why* they are thought about.

I remember that I was once in a company which included an important financier and collector of modern art who also "had," as a matter of course, a very fine country estate complete with dogs, horses, and prize poultry. I was chatting, not with him but with my neighbor on the other side, about pets, and for the want of anything better to say, remarked—quite untruthfully—that what I should really like to have was a hippopotamus. The financier heard this remark through one ear and he was alarmed—largely, I suspect, because I had a connection with one of his casual enterprises and he was afraid that I was insane. He turned suddenly towards me to demand: "Why on earth would you want a hippopotamus?" And I was inspired to make an answer which I thought would allay his fears. "Why, don't you see?" I said. "A hippopotamus would be the most expensive pet one could possibly have. The cost of keeping him would be enormous. I could say to myself: 'If I can have a hippopotamus, I could have any pet I could possibly want.' " Relief and comprehension took immediate possession of his countenance. "I see," he said, and turned back to his own companion. But he had revealed very clearly why he owned dogs and horses as well as some very costly examples of modern painting.

I am afraid that a great many people who boast of being, and in fact believe themselves to be, horse-lovers and dog-lovers actually love them no more than my financier loved his prize poultry or loves the hippopotamus which, for all I know, he may before now have bought just in order to show that he could actually have what I spoke of as an impossibility. Gérard de Nerval presumably did not really love the lobster he is said to have led about Paris on a ribbon to attract attention. I see no reason to suppose that some of the most passionate horse and dog fanciers who own, breed, and travel about from show to show love their prize-winners any more. The fact that a man is proud of his winning boxers no more proves that he loves dogs than the equally proud wearer of a mink coat demonstrates thereby her love of minks—which is not generally supposed to be the reason for wearing their skins. Professed cat-lovers are a good deal less numerous than professed lovers of dogs, and I suspect that there is a sound reason for their tendency to consider themselves morally superior. There is only one way of owning or even of "having" a cat. And it is the good way.

Last night I heard the first katydid of the season. I do not suppose that one can "have" a katydid even in the sense that I have a frog. Indeed I don't suppose anyone could even love a katydid or any other insect except, of course, in the sense that it has sometimes been supposed that God loves men— which is to say that He loves the race and wishes it well, in general and as a whole, without concerning Himself too much about any individual. I should very much regret the disappearance of all katydids, even of all those who inhabit this particular region. But I can't be very much exercised over the fate of any particular one. Two-legged creatures we are supposed to love as well as we love ourselves. The four-legged, also, can come to seem pretty important. But six legs are too many from the human standpoint. Nothing that has them can

be regarded with any sense of great intimacy. I have been
known, on occasion, when a katydid wandered down from the
treetops where they usually stay and fell under my hand, to
toss it casually to the pet ducks on the lawn. The lucky duck
was grateful, but the insect might find the act strange, coming
from a lover of nature. After all, the ducks could eat corn.

A friend, learned in such matters, tells me that St. Thomas
Aquinas answers the plaints of individuals who consider themselves ill-used by God because they are not so strong, or so
rich, or so fortunate as most people, by assuring them that the
Creation was an Act of Generosity, not an Act of Justice.
This means, as I understand it, that no one can claim anything as a right. Life itself is more than he had any reason
to expect, and the recipient of bounty has no right to complain that another pauper was given more than he. I confess
that I find this a little hard to take so far as I myself am
concerned. But I expect the katydid on the way to the duck
to understand it. He has had his life up to now. Besides, the
duck is bipedal if not *implumis,* and he has the superior claim.

These are complacent August thoughts; jungle thoughts
some might call them. And perhaps, considering nature's
state at the moment, they have every right to be. I have never
been south of the Tropic of Cancer and therefore have never
seen a real jungle; but descriptions often warn us that it is
green and somnolent—not, as the imagination tends to picture
it, lively or colorful. And in a year like this one, when rain
has been superabundant, a New England summer produces
a kind of jungle, or at least something a good deal more like
one than the August farther south or, *a fortiori,* like the summer in the more arid west, where heat means a sharp decline
in vegetative growth and produces something that suggests
the desert rather than the jungle.

In our part of the country, where roadsides and fields have
been kept artificially clear, there is even in the Jungletime of
August the color of sturdy weeds. But these, or at least the
abundance of them, are the result of unintentional cultivation.
They have taken advantage of our clearings, and many—the
goldenrod for example—are doubtless far more prevalent than
they were before the white man came. But in the woods and
the thickets where nature has her own way, there is nothing
but a jungle of leaves and branches almost as green, almost

as thick, and almost as unrelieved as anything the tropics could produce.

As in the jungle itself, something is flourishing wherever sunlight can fall, and we feel, as we never do in spring, that there is too much; an unnecessary repetition of the same thing, so blindly superabundant as to be almost frightening. What is the good of so much life which seems about to choke itself? Green, the most wonderful of all colors, is by now monotonous; is revealed as only the crude, fundamental stuff of a too exuberant life. The quaint fancy which led someone long ago to give one of our common birds a verb for a name —*vireo,* "I am green"—seems inevitable now. "I am green," "I am green," "I am green," seems all that Nature herself can say at this moment.

Only we, who look before and after, know that this is not the real jungle; that it is merely a phase during which our temperate world puts on its very respectable imitation and shows us what it could do if given the time. We can hardly imagine that the trees will ever be bare and the ground dead again. But we know what we cannot realize; know that all this exuberance will wither in a deadly breath when autumn strikes. Because we do know it, certain sights and certain voices now putting in their first appearance seem ominous, though they are gay enough in themselves.

There is, for example, the small matter of that katydid. Only long weeks of heat have brought him around to the amorous mood which made the peepers vocal nearly five months ago while they were still immersed in ice-water and thus undergoing, without effect, a sovereign, monkish remedy. For the katydid this is, in a sense, spring at last. But we know that once he has started to sing, the day is not far off when we shall hear the last hardy individuals of his species, barely able to shake off the numbing effects of cold, dragging out a few last chirps. His first song is, for us if not for him, less the beginning of something than a warning that a season is getting near its end.

So too there is something ominous about the various kinds of wild asters which begin to attract attention about the time the katydid begins to sing. They hint of the end though they are gay in themselves. Or are they, really? Through all its shades they repeat one color and that is the color of mourning. Their blooming is part of a grand ceremony, part of what is called in France (there usually with some tinge of exaggeration) the *pompes funèbres*. Someone is hanging purple on the doorpost of a summer.

1949

September

"Hurrying along like a caterpillar in the fall" is said to be—or to have been—a colloquial expression. I do not remember that I ever heard it from the lips of any speaker, but I know very well the creature who must have suggested the comparison. There are not many caterpillars about at this time of year for most kinds have either retired into a chrysalis or a cocoon to spend the winter or long ago turned into a moth or a butterfly which left eggs to survive the snows as best they may. There is, however, one common and conspicuous little fellow, very hairy in appearance and broadly banded in black and red-brown, who is plentiful enough and certainly does hurry along as though he needed to get somewhere quick.

As a matter of fact he does. People who notice sometimes call him "woolly bear" or "harlequin caterpillar," and this is rather a pity for he enjoys the rare privilege of being officially designated by a name not jaw-breaking but quite euphonious: *Isia isabella*. And whatever you call him, his air of *empressement* has more justification than that of most human hurriers. Not much time is left to find a cozy corner in which to curl up for the winter.

Why he chooses to spend the dead season in what looks like a dangerous and uncomfortable way instead of shutting himself up in a chrysalis or a cocoon probably no one will ever know. But that is what he has been doing for some millions of years, and the insects are conservative in a more thorough-going way than a human being can hope to imitate. When they insist that the old ways are best, they do not mean the ways of their youth, or of their fathers' day or even of their grandfathers'. They may mean the ways of the carboniferous age or even before.

In the spring, if all goes well, *Isia isabella* will come out of

22

hibernation and hurry along again as fast as he did in the fall because, once again, he can hardly meet the schedule imposed upon him by the rhythm of his own physiological process. He will snatch a little food—preferably a leaf of the plantain you have been careless enough to allow on your lawn—and then resign himself into a cocoon within which most of his body will dissolve before re-forming itself. Then he will emerge as a pretty enough little moth, pink and cream in color, but rather less striking than he was in his fur coat.

It is the air of urgency itself which strikes a responsive chord in me when I see him on a garden path in late September. His consciousness, if any, must be dim. He cannot know why he is in a hurry, only that he is. But I recognize in myself a similar vague uneasiness. My preparations for the winter have been made. My house is tight; there is fuel oil in the tank and some food in the cellar. But the confidence of summer has imperceptibly faded. Something impends. *Isia isabella* and I know in our nerves and our muscles that something pretty drastic is going to happen and we are not sure that the most we can do about it will be enough.

No doubt individual human beings vary in their psychology almost as much as the kinds of animals do. Your squirrel, for example, is stimulated into a fever of activity in autumn. He is excitable and irascible, quarreling with his fellows and taking time out to scold indignantly any two- or four-footed creature who invades his woods. But he is exuberant rather than hurried or uneasy. He seems confident that his store of nuts will hold out. Similarly many housewives burst into an autumn flurry of activity almost as remarkable as that of the spring, and some of them seem to enjoy it. Some men, even some of those whose desire to be useful about the house is sporadic, are suddenly inspired to take down screens and to put up storm windows. It is as though such purposeful activity released some tensions; as if it relieved, by yielding to them, some urges that rise in time with the rhythm of all Nature. "I feel it," says the subconsciousness; "something is going to happen." "Well," it answers itself, "I am doing something about it, aren't I?"

One day the first prematurely senile leaf will quietly detach itself in a faint breeze and flutter silently to the ground. All through the summer an occasional unnoticed, unregretted leaf has fallen from time to time. But not as this one falls. There is something quietly ominous about the way in which it gives up the ghost, without a struggle, almost with an air of relief. Others will follow, faster, and faster. Soon the ground will be covered, though many of the stubborner trees are still clothed. Then one night a wind, a little harder than usual, and carrying perhaps the drops of a cold rain, will come. We shall awake in the morning to see that the show is over. The trees are naked; bare, ruined choirs, stark against the sky.

To me there always seems to be something perverse about those country dwellers who like the autumn best. Their hearts, I feel, are not in the right place. They must be among those who see Nature merely as a spectacle or a picture, not among those who share her own moods. Spring is the time for exuberance, autumn for melancholy and regret. Season of mists and mellow fruitfulness? Yes, of course, it is that too. But promise, not fulfillment, is what lifts the heart. Autumn is no less fulfillment than it is also the beginning of the inevitable end.

No doubt the colors of autumn are as gorgeous in their own way as any of spring. Looked at merely as color, looked at with the eye of that kind of painter to whom only color and design are important, I suppose they are beautiful and nothing more. But looked at as outward and visible signs, as an expression of what is going on in the world of living things, they produce another effect.

"No spring, nor summer beauty hath such grace, as I have seen in one autumnal face"—so wrote John Donne in compliment to an old lady. But Donne was enamored of death. Send not to know for whom the leaf falls, it falls for thee.

To the physicist, red and green are primary colors. So are they also to the biologist, though in a different sense. They are the primary colors of life—the red of blood and the green of chlorophyll. Your animal keeps his primary color hidden. When we actually see it, open and naked, we shudder. If he flaunted his blood as vegetation flaunts its chlorophyll, if the animal sang red, red, red, as the plant sings green, green, green, it would be intolerable.

Man is conspicuously the connoisseur; presumably he alone experiments consciously with his sensations and learns to play delicately with the pleasure which is almost pain and the harmony which is almost discord. Perhaps that is the reason why he is almost the only animal whose blood shows clearly through the delicate skin, hinting that it flows red, red, red just below the covering just as the clothing of a woman hints of nakedness beneath. But, through the summer at least, the vegetable kingdom has known no such modesty. And because green is as cool as red is hot, we call the summer's leafiness calm and refreshing, indifferent to the fact that it is, in its own way, flaunting the crude stuff of its kind of life.

The colors of autumn are very different from that. Sometimes we think of them as brilliant but that is because we forget their true significance. Autumn colors, russet and yellow, are not primary colors in either the physicist's or the biologist's sense; not the colors of living but of dying. They mean, so the physiologist assures us, not that something has been added, but that something has been taken away. The thrifty tree has withdrawn into its permanent trunk the vital parts worth saving, and it delicately discards something that it would no longer be able to maintain. Spring was the time of expansion, this of retrenchment. There is nothing to do now but to lay low and hope for the best.

Most of us, as well as a great many of the creatures who feel the little premonitory shudder brought by autumn's first breath, will survive. Once our confidence has returned we will rejoice in a new way and take our pleasure in being snug, in feeling ourselves survive, even when the snow and the ice and the cold forbid us to do more than that. We even call the first chill of autumn "bracing," though the very choice of the adjective means something. It is against a stress or a blow that we "brace" ourselves, and no one ever needed to feel "braced" in the springtime. The pleasures we promise ourselves are those of effort and struggle. It will be the season for the stoic and the puritan as spring and summer were the season for the pagan.

And what of those very many creatures, among the insects especially, who know but one spring; for whom the fall is not a period of danger, of hardship, or of sleep, but inevitably the end which it has been for all their kind during millions of years? The little, delicate, pale green tree-crickets, for instance, who have sung so persistently for a few weeks and produced a volume of sound so incredibly great in proportion to their size. In their heyday they kept well under cover and were almost impossible to locate even when they were making their near presence conspicuous. Now they seem to gather in companies on the trunk of my apple tree waiting for the anaesthetizing chill.

Occasionally, also, you may see a solitary individual of this or some other short-lived species who has survived a little longer than he should. He moves sluggishly, perhaps utters an occasional low cheep, and moves into the failing warmth of the autumn sun like one of those last human survivors of a universal calamity whom imaginative writers have pictured as hopelessly prolonging life on a cooling planet which will never grow warm again. For these creatures the fact that spring will return in six or eight months is a fact as useless as it would be for a man in similar position who knew that the earth was to become habitable again in a million years. Indeed, our tree-cricket or our katydid would not live much longer if we moved him into artificial warmth and supplied him with food from our larder. He has got into the habit of dying at about this time. His whole life scheme is adjusted to the brevity of the season which favors him. Like a very old man he seems to die of nothing except death itself.

Of course such an insect does not know that he is going to die in the sense that a man can know that his end is imminent. Perhaps, indeed, even a man cannot really know that; cannot really grasp what it means. And the man has a brain, the insect a nerve mechanism so different from ours that it is infinitely more unlike that of the stupidest mammal than the brain of that stupidest mammal is unlike ours. Yet even sober and objective naturalists have been unable at times to refrain from speculating over the meaning of what we can only call, by inappropriate human analogy, the insect's "attitude toward death"—and especially of that attitude as it affects, or rather fails to affect, his obsession with the future welfare of his species. Men often say of an object or of an institution, or of their house or their government, or even of the solar system itself: "Well, I guess it will last out my time, and that is enough for me." But an insect would be as incapable of acting on that principle as he would be of saying he was going to.

Men, to be sure, commonly care about the welfare of their children. But they have seen those children and established some relation with them, whereas in the vast majority of cases the insect never sees his offspring and, in the case of many, many species—for instance, that of the crickets and grasshoppers we have been talking about—is dead the whole aeon of a winter before his children will hatch in the spring he can never see. It is true that the ants, the bees, and the wasps do actually take care of grubs which they seem surprisingly to recognize as potentially creatures like themselves; true, also, that some other multilegged beasts have some association with their young—as in the somehow repulsive case of the large wolf spider whom many have seen wandering abroad with the whole pullulating mass of her spiderlings piled on her back. But the rule is that eggs are laid and then abandoned; that, very frequently indeed, they are not hatched until long after the parent has succumbed to cold or to old age. And yet there is no business to which insects are so passionately devoted as to that of preparing, often very elaborately indeed, for the welfare of this progeny. It is very much as though a man were to consider it his chief business in life to arrange for the well-being, not of his children, but of some distant descendants a thousand years removed from him.

The ego of these creatures, their individualism, if you like, is more than under control; it is nonexistent. Here are your perfect citizens of the world state and the classless society. Automatically they consider the welfare of the race above their own, and they do not mind even if a thousand of their children die; do not mind even if—as is said to be the case with the wolf spider—some of their children eat the others up; provided only that a sufficient number survive. In respect to them, as in respect to some human zealots devoted to the cause of humanity at large, it is sometimes hard to tell where a laudable concern with the greatest good of the greatest number leaves off and mere brutality begins. Tennyson reproached Nature because: "So careful of the type she seems, so careless of the single life." He did not suggest that we should imitate her. But that is precisely what these insects do.

1949

November

Last week I had a visitor from the city and I am afraid that both of us were relieved when Monday morning came round at last. It has happened before, but neither of us can learn—or, more probably, can admit that he has learned. Under other circumstances we get along very well indeed. I respect him and I find him entertaining. I rather believe that he would say the same of me. But "nature puts him out." I think that there have been moments when he was on the point of suggesting that we pull down the shades.

What makes the case of this particular friend interesting is the fact that his aversion is a genuine aversion, not merely a negative failure to be interested in what nature has to offer. Your average city dweller, whether he be intellectual or merely cockney, can take a country week end in his stride; in fact may even enjoy it as an interlude. So far as possible he brings the city with him; comes loaded with bottles, possibly with books or magazines, and with the paraphernalia of some organized sport. What he dreads is mere emptiness, mere lack of occupation, and even with these artificial aids he cannot face more than a few days for the simple reason that his normal activities are interrupted and his normal interests no longer fed.

Such a man may be pitied, but there is nothing very mysterious or very interesting about his case. I know many such. Some of them actually own houses in the country, and sometimes genuinely believe that they are fond of what they innocently call "country life." But the friend of whom I am thinking at the moment belongs in quite another class. The one sort thinks he is indifferent to or even that he likes the out-of-doors because he does not really know what the out-of-doors is; my friend dislikes it, dislikes nature herself, just because

28

he does know—or at least senses—what she is and what she means.

He has never spoken, as another friend sometimes does, of his eagerness to get back to "God's concrete," but I know that he feels it. Even as he steps off the train at our rather bustling little station, he looks about warily as though he half expected to see hostile Indians, and by the time our automobile has stopped in front of my garage, he is definitely alarmed. He knows that I am not really going to ask him to clear the forest or, for that matter, to go for a walk. But the surroundings suggest the theoretical possibility of such things and they make him uneasy.

Outdoors in the summertime he tolerates my small lawn and mildly approves of the few flowers carefully confined to their beds. They are like the caged animals in a zoo, put on exhibition to satisfy public curiosity and therefore well enough in their way. But why, just beyond the confines of this lawn, are all these other trees and shrubs and herbs allowed, as it were, to run around loose? I do not think that he anticipates any definable danger from a bit of wild laurel or even from a squirrel, but they are obviously out of place. My modest little woodland, mostly unimpressive second growth, carries the threat, vague but disturbing, of the immemorial forest pushing in to surround him.

My friend has, in other words, got used to the assumption that nature has been tamed, that even plants are things that grow when, and only when, they are tended in pots on a window sill or a penthouse terrace. They are, in their way, as safe as pekinese or poodles. But out here they are actually growing on their own. I do not water them; the rain does. They do not even ask my permission to grow. They have a will and a competent self-reliance of their own. To what may such a state of affairs possibly lead? Just how safe are we against the possibility of a sort of revolt of the Helots? If nature looks as though she might be capable of seizing a favorable opportunity to take over, then he would prefer to be somewhere else. New York City might have time to prepare her defense while Connecticut was being engulfed.

This time I asked him to come in November because I thought the relatively dead season might prove reassuring. His enemies have even the season as their enemy. The chill blasts have given the impudent weeds and the bold, arrogant trees their come-uppance. The animals are lying low and we can stay in the house. We can keep warmer than they can and by means which are reassuringly the same as those of the city. Furnaces burn oil in Connecticut as well as in New York. This room is quite as comfortable as an apartment. Unfortunately, however, the object lesson did not really convince. My friend could not forget last summer's horrors. The trees, though bare, are not dead but sleeping. The hard brown earth may feel a little more like cement than it did before, but life will spring out of it again next May or June. Man does not own this land. The untamed seeds as well as the untamed insects and animal creatures are only biding their time. That time will come again.

And so, on Monday morning, we part, he relieved to be returning to the world where man has successfully imposed himself upon nearly everything which is visible; I happy to be allowed to remain where nearly everything reminds me that I am part of something neither myself nor wholly subject to me. I am not too intolerant of his attitude because I remember we belong now in two different, very significant categories, and that there is no telling to what ultimate extremes either his premise or mine might ultimately lead not only us as two individuals but the whole mass of those who agree with the one or the other.

The Reverend Sydney Smith who bewailed his sad fate when he found himself "twelve miles from a lemon" is the perfect example of the highly intelligent man whose dismay outside city limits is the result of nothing except the more negative failure to notice that there is anything there even possibly meaningful, for good or for evil. Some of the best of his sayings clearly proclaim that fact. Take, for instance: "I have no relish for the country; it is a kind of healthy grave." Or the remark about living in a place with only one post a day and therefore with no really fresh news: "In the country I always fear that creation will expire before tea-time." His present-day descendants are those who feel the same way if they do not get the latest bulletins by radio, "every hour on the hour." But to them the proper answer is Thoreau's: "I had no idea that there was so much going on in Heywood's meadow," and the real question is: What news is of greatest importance? Is the resurrection significant? If so, then why are there no bulletins to announce that the fat caterpillar who hung his green-and-gold sarcophagus not far from my study door has emerged in the form of a Monarch butterfly?

No, the real horror of the country for those who can feel it, and feel it as horror, is not the fact that it is empty or that nothing happens, but quite simply that there is so much here which is not man, so much happening here which may concern man deeply if, though only if, he is willing to admit that what does not concern him exclusively may be, for that very reason, far more significant than the things which only he knows about or cares about. If, as Sydney Smith feared, "creation" should come to an end before tea-time, the news would not be published in London any more than it would be published in Yorkshire. What London might know about before the counties did would be the fall of a government, the bombing of a city, perhaps the beginning of the end of "civilization." But "creation" includes a great deal more than what any such man-made catastrophe would put an end to. Thousands of living things would continue to lead what seems to be quite happy existences, entirely unaware that what we like to call the world had come to an end. The cockroach and the bird were both here long before we were. Both could get along very well without us, although it is perhaps significant that of the two the cockroach would miss us more.

No one, so it seems to me, can properly be called either a lover or a hater who does not find himself moved when in nature's presence by one or the other of these emotions and who does not, to some extent, recognize its source. Without being so moved he may enjoy fresh air and an open space for exercise. He may be glad to get away from crowds and may feel the peace of a successful escape. But if that is all, then he has not advanced beyond the mere Horatian ideal of retirement, has made no contact with nature in the sense in which those who love her for her own sake understand their love. Perhaps he is even capable of some purely aesthetic pleasure in the shape and color of hills or of trees. But if these are no more than shapes and colors, then he has no communion with anything except himself.

Everywhere, even in November, nature invites that communion. The bare trees raise their limbs toward heaven and permit us to interpret as well as to share that gesture. It is no mere *de profundis clamavi;* perhaps it is also not either adoration or a plea for intercession. Perhaps instead it is something rather like defiance. "We are alive," say the trees, "and you, O sky, are not. Without your light we would perish; unless the sun comes in time to shed its rays less obliquely upon us, we shall never awake from the sleep which now envelops us. But what you have the power to give, you yourself are without, you can have no share in. You represent the regular, the remorseless, the thing which endures so long that you are, as we count things, eternal. But we are part of the Great Rebellion against your exclusive rule.

"Enclosed within the cellulose walls of the little blocks out of which our great structure is made there is a jelly which is in many respects much more different from man's protoplasm than that protoplasm is from the protozoan jelly; but it is not utterly different. We and the animals took our separate routes long, long ago, but we started out together—as man with his microscope knows when he discovers under it little creatures that are neither plant nor animal but are both, living things for whom the distinction between flesh and vegetable tissue has as yet no meaning. And we are still, as tree and as man, alike in the very important fact that we are different from the stars or suns. You circle in what seems an endless regular dance, you provide for us not only a place to live but also a magnificent spectacle for our enjoyment. But you are without will and without sentience. And we have both. We can, as you cannot, assert ourselves. We are alive, I tell you, we are alive! And at least some of us know that we are."

Historical accounts make it clear enough that when Darwin and Huxley won their battle over *The Origin of Species* and *The Descent of Man,* the most they achieved was a reluctant, shamefaced confession that man is a part of nature and must admit his blood relationship with other living things— very much as a proud family might admit, when faced with the evidence of some genealogist, that it has had its obscure and humble branches.

No doubt this was in part because the popular mind made the issue simply the question whether or not the caged ape in the zoo was to be recognized as a brother; and perhaps its attitude might have been different if it had realized—as comparatively few seem to realize even today—that it was not having foisted upon it some disreputable "poor relation" but offered, instead, admission into a great fellowship: the privilege of considering itself a part of nature's great family. And if the thing had been seen in that light, then perhaps mankind would have been ready, not merely to admit, but proudly to claim, its privilege.

On this earth, perhaps throughout the whole universe, the most fundamental of all antimonies, the most crucial of all struggles, is that between life and death—or, as it might be more true to say, between life and not-life. And who, capable of realizing this fact, or of seeing himself as part of the Great Rebellion of the animate against the inanimate, can fail to find comfort in the fact that it is not alone in him that the one protagonist is embodied; perhaps even that the ultimate issues do not depend upon his success or his failure alone? Consider again the November trees which lift their arms to say that they have only temporarily yielded; that next spring they will again assert their determination to live. Those trees, like the frog now sleeping under the mud, are on our side.

1949

The Miracle of Grass

Of all the green things which make up what Goethe called "the living garment of God," grass is one of the humblest, the most nearly omnipresent, and the most stupidly taken for granted—a miracle so common that we no longer regard it as miraculous.

To some (poor things) it is merely what you try to keep the dandelions out of, or what you strike a golf ball across. But even such are paying some tribute to it. To those of us a little more aware of the great mystery of which we are a part, its going and its coming, its flourishing and its withering, are a sort of soft ostinato accompaniment in the great symphony of the seasons.

Even in the arid Southwest it springs up bravely for a few short weeks. In California the brown hills turn to emerald almost overnight. And in the gentler, more circumspect East, one hardly knows when the great awakening took place. So imperceptible, but ineluctable, is its progress that those of us who watch for it never quite catch the very moment when the transformation occurs. While our backs are turned it is alive again, and no other phenomenon of spring is at once so quiet and so all-enveloping. If there are astronomers on Mars peering at us as our astronomers are peering at their planet, they must see, much more dramatically, what is usually observed there by earthly astronomers. Martian vegetation is perhaps only a dry lichen much like what we see clinging on the bare rocks near the summits of our highest mountains. But ours is a green carpet, soft to the feet, restful to the eye, and announcing to all living things that spring is here again.

What is this thing called grass? "Why," says the botanist, "that is a question easy to answer. Grass, properly so-called, is any one of the numerous genera and species which compose that family of monocotyledonous flowering plants long

known as the Gramineae. Unfortunately, its early evolution-
ary history (like that of all the flowering plants) is obscure
since the fossil record is scanty. But at least we can say with
reasonable certainty that no grass carpeted the earth in that
long ago when the first air-breathing animals crawled out of
the water. Also that it was not until the cool weather of the
Miocene (say a mere forty million or so years ago) that it
became a dominant plant and thus made possible the flourishing of the herbivorous mammals over a more peaceful earth
where the bellowing of the dinosaurs had given way to the
lowing of herds. Then, only yesterday as world history goes,
grass conferred upon our own species that tremendous blessing called wheat."

For a less dusty question and answer we must turn to the
poets, many of whom have had their say, though only Walt
Whitman put grass at the center of a magnum opus.

A child said, "What is the grass?" fetching it to
    me with full hands;
I guess it must be the flag of my disposition, out
    of hopeful green stuff woven.
Or I guess it is the handkerchief of the Lord,
A scented gift that Remembrancer designedly dropped,
Bearing the owner's name some where in the corners,
    that we may see and remark, and say, "whose?"

Few today have time for such meditations or for such quiet
pleasures. Most of us are too desperately busy seeking recreation, entertainment, and amusement ever to experience that
joy for which all the other things are but disappointing substitutes—as essentially ersatz as plastic for china, neon lights for
dawn and sunset, or the corner grocer's cottony horror offered us in place of that other great gift of grass called bread.
"Joy be with you," people used to say when parting from
a friend. Now the modish farewell is, "Have fun!" Sometimes those thus sped away actually do have fun; often they
do not; and even the most successful in this enterprise are
not too much to be envied. Those of us who want something
more than fun, whether it be the exaltation of great art or the
mystical experience of "belonging" to something greater than
one's self, are a little afraid of being called highbrows or
"nature lovers" because neither grass nor Wordsworth's

meanest flower that blows are what we call "fun things." They can be something much more rewarding, nevertheless.

Henry David Thoreau once explained that he did not drink wine because he was afraid it might "spoil his taste for water." Henry loved to shock by "going too far" in defending what he wanted to defend, and perhaps he was going too far when he said that. If ours were an age tending toward the puritanical and the ascetic, he might be a dangerous influence, persuading us to surrender in the name of simplicity things much worth having. But since our manners and our morals are not, whatever else they may be, puritanical or ascetic, his voice is more worth hearing than that of those who call for more complexity, for madder music, and for stronger wine. Both of these last pay diminishing returns.

We boast that this is the age of abundance, and the proudest achievement of our best-intentioned men is that, for the first time in history, abundance has been democratized or, to put it somewhat sourly, that now as never before nearly everybody can have rather too much of many things not worth having. Deprivation can kill joy, but so, almost as certainly, can superfluity, for though we always want more, the limiting factor is ultimately what we can take in. More toys than he can play with are a burden, not a blessing, to any child be he five or fifty. It is disastrous to own more of anything than you can possess, and it is one of the most fundamental laws of human nature that our power actually to possess is limited.

In 1689 Louis XIV ordered the following for his garden at Versailles: 87,000 tulips, 800 tuberoses, 400 lilies, and 83,000 narcissus. In this egalitarian age there are not very many individuals likely to be able to be quite that absurd. But there are many who can and do make the same mistake for the same reason. You just can't take in or possess that many tulips, and if you are foolish enough to try, you will miss the violet by the mossy stone, and even more surely the "thought too deep for tears" which one violet or one tulip might inspire.

"The happiness of the great," wrote Francis Bacon, "consists only in thinking how happy others must suppose them to be." In Bacon's time the term "status," so beloved of present-day sociologists, had not been invented, but Bacon had grasped the concept behind it. The desire for status is the same desire to be envied which Bacon had in mind, and it was what Louis XIV also was aiming at. "It will be evident to all," so he said to himself, "that no one else in all the world can have as many tulips as I can, and they will envy me—though, God knows, the whole eighty-seven thousand of them look dull enough to me."

When grass becomes merely "a lawn," it is in danger of becoming what that sour economic Puritan Thorstein Veblen said it always was, namely a "status symbol," a display of conspicuous expenditure meant to demonstrate that its owner can afford to waste in mere display what might be used to produce wheat or vegetables. Veblen was wrong, because a lawn can also demonstrate a great truth which economists are prone to forget, namely, that beauty may be its own excuse for being. But a lawn *can* be what he called it, and there is no greater paradox than this transformation of the humblest and most unshowy of green things into a status symbol. Of course, neither your lawn nor mine (when in Connecticut I had one) is that. But just to be sure that it isn't, a salutary experience can be had if we ask ourselves from time to time what our real reason for having it is.

If we have any doubts an experiment might be worthwhile. Lie down upon your lawn to see what happens. And while I would not advise that all lawns be surrendered to dandelions, I would suggest that you ask yourself, when one of these gay little miracles raises its flower toward the sun, whether you reach for the weed killer without first remembering Whitman's tribute:

> Simple and fresh and fair from winter's clothes
>   emerging,
> As if no artifice of fashion, business, politics,
>   had ever been,
> Forth from its sunny nook of sheltered grass—
>   innocent, golden, calm as the dawn,
> The spring's first dandelion shows its trustful
>   face.

"All flesh is grass." For once the apostle and the scientist seem to be in agreement though they were not saying the same thing. To St. Peter all flesh is grass because man, too, "withereth and the flower thereof falleth away." To the biologist all flesh is grass in a more literal sense. No animal, man included, could exist if it were not for the fact that green plants mediate between him and the inanimate materials of the earth. They alone have the power of rising by one step the relative simplicity of the mineral to the complexity of the proteins indispensable to him. Where they leave off his mysterious metabolism takes over. What was mineral but became protein now becomes that even more mysterious thing called protoplasm. And protoplasm is the base of all man's life, thought, imagination, and ideals.

In time, a man passes away, he also withers and the flower thereof falls away, protoplasm descends the scale again to the merely mineral, and grass picks it up once more to repeat the cycle. The process began some billions of years ago and must continue as long as life lasts.

Which of the two truths is the most profound and the most important? The moral truth of the apostle, or the strange, inhuman truth of the biologist. One is as old as civilization, the other almost as new as yesterday. And perhaps just because it is uniquely ours we tend to value it most highly. But we may be wrong. Many civilizations, some of them glorious, were created and then destroyed by men who were innocent of chemistry. But they could not have been what they were had they not known what Peter and what Whitman knew. It is just possible that our civilization will fail because we do know one kind of truth and, in our pride, forget the other.

> And now it seems to me the beautiful uncut hair
>   of graves.
> It may be you transpire from the best of young
>   men,
> It may be if I had known them I would have loved
>   them.
> It may be you are from old people, or from offspring
>   taken soon out of their mother's laps,
> And here you are the mother's laps.
> This grass is very dark to be from the white heads
>   of old mothers,
> Darker than the colorless beards of old men,
> Dark to come from under the faint red roofs of
>   mouths.

1962

Why I Came

A "tour" is like a cocktail party. One "meets" everybody and knows no one. I doubt that what is ordinarily called "travel" really does broaden the mind any more than a cocktail party cultivates the soul. Perhaps the old-fashioned tourist who used to check off items in his Baedeker lest he forget that he had seen them was not legitimately so much a figure of fun as he was commonly made. At best, more sophisticated travelers usually know only the fact that they have seen something, not anything worth keeping which they got from the sight itself. Chartres is where the lunch was good; Lake Leman where we couldn't get a porter. To have lived in three places, perhaps really to have lived in one, is better than to have seen a hundred. I am a part, said Ulysses, of all that I have known—not of all that I have visited or "viewed."

In defense of cocktail parties it is commonly said that they are not ends in themselves but only, more or less frankly, occasions on which people offer themselves for inspection by their fellows. Young men and young women attend in order, as they say, "to look 'em over"; older people in order, as they more sedately put it, on the chance of meeting someone whose acquaintance they would like to cultivate. Something of the same sort is the most that can be said in defense of the tour. Of some spot of earth one may feel that one would like it if one could really see or really know it. Here, one may say, I should like to stay for a month, or a year, or a decade. It could give something to me and I, perhaps, something to it—if only some sort of love and understanding. More rarely—perhaps only once, perhaps two or three times —one experiences something more like love at first sight. The desire to stay, to enter in, is not a whim or a notion but a passion. *Verweile doch, du bist so schön!* If I do not somehow possess this, if I never learn what it was that called out, what it was that was being offered, I shall feel all my life that I have missed something intended for me. If I do not, for a time at least, live here, I shall not have lived as fully as I had the capacity to live.

A dozen years ago, on a trip undertaken without much enthusiasm, I got off the train at Lamy, New Mexico, and started in an automobile across the rolling semidesert toward Albuquerque. Suddenly a new, undreamed-of world was revealed. There was something so unexpected in the combination of brilliant sun and high, thin, dry air with a seemingly limitless expanse of sky and earth that my first reaction was delighted amusement. How far the ribbon of road beckoned ahead! How endlessly much there seemed to be of the majestically rolling expanse of bare earth dotted with sagebrush! How monotonously repetitious in the small details, how varied in shifting panorama! Unlike either the Walrus or the Carpenter, I laughed to see such quantities of sand.

Great passions, they say, are not always immediately recognized as such by their predestined victims. The great love which turns out to be only a passing fancy is no doubt commoner than the passing fancy which turns out to be a great love, but one phenomenon is not for that reason any less significant than the other. And when I try to remember my first delighted response to the charms of this great, proud, dry, and open land I think not so much of Juliet recognizing her fate the first time she laid eyes upon him but of a young cat I once introduced to the joys of catnip.

He took only the preoccupied, casual, dutiful sniff which was the routine response to any new object presented to his attention before he started to walk away. Then he did what is called in the slang of the theater "a double take." He stopped dead in his tracks; he turned incredulously back and inhaled a good noseful. Incredulity was swallowed up in delight. Can such things be? Indubitably they can. He flung himself down and he wallowed.

For three successive years following my first experience I returned with the companion of my Connecticut winters to the same general region, pulled irresistibly across the twenty-five hundred miles between my own home and this world which would have been alien had it not almost seemed that I had known and loved it in some previous existence. From all directions we crisscrossed New Mexico, Arizona, and southern Utah, pushing as far south as the Mexican border, as far west as the Mojave Desert in California. Guides led us into the unfrequented parts of Monument Valley and to unexplored cliff dwellings in a mesa canyon the very existence of which was nowhere officially recorded at the time. We climbed the ten-thousand-foot peak of Navajo Mountain to look from its summit across the vast unexplored land of rocks which supported, they said, not one inhabitant, white or Indian. Then one day we were lost from early morning to sunset when the tracks we were following in the sand petered out to leave us alone in the desert between Kayenta and the Canyon de Chelly.

To such jaunts the war put an end. For seven years I saw no more of sand and sunshine and towering butte. Meanwhile I lived as happily as one could expect to live in such years. The beautiful world of New England became again my only world. I was not sure that I should ever return to the new one I had discovered. Indeed it receded until I was uncertain whether I had ever seen it at all except in that previous existence some memory of which seemed to linger when, for the first time in this one, I met it face to face. Now and then, on some snowy night when the moon gleamed coldly on the snow, I woke from a dream of sun and sand, and when I looked from my window moon and snow were like the pale ghosts of sand and sun.

At last, for the fifth time, I came again, verifying the fact that remembered things did really exist. But I was still only a traveler or even only the traveler's vulgar brother, the tourist. No matter how often I looked at something I did no more than look. It was only a view or a sight. It threatened to become familiar without being really known and I realized that what I wanted was not to look at but to live with this thing whose fascination I did not understand. And so, a dozen years after I first looked, I have come for the sixth time; but on this occasion to live for fifteen months in a world which will, I hope, lose the charm of the strange only to take on the more powerful charm of the familiar.

Certainly I do not know yet what it is that this land, together with the plants and animals who find its strangenesses normal, has been trying to say to me for twelve years, what kinship with me it is that they all so insistently claim. I know that many besides myself have felt its charm, but I know also that not all who visit it do, that there are, indeed, some in whom it inspires at first sight not love but fear, or even hatred. Its appeal is not the appeal of things universally attractive, like smiling fields, bubbling springs, and murmuring brooks. To some it seems merely stricken, and even those of us who love it recognize that its beauty is no easy one. It suggests patience and struggle and endurance. It is courageous and happy, not easy or luxurious. In the brightest colors of its sandstone canyons, even in the brighter colors of its brief spring flowers, there is something austere.

Within the general area which called to me there is the greatest variety possible, once one grants the constant factors: much sun and little rain. The most spectacular part is the high region to the north, where the plateau is at about five thousand feet and mountains, here and there, rise to reach twelve thousand. Across the southernmost and most frequented part of this northern plateau the Grand Canyon cuts its way, and to the northeast of the canyon, in the region given over mostly to the Indian reservations, rock sculpture becomes most fantastic. It is here that the windblown sand has carved the rock—red and yellow and white—into the isolated "monuments" which stand out in the clear air to produce "objects in space" which the nonobjective sculptor can hardly hope to imitate, at least on so grand a scale.

To the south, when one drops off the plateau—and for many miles there is no descent other than that of an almost literal drop—one lands in an extension of Mexico's Sonoran Desert. Curious little heaps of mountain—the remains, I suppose, of what were once ranges—are scattered here and there over the otherwise flat land. This is the country of cactus and mesquite and creosote bush. Hotter in summer, warmer in winter, than the higher parts, it is the region most properly called desert country. It is also less varied than the other, less tumultuously exciting, and more fit for the kind of human habitation we know. It is capable, as the northern part is not, of being taken possession of by human beings and used to support a moderate population.

Yet something—perhaps something more than the grand common factors of much sun and little rain—links the two regions, makes them part of the same world, enables them to exercise some kindred charm. But what, I ask myself again, is the true nature, the real secret of that charm? I am no simple stoic. Hardship and austerity do not in themselves make an inevitable appeal to me and they are not only, not even principally, what I seek here. Everywhere there is also some kind of gladness.

Perhaps some of this glad charm is physical. To many people at least, dry warmth gives a sense of well-being and is in its own way as stimulating to them as the frosty air of the north is to others, caressing rather than whipping them into joyous activity. Some more of the charm is, I am sure, aesthetic. The way in which both desert and plateau use form and color is as different from the way in which more conventionally picturesque regions use them, as the way of the modern painter is different from that of the academician. But there is also, I am sure, a spiritual element. Nature's way here, her process and her moods, corresponds to some mood which I find in myself. Or, if that sounds too mystical for some tastes, we can, perhaps, compromise on a different formulation. Something in myself can be projected upon the visible forms which nature assumes here. She permits me to suppose that she is expressing something which another much-loved countryside left, for all the richness of the things it did express, unsaid, even unsuggested. To try to find out what that may be is the reason I have come once more to look at, to listen to, and this time if possible, to be more intimately a part of, something whose meaning I have sensed but not understood.

1952

The What and the Why
of Desert Country

On the brightest and warmest days my desert is most itself because sunshine and warmth are the very essence of its character. The air is lambent with light; the caressing warmth envelops everything in its ardent embrace. Even when outlanders complain that the sun is too dazzling and too hot, we desert lovers are prone to reply, "At worst that is only too much of a good thing."

Unfortunately, this is the time when the tourist is least likely to see it. Even the winter visitor who comes for a month or six weeks is most likely to choose January or February because he is thinking about what he is escaping at home rather than of what he is coming to here. True, the still warm sun and the usually bright skies make a dramatic contrast with what he has left behind. In the gardens of his hotel or guest ranch, flowers still bloom and some of the more obstreperous birds make cheerful sounds, even though they do not exactly sing at this season. The more enthusiastic visitors talk about "perpetual summer" and sometimes ask if we do not find the lack of seasons monotonous. But this is nonsense. Winter is winter even in the desert.

At Tucson's twenty-three hundred feet it often gets quite cold at night even though shade temperatures during the day may rise to seventy-five or even higher. Most vegetation is pausing, though few animals hibernate. This is a sort of neutral time when the desert environment is least characteristically itself. It is almost like late September or early October, just after the first frost, in southern New England. For those who are thinking of nothing except getting away from something, rather than learning to know a new world, this is all

44

very well. But you can't become acquainted with the desert itself at that time of year.

By April the desert is just beginning to come into its own. The air and the skies are summery without being hot; the roadsides and many of the desert flats are thickly carpeted with a profusion of wild flowers such as only California can rival. The desert is smiling before it begins to laugh, and October or November are much the same. But June is the month for those who want to know what the desert is really like. That is the time to decide once and for all if it is, as for many it turns out to be, "your country."

It so happens that I am writing this not long after the twenty-first of June and I took especial note of that astronomically significant date. This year summer began at precisely ten hours and no minutes, Mountain Standard Time. That means that the sun rose higher and stayed longer in the sky than on any other day of the year. In the north there is often a considerable lag in the seasons as the earth warms up, but here, where it is never very cold, the longest day and the hottest are likely to coincide pretty closely. So it was this year. On June 21 the sun rose almost to the zenith so that at noon he cast almost no shadow. And he was showing what he is capable of.

Even in this dry air 109° Fahrenheit in the shade is pretty warm. Under the open sky the sun's rays strike with an almost physical force, pouring down from a blue dome unmarked by the faintest suspicion of even a fleck of cloud. The year has been unusually dry even for the desert. During the four months just past no rain—not even a light shower—has fallen. The surface of the ground is as dry as powder. And yet, when I look out of the window, the dominant color of the landscape is incredibly green.

On the low foothills surrounding the steep rocky slopes of the mountains, which are actually ten or twelve miles away but seem in the clear air much closer at hand, this greenness ends in a curving line following the contour of the mountains' base and inevitably suggesting the waves of a green sea lapping the irregular shore line of some island rising abruptly from the ocean. Between me and that shore line the desert is sprinkled with hundreds, probably thousands, of evenly placed shrubs, varied now and then by a small tree—usually a mesquite or what is called locally a cat's-claw acacia.

More than a month ago all the little annual flowers and weeds which spring up after the winter rains and rush from seed to seed again in six weeks gave up the ghost at the end of their short lives. Their hope of posterity lies now invisible, either upon the surface of the bare ground or just below it. Yet when the summer thunderstorms come in late July or August, they will not make the mistake of germinating. They are triggered to explode into life only when they are both moist and cool—which they will not be until next February or March when their season begins. Neither the shrubs nor the trees seem to know that no rain has fallen during the long months. The leathery, somewhat resinous, leaves of the dominant shrub—the attractive plant unattractively dubbed "creosote bush"—are not at all parched or wilted. Neither are the deciduous leaves of the mesquite.

Not many months ago the creosote was covered with bright yellow pealike flowers; the mesquite with pale yellow catkins. Now the former is heavy with gray seed and on the mesquite are forming long pods which Indians once ate and which cattle now find an unusually rich food.

It looks almost as though the shrubs and trees could live without water. But of course they cannot. Every desert plant has its secret, though it is not always the same one. In the case of the mesquite and the creosote it is that their roots go deep and that, so the ecologists say, there is in the desert no wet or dry season below six feet. What little moisture is there is pretty constant through the seasons of the year and through the dry years as well as the wet. Like the temperature in some caves, it never varies. The mesquite and creosote are not compelled to care whether it has rained for four months or not. And unlike many other plants they flourish whether there has been less rain or more than usual.

Those plants which have substantial root systems but nevertheless do not reach so deep are more exuberant some years than others. Thus the Encelia, or brittlebush, which, in normal years, literally covers many slopes with thousands of yellow, daisy-like flowers, demands a normal year. Though I have never seen it fail, I am told that in very dry years it comes into leaf but does not flower, while in really catastrophic droughts it does not come up at all, as the roots lie dormant and hope for better times. Even the creosote bush, which never fails, can, nevertheless, profit from surface water, and when it gets the benefit of a few thunderstorms in late July or August, it will flower and fruit a second time so that the expanse which is now all green will be again sprinkled with yellow.

On such a day as this even the lizards, so I have noticed, hug the thin shade of the bushes. If I venture out, the zebratails scurry indignantly away, the boldly banded appendages which give them their name curved high over their backs. But I don't venture out very often during the middle of the day. It is more pleasant to sit inside where a cooler keeps the house at a pleasant eighty degrees. And if you think that an advocate of the simple life should not succumb to a cooler, it is you rather than I who is inconsistent. Even Thoreau had a fire in his cottage at Walden and it is no more effete to cool oneself in a hot climate than it is to get warm before a stove in a cold one. The gadget involved is newer, but that is all.

In this country "inclemency" means heat. One is "sunbound" instead of snowbound and I have often noticed that the psychological effect is curiously similar. It is cozy to be shut in, to have a good excuse for looking out of the window or into oneself. A really blazing day slows down the restless activity of a community very much as a blizzard does in regions which have them. Without the one or the other any society, I imagine, would become intolerably extroverted. Where there is either, a sort of meteorological sabbath is usually observed even by those who keep no other.

In Connecticut the chickadees came to see me when I did not go to see them. In Arizona the desert birds do the same, though the attraction—which was certainly not me in either case—is water rather than food. A curve-billed thrasher, his threatening beak half-open like the mouth of a panting dog, approaches defiantly, scattering the smaller birds as he comes. A cactus wren, the largest and boldest of the wren tribe, impudently invades my porch and even jumps to a window sill to peer at me through the glass. And as I know from experience, he will invade even the house if I leave a door open and will carry away for his nest any material available. Only the large white-winged dove does not seem to notice that this is an unusually warm day. He will fly away to Mexico at the first hint that summer is over and now, when the temperature in the sun must be at least 120 degrees, he seems to be saying, "But we don't call this hot in Campeche." From my window I see also the furry and the scaly as well as the feathered. A jack rabbit approaches cautiously and after looking carefully about dares to lower his head long enough to take a long drink; a few minutes later a lizard does the same. What did either do before I kept a vessel always full? Most of the time, I imagine, they did without. But like human beings who have access to conveniences and luxuries, they probably prefer to do with.

Obviously the animals and plants who share this country with me take it for granted. To them it is just "the way things are." By now I am beginning to take it for granted myself. But being a man I must ask what they cannot: What *is* a desert and why is it what it is? At latitude thirty-two one expects the climate to be warm. But the desert is much more than merely warm. It is a consistent world with a special landscape, a special geography, and, to go with them, a special flora and fauna adapted to that geography and that climate.

Nearly every striking feature of this special world, whether it be the shape of the mountains or the habits of its plant and animal inhabitants, goes back ultimately to the grand fact of dryness—the dryness of the ground, of the air, of the whole sum-total. And the most inclusive cause of the dryness is simply that out here it doesn't rain very much. In desert country everything from the color of a mouse or the shape of a leaf up to the largest features of the mountains themselves is more likely than not to have the same explanation: dryness. So far as living things go, all this adds up to what even an ecologist may so far forget himself as to call an "unfavorable environment." But like all such pronouncements this one doesn't mean much unless we ask "unfavorable for what and for whom?" For many plants, for many animals, and for some men it is very favorable indeed. Many of the first two would languish and die, transferred to some region where conditions were "more favorable." It is here, and here only, that they flourish. Many men feel healthier and happier in the bright dry air than they do anywhere else. And since I happen to be one of them, I not unnaturally have a special interest in the plants and animals who share my liking for just these conditions. For five years now I have been amusing myself by inquiring of them directly what habits and what adjustments they have found most satisfactory. Many of them are delightfully ingenious and eminently sensible.

To find an animal which refuses to live anywhere *except* in the desert; to find one which is, in his own peculiar way, very demanding even though what he demands is what most animals would not have at any price, I do not have to go far. Indeed, I do not have to go far from my doorstep. And it happens that I intruded upon this perfect desert dweller at a dramatic moment only a few days ago when I stepped out in the early morning and was startled by a large chicken-sized bird—if you can still call him a bird—who was dashing madly back and forth at right angles to my line of vision. His headlong plunges were so like those of a frenzied hen who seems to be rushing madly in all directions at once, that for a moment I thought I had frightened him out of his wits. As it turned out, he was merely too busy at the moment to acknowledge my presence.

As to *what* he was, that question could be answered by even the most unobservant person who has ever driven a highway in the desert. He was one of the commonest, as well as perhaps the most remarkable, of all desert birds—namely a road runner—nearly two feet of relentless energy from the tip of his wicked bill to the tip of the long, expressive tail which may trail the ground when he is calm or depressed, or be raised almost as straight up as the tail of a confident cat when he is happily angry, as indeed he seems to be a good part of the time. From his bold bad eye to his springy tread everything proclaims him "rascal," and he has, in truth, a number of bad habits. But there is also something indescribably comic about him, and he illustrates the rule that comic rascals have a way of engaging the affection of even the virtuous. Nearly everybody is curiously cheered by the sight of a road runner. In the old days the cowboys used to be amused by his habit of racing ahead of their horses and they gave him his name. The Mexicans of Sonora call him affectionately "paisano" or "countryman."

My specimen, far from having lost his wits, had them very much about him. Suddenly he arrested his mad career, stabbed with lightning rapidity at the ground and, crest erect, lifted his head triumphantly—with a good-sized lizard in his beak. No one who has ever seen one of our lizards run would like to be assigned the task of chasing it from bush to bush and then nabbing it with a hand. But catching lizards is all in a day's work for a road runner and mine was merely collecting some for his breakfast. His diet is varied from time to time by a snake, or even an insect, if the insect happens to be large enough to be worth the effort of a leap from the ground to take him on the wing, as I have seen a zooming dragonfly taken. Responsible observers say that when the lizard tries his usual trick of surrendering his tail so that the rest of him may make a safe getaway, the road runner, unlike some other predators, is not to be fooled. He merely takes a firmer grip on the body and collects the discarded tail later. Scorpions are also quite acceptable as tidbits.

Inevitably such a creature is the center of many legends. There seems to be no doubt that he takes the killing of rattlesnakes in his stride, but old-timers insist that he sometimes first surrounds the snake with a circle of spiny cactus joints so that the snake cannot get away. In fact, only a few weeks ago a friend told me that one of *his* friends had seen a slight variation on this performance when a road runner walled the snake in with small stones before attacking him. But like the milk snake milking a cow and the hoop snake rolling merrily along with his tail in his mouth, this remarkable performance seems never to be witnessed by anyone with a professional interest in natural history and it is usually a friend of a friend who was on the spot. The situation seems much the same as that with ghosts. You are most likely to see them if you are a simple person and have faith.

As a matter of fact, however, you do not always have to be a simple or ignorant person to believe what the simple tell you. A well-educated man recently passed on to me the old superstition that the Gila monster, our only poisonous lizard, owed his venom to the unfortunate fact that nature had not provided him with any orifice through which the waste products of metabolism could be discharged, and that poisons therefore inevitably accumulated. One need only turn a Gila on his back to dispose of this legend which is sufficiently improbable on the face of it. Most of the people who repeat it have pointlessly taken part in the attempt to exterminate these creatures but have obviously never looked at the bodies of their victims.

Of course it may just possibly turn out that the road runner really does fence his victims in. Stranger things do happen and the evidence against it is necessarily only negative. But the "paisano" is odd enough without the legends. Almost everything about him is unbird-like at the same time that it fits him to desert conditions. He is a bird who has learned how not to act like one.

Though he can fly—at least well enough to get to the top of a mesquite if there is some really urgent reason for doing so—he would rather not, trusting to his long legs to catch his prey and to get him out of trouble. The sound which he makes is like nothing on earth, least of all like a bird. One writer describes it as a sort of modified Bronx cheer, which is right enough since it seems to be made by the raucous expelling of air accompanied by a rapid gnashing of the bill —if a bill can be gnashed. Like the bird himself, the sound is derisive, irascible, ribald, threatening, and highly self-confident. As befits a no-nonsense sort of creature, the road runner is content to dress himself in neutral, brown-speckled feathers, but there is a line of red cuticle behind his eye which he can expose when it seems desirable to look a bit fiercer than usual.

Sociologists talk a great deal these days about "adjustment," which has always seemed to me a defeatist sort of word suggesting dismal surrender to the just tolerable. The road runner is not "adjusted" to his environment. He is triumphant in it. The desert is his home and he likes it. Other creatures, including many other birds, elude and compromise. They cling to the mountains or to the cottonwood-filled washes, especially in the hot weather, or they go away somewhere else, like the not entirely reconciled human inhabitants of this region. The road runner, on the other hand, stays here all the time and he prefers the areas where he is hottest and driest. The casual visitor is most likely to see him crossing a road or racing with a car. But one may see him also in the wildest wilds, either on the desert flats or high up in the desert canyons where he strides along over rocks and between shrubs. Indeed, one may see him almost anywhere below the level where desert gives way to pines or aspen.

He will come into your patio if you are discreet. Taken young from the nest, he will make a pet, and one writer describes a tame individual who for years roosted on top a wall clock in a living room, sleeping quietly through evening parties unless a visitor chose to occupy the chair just below his perch, in which case he would wake up, descend upon the intruder, and drive him away. But the road runner is not one who needs either the human inhabitant or anything which human beings have introduced. Not only his food but everything else he wants is amply supplied in his chosen environment. He usually builds his sketchy nest out of twigs from the most abundant tree, the mesquite. He places it frequently in a cholla, the wickedest of the cacti upon whose murderous spines even snakes are sometimes found fatally impaled. He feeds his young as he feeds himself, upon the reptiles which inhabit the same areas which he does. And because they are juicy, neither he nor his young are as dependent upon the hard-to-find water as the seed-eating birds who must sometimes make long trips to get it.

Yet all the road runner's peculiarities represent things learned, and learned rather recently as a biologist understands "recent." He is not a creature who happened to have certain characteristics and habits and who therefore survived here. This is a region he moved into and he was once very different. As a matter of fact, so the ornithologists tell us, he is actually a cuckoo, although no one would ever guess it without studying his anatomy. Outwardly, there is nothing to suggest the European cuckoo of reprehensible domestic morals or, for that matter, the American cuckoo or "rain crow" whose mournful note is familiar over almost the entire United States and part of Canada—not excluding the wooded oases of Arizona itself. That cuckoo flies, perches, sings, and eats conventional bird food. He lives only where conditions are suited to his habits. But one of his not too distant relatives must have moved into the desert—slowly, no doubt—and made himself so much at home there that by now he is a cuckoo only to those who can read the esoteric evidences of his anatomical structure.

Despite all this, it must be confessed that not everybody loves the road runner. Nothing is so likely to make an animal unpopular as a tendency to eat things which we ourselves would like to eat. And the road runner is guilty of just this wickedness. He is accused, no doubt justly, of varying his diet with an occasional egg of the Gambel's quail, or even with an occasional baby quail itself. Sportsmen are afraid that this reduces somewhat the number they will be able to kill in their own more efficient way and so, naturally, they feel that the road runner should be eliminated.

To others it seems that a creature who so triumphantly demonstrates how to live in the desert ought to be regarded with sympathetic interest by those who are trying to do the same thing. He and the quail have got along together for quite a long time. Neither seems likely to eliminate the other. Man, on the other hand, may very easily eliminate both. It is the kind of thing he is best at.

In the plant world the road runner's opposite number is certainly the cactus. To most people—and quite properly—it is the desert plant par excellence. Many kinds are, like the road runner, at home in the desert and nowhere else. Like the road runner also they belong to a family of pioneers which moved into arid America and changed itself radically to meet the new conditions. Most of the cuckoo tribe live by following other habits in other environments. The relatives of the desert cacti do the same.

Members of the Sonoran branch of the family come in all shapes and sizes from tiny two-inch pincushions full of pins to the giant saguaro which towers sometimes seventy-five feet, weighs six or seven tons, and lives for as much as two hundred years. Some eleven sorts of cactus have been found only in Arizona; other kinds are more widespread. But they all have the same general characteristics and employ very similar devices in their determination to make a good best of desert living.

Most have the succulent stems which store water, when they can get it, to be saved for a non-rainy day—or month, or even year. Leaves are vestigial or completely absent because too much moisture would evaporate from them, and the stems are green with chlorophyll so that they can perform the functions of leaves. These stems are also often coated with wax to economize water still further and usually they are provided with formidable spines—partly to discourage animals which would be only too glad to use the succulence for their own purposes, partly because spines limit the free circulation of the hot, desiccating atmosphere, perhaps also because they provide broken shade to the surface of the plant.

All these devices have been independently invented by other plant families which also moved into the desert. Succulence, waxy coatings, and reduced or absent leaves are common. To the layman, indeed, any plant which exhibits all these characteristics is commonly called "a cactus," though he is often wrong because the true cactus is a member of a family strongly marked in other ways. That graceful spray of ten-foot wands tipped with flame-colored flowers and called ocotillo is no more a cactus because it has spines and bears no leaves except during wet weather than a butterfly is a bird because it has wings.

In the case of the butterfly and the bird two quite different creatures learned to fly by inventing wings. In the case of the ocotillo and the cactus two different kinds of plants discovered the same methods of economizing on water. Nevertheless, true cacti are common enough and a number of species are growing within a few feet of my door. The why and wherefore of their diverse shapes and habits is an interesting subject, but at the moment we are concerned rather with the general methods by which cacti have learned to live in the desert.

The question might be asked of any one of a dozen sorts, but we may as well address it to the giant saguaro. For one thing, it is in many ways among the most remarkable of all. For another, not even the most casual visitor to the region where it grows can have failed to be aware that it is unlike anything to be seen elsewhere. There must be few Americans who are not at least vaguely familiar with drawings or paintings or photographs of the saguaro towering starkly over the desert and stretching out its grotesquely extended arms. As a matter of fact, artists and cartoonists have established it as a conventional symbol of location. When you see a saguaro that means "Scene: The Desert" just as the Eiffel Tower means "Paris" or the Public Library lions mean "New York." Actually it has been employed far too widely for even reasonable accuracy. To many artists it seems to mean not only "desert" but "any desert," though the truth is that the saguaro's range is extraordinarily limited. There are some in northern Mexico; there are also a very few in California just across the Colorado River from Arizona. But, except for these, there are no others anywhere in the world and the symbol ought to mean not "desert" but "the Sonoran Desert of southwestern Arizona and northern Mexico." To the traveler approaching from the east or the north, the first sight of a saguaro standing sentinel is the announcement, "I have arrived."

Under the special conditions prevailing where it flourishes best—loose rocky soil, low rainfall, and high temperature—no other growth achieves such a height or such a bulk. Inevitably the saguaro suggests some strange kind of tree, not a succulent plant, and its weight is tremendous. As we said a few minutes ago, it may tower fifty feet and may weigh 12,000 pounds. Indeed, fully grown plants are quite commonly not much smaller. Yet they are obviously, in everything except size, very much like other members of the sometimes quite modest cereus subgroup of the cacti. The waxy green skin is tender; the flesh is pulpy and moist, though the moisture contained is too bitter to drink. In spring when a little circle of white flowers opens at the tip of one or more of the arms, the flowers are unmistakably cactus flowers. When the red fruits follow they look like many other cactus fruits, even very much like the familiar prickly pear sometimes sold in fruit stores.

Yet everything about the saguaro is somehow odd. The seeds, like most cactus seeds, are tiny. The disproportion between the acorn and the oak is not nearly so great. And they grow with extraordinary slowness. After two or three years a seedling is only a few millimeters high; after ten years, less than an inch. From then on the rate of growth is variable, but a three-foot specimen may be twenty to fifty years old. In middle age (or shall we say adolescence) it will grow faster, but it will take about a century to reach maturity, after which an individual may have another hundred years to live. Planting a tree is often taken as a symbol of the farseeing and the unselfish. One puts an acorn in the ground with a certain sense of demonstrating both faith in and concern for a future other than one's own. But if anyone ever planted a saguaro for the sake of future generations, he was carrying such faith and such concern to fantastic limits.

Yet in favorable areas the saguaros form veritable forests; thousands of specimens covering hundreds of acres grow almost as close together as giant trees do. Obviously the saguaro is extremely well suited to what it is suited to. There is no suggestion that it would prefer any other environment. Indeed, the fact that it is so restricted in its distribution, that it does not tolerate introduction into other parts of the world, is proof enough how perfectly it has adapted itself. What makes it so fit to live just here?

The most uninstructed visitor who saw a forest of these giants for the first time would almost certainly assume that their roots go very deep down. If he happened to know something about the habits of certain other desert plants— how, for example, a yucca no more than six or eight feet high may send a root forty feet below the surface in search of water—he would probably suppose that the saguaro must reach half the way to China. But he couldn't be more wrong. The taproot of a huge specimen is seldom more than three feet long and seems ridiculously inadequate. As a matter of fact, the saguaro is so insecurely anchored that it often meets its end by being blown over in a storm, and wanton horsemen have been known to destroy in a few moments a century of slow living with a tug upon a lasso.

Yet there is method in the saguaro's seeming madness. It does not go deep for water because where it grows there usually isn't any. In fact its preferred areas are those buried under the loose rocky detritus of disintegrating mountains and therefore the very ones which are the despair of the well digger. But the saguaro has learned that when the occasional torrential rains do come, the water does not run off as quickly as it does on the hard-backed flats because it sinks a few inches into the rocky soil. And while the saguaro was learning that, it was also learning how to take advantage of the fact. It sends out a network of lateral roots only eight to twenty inches below the surface but as much as ninety feet in length, so that the great trunk rises from the center of a sort of huge disk just below the surface.

Thanks to this arrangement, it is ready to take full advantage of the occasional periods when these roots are bathed in water. Moreover, the trunk is longitudinally accordion-pleated and as moisture is absorbed the pleats unfold. As much as a ton may be absorbed after a single downpour and the supply, carefully hoarded, can last if necessary for a full year.

In fact the saguaro cannot live where rains are frequent

because, for one thing, it may take up so much water as to burst itself open. Even when growing under ideal conditions, it may have a moisture content of from seventy-five to ninety-five percent of its green weight. In a saguaro forest the large plants are usually fifteen or twenty feet apart, because each needs a considerable area from which to draw water, and the mature specimens are those which have successfully defended the plot of ground to which a seedling staked a claim perhaps a century ago. In a deciduous forest the contest between individuals is literally for a place in the sun. Where the saguaro grows there is enough of that for everybody. But every individual must protect his water rights in his own area.

For all the soft succulence of the saguaro's trunk, for all the fact that it is not, like a tree, predominantly woody, there is nothing weak about its structure. It may sway in the wind like an oak or an elm; in a storm, branching "arms" may sometimes break off, or the whole may be uprooted. But the massive trunk is surprisingly strong. Indeed, when you realize that the flesh beneath the waxy skin is soft and pulpy, it is astonishingly so.

Examine the skeleton of a dead specimen lying on the desert and the mystery is explained. The soft part decayed rapidly but there remained the almost indestructible woody "ribs," each as long as the saguaro was high. Among the many remarkable discoveries of this cactus was the discovery of the principle of "reinforcement" which man now takes advantage of when he embeds steel rods in his concrete walls. The center of the saguaro is pulpy and so is the outer flesh. But imbedded in this pulp is a cylinder of closely placed rods which give the whole a flexible strength. Since the time before history, Pima and Papago Indians living in the saguaro country have used these rods to construct wooden shelters which must be as immune to decay as cypress.

In another way also, the saguaro finds that its ability to produce either pulpy or extraordinarily hard tissue comes in handy. It is very much subject to the attack of woodpeckers. In fact one species of the latter, the gilded flicker, seldom nests in anything except a hole which it has excavated in the saguaro, and its range is almost coextensive with that of the giant cactus. Moreover, this particular bird insists upon digging a new home ever so often, leaving abandoned dwellings to be used by quite a few other species of nesting birds—by cactus wrens, elf owls, and others, even sometimes, as I have happened to observe, by honeybees who have left their man-made hive. The result of all this is that there are very few mature saguaros which do not have from one to a dozen cavities in their trunks. But the saguaro handles this situation very successfully. The wound inflicted by the flicker is quickly sealed off by a layer of extraordinarily tough scar-tissue. Not infrequently one finds among the bleached ribs of some long dead saguaro a curious boot-shaped receptacle which represents the lining of a flicker's nest. The Sonoran Desert must be one of the few places in the world where one may come home from a walk carrying a hole—and a very durable one at that.

For plants which grow only in one or more isolated and very restricted areas the botanists have a word: "endemic." Endemics contrast most sharply with "cosmopolitans" which sometimes almost circle the globe, somewhat less sharply with other species or genera which cover large areas without being actually cosmopolitan. But there are few species whose endemism is more striking than that of the saguaro which is limited to this one small area. And there are few if any endemics which are so striking a feature of the one region where they are at home.

Both cosmopolitanism and endemism present problems for the evolutionist and the plant geographer. How did the cosmopolitans spread from, say, Africa to South America? Why haven't those endemics which are found only in one place set forth to colonize others? How did those which exist in several widely separated but restricted areas come to have this "discontinuous distribution"?

The answers to those questions when either found or guessed at are various. Obviously a plant species or genus can't migrate past barriers which it cannot cross. A plant adapted, for instance, to desert conditions obviously can't get to another desert thousands of miles away across a damp, humid stretch any more than a moisture-loving plant can cross a desert from one moist region to another. If, as happens to be the case, there are very closely related cosmopolitan genera in Africa and in South America, they must have made their way from one continent to another via some land connections either now or once existing. No less obviously, if endemics are "discontinuously distributed" in several small, widely separate areas, that presents a different problem. And in some cases at least they probably represent "relics"— surviving patches of some once large continuous distribution.

All this is part of a very large and complicated subject into which we need not try to enter very deeply. But once one has turned from astonishment at the saguaro as an individual to contemplate the fact that it is not to be found anywhere except in this one region where it is so very abundant indeed, one cannot help wondering why that should be. Were there ever saguaros anywhere else? Are they "relics" or did they first develop here and never get any farther?

Such questions cannot be answered fully and positively, but some very probable guesses can be made. No remains of a saguaro, fossil or otherwise, have ever been found except in this region. By itself that is not very strong evidence because fossil cacti of any kind are almost unknown. But certain other facts can be added. The cactus is an American family so there can't be much doubt that the saguaro originated in this hemisphere. It is so highly specialized that it will not flourish except under the very special conditions which it finds in this one kind of desert. If it ever colonized a larger area, it must have been one which was at that time almost precisely what the Sonoran Desert is now. And for all these reasons it seems a fairly safe guess that there never were any saguaros in any place very far from where they are now found.

Look again, therefore, at any one of the thousands to be seen in southern Arizona. Probably nowhere else was one ever seen. They represent about as close an approximation to a "special creation" as one is likely to find. They certainly look improbable, and in a sense they were improbable—until, for some reason which evolutionists don't even pretend to understand fully, an organism's ability to vary produced at last this strange plant perfectly adapted to the narrowly defined conditions which existed right here. The first known mention of the saguaro is said to be in 1540. Surely the botanical Cortez who first saw it must have felt "a wild surmise."

1955

The Mouse That Never Drinks

For several years I was on quite intimate terms with the common house mouse and I attempted to celebrate his charm in print. There is, therefore, nothing odd in the fact that I have recently been associating with the so-called kangaroo rat of the desert, who is, really, more mouselike than ratlike. I keep a pair of them in a glass case from which they enjoy frequent sorties to sit on the palm of my hand, rest in my pocket, or run through paper tubes which they seem to accept as easily recognizable substitutes for an underground passageway.

So far as I am concerned there is, I say, nothing odd about this. But there is something very odd indeed about my companions. In fact the kangaroo rat is famous as "the mouse that never drinks," and because of his incredible abstention from all potations, he has attracted the attention—considerably more unwelcome than mine—of laboratory scientists who have analyzed his blood, examined his urine, and imposed fantastically abnormal conditions upon him to force him to break his inveterate teetotalism.

They find that it can be done. But it is not certain that in nature he ever does so. Obviously he is the most triumphant imaginable example of adaptation to the most characteristic desert difficulty, the absence of water. It is no wonder that the largest of all the kangaroo rats lives in Death Valley, the hottest and driest spot in the United States, where it sometimes never rains at all for a year and more. To get along without is the most radical solution in any economy of scarcity.

In the appearance of the sleek little creatures there is nothing to suggest the underprivileged. Their manner is exuberant and, unlike many desert plants, they do not look at all desiccated—which as a matter of fact they are not. You would never suspect that they did not drink like any other flourishing animal. In fact it is hard to believe that they don't. And to realize fully just how extraordinary that fact is one should know them personally as well as technically. But let us begin with technicalities.

From the zoologist's standpoint the kangaroo rat is actually neither a rat nor a mouse because he belongs to a different order of the rodent family, one of the reasons being that he has twenty teeth while both Rattus and Mus have to get along with only sixteen. Still, his general appearance is mouselike enough. He has thick, silky brown hair and a pointed be-whiskered nose. His crowning glory—worn at the opposite end from that on which crowning glories are usually worn—is a handsome tail half again as long as all the rest of his body and with a furry banner at the end, much like that on the tail of a lion. Moreover, this tail turns out to be very useful as well as ornamental.

Actually there are some sixteen different species of kangaroo rats resident in the arid parts of the West and one of them, also found about Tucson, goes in for a fine decorative touch by choosing to have his banner a contrasting white. Mine, whose scientific name is *Dipodomys merriami,* is the smallest of the tribe and consists of about four inches of body with six or more of tail. I choose him rather than his larger cousin because he happens to be the one whose independence of any external water supply has been tested and vouched for by relentless laboratory experimenters.

Dipo's large black eyes are a clear enough indication that his habit is nocturnal, and the casual traveler ordinarily sees him only as some sort of small rodent hurrying across the road in the headlights of an automobile. In nature he makes extensive burrows entered through many surface holes and usually under a considerable mound of earth, perhaps fifteen feet in circumference and often so thoroughly tunneled just below the surface that it will collapse if one attempts to walk across it.

Other desert rodents, ground squirrels and gophers, make similar holes, but the Dipo's residence is usually recognizable by the fact that the mound is elevated well above the surrounding surface of the ground. Apparently, however, he does not always have this well-constructed home to himself. It seems that rabbits sometimes enlarge one of his entrances and move in. So probably does an occasional snake, who cannot be a very welcome house guest. Moreover, though Dipos probably have a home base, they take refuge in the nearest hole when danger threatens and they must often be surprised by what they find there.

In Australia there is also a kangaroo rat which really is a kangaroo—a marsupial that is, complete with a pouch in which to carry its young. Sticklers say it should be called rather a "rat-kangaroo" just as, so these same sticklers insist, an aviator ought to be called a "manbird" and only an ornithologist a "birdman." But, in any event, Dipo is a rodent, not a marsupial, and the only true American marsupial, the 'possum, does not live in the arid Southwest. Nevertheless Dipo gets his common name from the obvious fact that he *looks* like a kangaroo—because of his long tail, his stubby little forelimbs which are not much good for walking, and his habit of sitting or jumping on his long hind legs. Like a real kangaroo he will also box with a neighbor while sitting on his tail and striking out with his hands.

In the gobbledygook of technical description, all the species of Dipodomys are said to be "admirably adapted to a bipedal, saltatory existence." In other words, they jump on their hind legs! Even in captivity and though normally rather placid creatures, they may, when some not-too-amiable brush between one and another takes place, suddenly begin to bound erratically a foot and a half high and to land after each bound no one can predict where. But why? The ability to do without water is obviously a very useful accomplishment for a desert dweller. What good are a disproportionately long tail and the ability to make prodigious, unpredictably erratic leaps?

There must be some reason, because in other faraway deserts, those in Africa for instance, other creatures have adapted themselves to the same "bipedal, saltatory existence." The African jumpers and the American are not descended from a common ancestor who just happened to develop this habit. The African jerboa, even though he looks and acts like a kangaroo rat and is also a rodent, is not even very closely related. His analogue of the Australian desert is also not descended from either of the other two long-tailed, short-forelegged desert creatures. Plainly we are again faced with a case of "convergence" like that of the desert cacti of America and the desert Euphorbias of Africa. Two different animals and two different plants have independently developed useful tricks for living in arid country. And the tricks are so similar that the two organisms have come to look very much alike. But the utility of the devices is evident in the case of the plants, not nearly so evident in that of the animals. Still, though no one is quite sure what the answer to the riddle is, a guess seems pretty probable.

Dipo can walk, or rather hobble, when he wants to. When he is tranquil that is usually what he does. But when he becomes excited or afraid, he begins to bound, switching his tail in the air as he leaps. And it is the switch of the long tail which makes his course unpredictable. Whether or not he himself knows where he is going to land is a question; certainly nobody else does. And that must be a great help when being pursued by a predator, especially an owl or a hawk. When one of them swoops at a Dipo, the Dipo usually turns out to be somewhere else. That must have saved many a life in Africa and Australia as well as in America. And if you accept the most mechanical theory of evolution, then the more erratically a rodent leaped and the longer tail he had, the better were his chances to survive and to hand on his longer tail to a goodly number of progeny.

Other kinds of rodents didn't develop in the same direction because most of them live where cover is available. But in the desert cover is scarce and the ability to elude capture by unpredictable movement much more important. On this assumption the tuft at the end of the tail, which is as characteristic of the jerboa as it is of the kangaroo rat, simply makes the tail more effective as a rudder. One observer reports that a captive Dipo who had lost a considerable part of his tail in some accident still leaped high but landed any old way instead of on his feet.

Among themselves Dipos seem rather quarrelsome. Mine, the merriami, are said to be the most peaceable of the tribe, and it is also said that for that reason several individuals of this species can be kept together in captivity. I have not found it so. My pair, even though they are male and female, have to be kept separated most of the time or they will soon take to boxing and from boxing to biting in a manner alarming to anyone anxious to keep them in good health. They seem, on the other hand, to have little fear of man and no tendency, even under provocation, to be aggressive toward him. They will run away if you approach them at liberty, but once caught, they will rest quietly on a human hand and, in fact, often come to it if one reaches down into a cage. It is said that even when roughly handled, merriami, at least, will make no attempt to bite, and mine have showed no resentment even when, on occasion, I have had to end a fight quickly by lifting one suddenly by the tail. Obviously they are very satisfactory pets, requiring a minimum of care. With a hopper of seeds there is no reason, so far as I can see, why they might not be left unattended for weeks. At least there is no water problem to be met. Mine have had none during the three months I have had them. And that brings us to Dipo's most extraordinary claim to fame.

How absolute is the independence of water? How is the seemingly impossible accomplished? The closer these questions are pushed, the more surprising the answers are.

To begin with, one should realize that many desert animals, like many desert plants, can get along on far less water than would suffice for the survival of most creatures. Sometimes it is said that even the jack rabbit does not drink, though this is so far from being absolutely true that I have often seen him taking a long draught from my birdbath. Quite possibly he can get along for a long time without any water, possibly he can get along indefinitely, but he drinks gladly and deep when he gets a chance. What is more important, the jack rabbit eats succulent green food when he can get it and is a great depredator of flower gardens when he gets a chance at them. With him it is not a question of doing with-

out water but simply of getting the comparatively little which is indispensable from his food instead of in liquid form.

The same is true in the case of many desert creatures. The road runner also visits the birdbath, but since he eats such other animals as snakes, lizards, and mice which have a good deal of water in their blood, he is in much the same position as the rabbit who likes a tender watery morsel when he can get it. The pack rat, another desert dweller, can, it has been demonstrated, get along without drinking at all. But he also must have succulent food. Dipo, on the other hand, belongs in an entirely different class. It is not only that he can get along without water. He will not take it if it is offered to him. And he does not have to have any succulent food either. *He can live indefinitely on the driest of dry seeds.*

This fact has been abundantly demonstrated by brutally thorough and rigorously controlled experiments. Kept under desert conditions of heat and of dryness for fifty-two days and fed on an exclusive diet of dried barley seeds, *Dipodomys merriami* not only lived but, when subjected to a post-mortem examination, showed no diminution in the proportion of water to total body weight; and that remained true even of those of the victims who gained in total weight during the course of the experiment. "Control" individuals who were given access to watermelon during the same period and who ate some of it retained no more water in their blood or tissues than did those who had eaten only dry food. As a matter of fact, *Dipodomys* needs to maintain the same water content in his blood as other rodents and will die from dehydration at about the same degree of deficiency in this respect.

The secret, then, is not merely the one we have met so often—rigid economy in the expenditure of water. In the first place, you cannot save what you have not been able to get. In the second place, *Dipodomys* isn't even as stingy in this respect as some other creatures. Unlike some insects and all birds, he does not save water by voiding uric acid only in solid form, though his urine is about twice as concentrated as that of the white rat, and when fed on dry food his excrement is forty-five percent water as compared with sixty-five percent for the white rat. He does save in another way because, unlike most mammals, he uses no water for heat regulation either by sweating from the pores of the skin or from the mouth by panting. As pitiless experimenters have demonstrated, only when subjected to heat of a nearly fatal degree will he slobber slightly at the mouth, thus using a little of the precious water to try to save himself in extremity. And one reason for his nocturnal habit probably is that he can keep relatively cool in his burrow during the day, thus avoiding the risk of being called upon to pant.

But no economy can explain a complete getting along without. Dipo's secret is simply—if you can call it simple—that he *manufactures* his own water from the dry materials present in starchy foods. In one sense the chemistry is elementary enough. Starch is a hydrocarbon and therefore contains hydrogen. Oxygen is abundant in the air he breathes. And as every high school student of chemistry knows, water is H_2O—or a chemical combination of one part oxygen with two parts hydrogen. You can make it by one of the simplest of laboratory experiments if you explode a mixture of the two. But you can't do it effectively enough in your own body, as Dipo does, who takes it all in a day's work. The result is what the biochemists call "the water of metabolism" and for Dipo, with his very unusual metabolism, it is no doubt a routine matter. The only way you can force him to drink is to feed him on a diet so largely protein that he does not get enough hydrocarbon to furnish him with hydrogen. In that unhappy state he will drink water—I wonder if it tastes very nasty—when it is given him.

If in one sense this is all simple enough, in another it is as mysterious as anything very well could be. Dipo "evolved" the capacity to produce water of metabolism sufficiently to supply his needs and they are quite as great as those of many other desert creatures. It is obviously a gift with great "survival value." But why didn't all the creatures, some of which certainly sometimes perish of thirst, "evolve" it too? What inborn capacity, if that is what it was, made him potentially independent of an external water supply?

Moreover, while Dipodomys was evolving his unusually effective gift for manufacturing water internally, he had also to evolve at the same time a certain special efficiency in an organ which is part of the standard equipment of all except the very simplest animals, and actually has at least an analogue even in the one-celled protozoa: namely the kidney. One authority on this organ, Dr. Homer W. Smith, Professor of Physiology at the New York University College of Medicine, enthusiastically maintains that the whole story of evolution can be told in terms of the evolution of the kidney. He has also the highest admiration for Dipo's renal equipment.

Most of us, it seems, do the kidney, whether our own or that of other animals, less than justice. We think of it as merely an organ of excretion, but it is actually far more than that. It is responsible for that "internal environment" in which all our vital organs and the very cells themselves live, isolated from the air which would be fatal. Ever since the days of the first vertebrates it has had a very difficult job to accomplish. So far as the invertebrate animals which still live in the sea are concerned, they have the same salt content as that of the sea itself, and all their rudimentary kidneys have to do is to get rid of any excess solids, including salt. But all vertebrates, including of course all those which live on land, have to maintain in their bodies blood of a density which must not vary except within small limits and which, as it happens, is considerably less dense than that of sea water.

There are those who believe that its density corresponds to that of the once less salty sea at the time when the first vertebrates developed. But however that may be, the kidneys have to see to it that the density remains constant by eliminating excess water or excess minerals as the case may be. To get rid of excess salts they must deliver to the bladder for excretion a fluid much denser than the blood. But there is a limit to what they can do in preparing this concentrated fluid. Men and nearly all animals will quickly die if they drink a quantity of sea water, because it is far denser than any fluid their kidneys can concentrate and it simply increases that oversaltiness of the blood of which thirst is a sign. So far as is known, only one animal can drink sea water, for though sea birds have sometimes been assumed capable of it, they probably are not. The one animal who can—as the reader has probably guessed—is our hero Dipodomys.

He does not want to waste water merely to get rid, as he must, of excess mineral matter. Hence he has developed an unparalleled capacity to concentrate urine. Man cannot concentrate a fluid to more than 4.2 times the osmotic concentration of his blood plasma, but the kangaroo rat is capable of concentrating to 17 times the density of his blood and that is considerably denser than sea water. Hence if he is forced by a special diet to drink when only sea water is available, he can quench his thirst with that.

You and I may be amazed at this feat without being greatly stirred by it. But to a man with Dr. Smith's enthusiasm for the kidney it implies a feat worthy of the highest admiration, and with real fervor he lets himself go with a flat statement: "The kidney of the kangaroo rat can concentrate to the greatest extent of any known animal."

Feeling that I have, perhaps, not admired Dipo sufficiently for this particular talent, I let him stand for a few minutes in the palm of my hand. I see again that he is an unusually attractive little beast but that there is nothing in his external appearance to reveal what a physiological marvel he is. Nor does he himself seem to be aware of it. Like any ordinary mouse he seems a very modest little creature. Why should the heart of mortal man, or the kidney of mortal mouse, be proud? God, the blind chance which is responsible for all evolution, or, perhaps, something somehow in between, has given him the kidneys he needs to live comfortably in the desert. Whether man and mouse want much or little here below depends on how you look at it. But both sometimes get what they want.

There are three conventional ways of meeting the water problem—by economizing, by storing, and by lying low. Dipo introduces us to the fourth and most radical method: making your own. Certain other animals probably make some, but so far as is known, the kangaroo rat is the only one who can make enough to be entirely independent.

Making your own is not only the most radical solution; it is also the only one of the four which is not adopted to a greater or lesser degree by both plants and animals. In other words, no plant can exist, as Dipo can, without some external source of water. In the damp air of the tropics many plants grow upon trees, have no roots in the ground, and depend upon rainfall or dew. But no plant in the desert can do that because rainfall is too infrequent and dew nonexistent, except perhaps in winter. In air so dry, the dew point is usually at a below-freezing temperature—which is certainly not to be looked for except during the early mornings of midwinter. And no plant of either the desert or the tropics can imitate Dipo's feat. Plants do not eat hydrocarbons from which the kangaroo rats make their water. As a matter of fact, plants make hydrocarbon and to do that you have to use up water, not create it.

Moreover, though all of the three less radical solutions have been hit upon by both plants and animals, they do not seem to be equally characteristic of both. On the whole, plants tend to store as well as to economize; on the whole, animals tend to have little or no provision for storing. They can get along on little and hence go long periods without replenishing the supply, but that is principally because they use so little, not because they put aside a supply to be drawn upon. Dipo doesn't. Even his blood is not unusually watery at any time.

There is, however, at least one desert animal who may violate the general rule and is worth mentioning for that reason, as well as for some others. He is the desert tortoise, a great lumbering fellow, scaly skinned and hard backed, who may be almost a foot in length, eight inches wide, and stand five inches off the ground. He is a formidable-looking creature who appears, as most turtles do, not only very ancient as a type, but almost equally ancient as an individual. He also looks rather threatening, though he is actually completely inoffensive—which all turtles certainly are not, as anyone who has ever had any experience with a snapper well knows. Though quite frequently found in very dry, cactus-covered desert areas, he is always a surprise when one comes across him crawling slowly along or holed up headfirst in some little recess under a rock.

It is also surprising to discover that, despite his robustious appearance, he is a vegetarian who favors salads of one sort or another and in captivity eats lettuce with as much enthusiasm as turtles show for anything. He sleeps in the shade at midday and he sleeps through most of the winter. Moreover, he seems to have been born old as well as resigned and wise. If you should happen across one, you will see that he is a kind of box-turtle, though the front of his under shell is not hinged and he cannot shut himself in completely. You may be puzzled by a curious triangular projection in front and wonder what he uses it for. He uses it to fight with when a tank battle between two individuals takes place.

This turtle, of course, gets his water from the succulent vegetables he eats. But the most remarkable thing about him is the way in which he stores it up against a rainless day. Just under his upper shell is an unusually large bladder which in good times is full of water to be drawn upon as needed. Obviously he could be called the camel of our deserts. As a matter of fact, I shouldn't be at all surprised if he could far outdo the real camel's somewhat overpublicized ability to go for a long time without a drink.

Among animals, then, Dipo and the desert tortoise represent two ultimates in adaptation. What plant, I have been wondering, should get first prize in this same category? Some might say "the barrel cactus" which, even under conditions of extreme aridity, may hold in its pulpy center enough water to save a human life. But water storage to a greater or less degree is common among the cacti and my candidate is one which stores little water and yet represents a sort of ultimate in the twin arts of economy and lying low.

Wander down into the driest desert region in northern Sonora, Mexico, and you are likely to find lying about under thorny bushes certain amorphous masses of grayish wood eight inches or more in diameter. They look rather like a gnarled bur from some old apple tree; they have neither roots nor stems, and they seem about as dead as anything could be. Pick one up and you will find it heavy as well as dry, and quite hard—as little like a living plant as anything you can imagine.

This, however, is the resting stage of *Ibervillea sonorae,* a member of the gourd family. Sometimes toward the end of May, it comes to life by sending out a few shoots upward and a few roots downward. It "knows" that Sonora's one season of scanty rainfall is about due and that it must be prepared to take advantage of it. If the rain does come, flowers and fruits appear before the whole thing dries up again into a state of suspended animation which seems almost as complete as that of a seed. At best, *Ibervillea* is not much to look at: a few straggling stems, small yellow flowers and, finally, a small berry-like fruit rather like a small, soft gourd. Moreover, membership in the gourd family is revealed by the structure of the flowers which, as in most gourds and melons, are "monoecious," i.e., separately sexed as male and female though both sorts are borne on the same plant.

Some years ago a specimen of *Ibervillea* was placed on exhibition in a glass case at the New York Botanical Garden. There was no intention to have it grow, but it showed what it is capable of. For seven years, without soil or water, simply lying in the case, it put forth a few anticipatory shoots and then, when no rainy season arrived, dried up again, hoping for better luck next year.

My specimen, transplanted to a situation somewhat like its native one, has put forth its stems at the appropriate time. Just how much it could endure I do not know. I would be less reluctant to find out than I would be to feed my Dipos an abnormal diet, deprive them of water and bake them with heat until they frothed at the mouth, and then note whether those given sea water would survive while those which were denied even that died. But I would be reluctant to push to its limits even a vegetable. It is enough for me to know without experimentation that the vegetable psyche—if there is any such thing—is even more patient, persistent, and enduring than the animal.

1955

II. OTHER LIVES

Has God, thou fool! work'd solely for thy good,
Thy joy, thy pastime, thy attire, thy food? . . .
Is it for thee the lark ascends and sings?
Joy tunes his voice, joy elevates his wings.

ALEXANDER POPE

Man and Beast

Whenever men stop *doing things* long enough to *think about them,* they always ask themselves the question: "What am I?" And since that is the hardest of all questions to answer they usually settle for what looks easier—"If I don't know what I am, then can I tell what I am like?"

To that there are three common answers: "Like a god," "Like an animal," and "Like a machine." Perhaps there is some truth in all, but the most evidently true is the second.

Man does not know how much he is like a god because he does not know what a god is like. He is not as much like a machine as he nowadays tries to persuade himself, because a machine cannot do many of the things he considers of supreme importance. It cannot be conscious; it cannot like, dislike, or desire. And it cannot reproduce its kind.

But man is so much like an animal—which can do all these things—that even the most convinced proponents of the other two answers always admit that he is something like an animal too.

Primitive man acknowledges the likeness by adopting an animal "totem," and by inventing legends which recall a time when the community was closer and more openly manifest. The most otherworldly of theologians regretfully admit that the most precious part of man, his nonanimal soul, inhabits an animal body. The naturalistic nineteenth century concluded that it was from an animal that man himself had "descended."

That he did in fact so descend (or ascend) is almost certainly true whether or not this is the whole truth about him and whether or not the inferences commonly drawn are correct or adequate. If we are going to accept also the now usual assumption that man is *nothing but* an animal, then we ought to be sure that we know what an animal is capable of before we agree to the more cynical conclusions to be drawn from the common belief. The simplest purpose of this book is to suggest by concrete illustrations what being "like an animal" means, and it will stress what might be called the privileges rather than the limitations involved.

Those indignant Victorians to whom the zealous apostles of Darwin expounded their theory of the Descent of Man did not see the matter in this light. Their reaction was not unlike that of a man whose cherished pedigree has been challenged. Did not the Darwinian iconoclasts banish God from his family tree and put an ape in His place? Was not the inevitable consequence to suggest that man's qualities were not those of the noble forefather he had chosen for himself but rather those which might be expected from the base blood now said to flow in his veins?

Though we are inclined to make fun of Victorian fears, they were not entirely unjustified. Psychology, ethics, and philosophy really have tended more and more to interpret man almost exclusively in terms of what the Victorians called his baser or animal nature, and those whose business it is to contemplate or to judge him have been more and more inclined to exclaim "How like a beast" instead of "How like a god." So insistently have they stressed the less attractive aspects of both the human being and the animal that man is often driven either to despair of himself or to a cynical acquiescence in the infamy of nature.

But not everything about the beast is beastly and this large consolation is one of the things the present book offers its readers. To be an animal is to be capable of ingenuity and of joy; of achieving beauty and demonstrating affection. These are surely not small things, though there is danger that we are forgetting how far from small they are. They are godlike attributes whether or not there is anything else godlike in the universe. To be alive at all, even if only as an amoeba is alive, is to be endowed with characteristics possibly unique and certainly exceptional throughout that vast expanse of space which extends for billions of light years beyond us, farther than telescopes—and much farther than thought—can reach.

In an attempt to understand them we shall draw upon both what the biological sciences have learned and, also, upon those direct experiences the sympathetic observer can have. We shall try first of all to look with unprejudiced eyes at specific examples of animal behavior. At the same time we shall also do a little more than that. We shall ask not only what the animal is doing but also how "aware" it seems reasonable to suppose that he is.

Science often objects to any such procedure. It sometimes insists that "behavior" is the only thing we can really know and that we should stop there. If we do not, so it often says, we run the risk of attributing to animals thoughts and feelings they do not have. Sometimes it says even that the safest assumption of all is that they have no thoughts or feelings of any kind, that they are almost, or absolutely, automata. But that assumption is actually no "safer" than the other. We have never entered into an animal's mind and we cannot know what it is like, or even if it exists. The risk of attributing too much is no greater than the risk of attributing too little.

It would, of course, be very reckless to assume that an animal's consciousness is exactly like ours. We do belong to a unique species and probably have both the keenest intelligence and the most vivid emotions (though not the keenest senses) in the whole animal kingdom. But if we really are animals, then the difference is hardly likely to be as great as the difference between sentience and automatism. If our consciousness "evolved," it must have evolved from something in some degree like it. If we have thoughts and feelings, it seems at least probable that something analogous exists in those from whom we are descended.

There are, I think, good reasons for believing that in the simpler animals consciousness is almost inconceivably dim. There is some reason for guessing that in some others, notably the insects, it has grown dimmer than it once was. But there is no good reason for doubting that many of the "higher" animals have some kind of very acute awareness which manifests itself in striking ways.

Probably their emotions are much more like ours than their thoughts can be. A dog certainly smells more keenly than we and perhaps he can be almost as happy or unhappy, as joyous or as fearful. But his intellectual insight is demonstrably not very keen. Perhaps we live in a world that is first of all a world of thoughts; he is in a world of odors, sounds, sights, and emotions. But at least his world, like ours, is a world of consciousness.

1956

The Harmless Necessary Mouse

Mr. James Thurber once complained that in his household they seemed "to have cats the way other people have mice"; but with me it was once the other way around. We had mice the way other people have cats.

In the beginning it was the war and the refugee problem which was responsible. One of the laboratories in Cambridge University had maintained for a long time a family of noble rodents which, like many other noble families, was perfectly ordinary in every respect except the fact that the family tree was a matter of careful record. Students of heredity did not want the line broken if Cambridge should be bombed out or meet other wartime disasters.

Accordingly the heads of the family were shipped over to a geneticist at Columbia University where they proceeded immediately to the chief business of a mouse's life—prompt, immoderate, and continuous reproduction. In a few weeks the descendants had become ancestors and two of the original refugees were presented to me. They were no longer of any Importance to Science because a geneticist, though he sounds very much like a genealogist, is really the opposite. The one is interested only in ancestors and the other only in descendants.

My two were white—albinos, that is—and were supposed both to be females—which indeed they were, though I had momentarily what looked like good reason for doubting the fact. I soon discovered that both, though very tame and charming, were, perhaps just because they represented a well-known family, rather unenterprising. Settled on top of a card table, provided with sleeping quarters and several tunnels constructed of Christmas cards, they were apparently quite content and made no move to climb down.

After they had been settled there for some weeks, I left

them in charge of the maid, while I went away on a visit. A few days later a long-distance telephone call informed me that one had given birth to a litter of nine. Since I was at that time shamefully ignorant, I had to go to an encyclopedia to confirm my guess that the mother had been with me too long already to have been in an interesting condition when I received her. Obviously her companion must be the father. "This," I said to myself, "reveals a nice state of affairs. The Professor of Genetics at Columbia can't tell a male from a female and that is carrying delicacy too far, at least for a scientist." But my indignation was short-lived. Two days later came another long-distance call. The other mouse had just given birth to a numerous litter.

Now, parthenogenesis, or virgin birth, is common enough among certain insects, but it would be almost as surprising in a mouse as it would be in a human being. Even the proudest families which find themselves threatened with extinction cannot do it that way. Some proletarian, living unsuspected in my wainscoting, had obviously exhibited the enterprise which the aristocrats lacked. This humble Romeo had climbed the balcony instead of waiting for his Juliet to come down.

Now, I exclaimed jubilantly, I shall have an opportunity to check up on Mendel for myself. The babies, still pink and naked, gave no clue. But if they had really been fathered as I suspected, then when the fur appeared it would be in every case plain mouse-gray. Albinism is a recessive characteristic and therefore would not appear in any issue of this first cross, though, of course, if inbreeding continued, approximately one-fourth of the second generation would be white, the other three-fourths gray.

Before long it was evident that Mendel and I were both right so far as this first generation was concerned, and, before very much longer, so far as the next was concerned also. Within a year I knew mice very well indeed, not only scientifically but personally. We were having mice the way other people have kittens. And very much like kittens they are, too, except that one has them even more frequently and more abundantly than kittens can be supplied by the most assiduous mother cat.

The unauthorized love match between the aristocratic lady and the man of the people turned out fine. The succeeding generations inherited the tameness and gentleness of the mother with the enterprise of the father. Soon a sort of family village had to be founded—a large, screened cage two stories high with separate boxes for the families set up by the grandchildren, a community dining hall, and a community playground, complete with a miniature version of the old-fashioned squirrel wheel in which young and old delighted to ride. Mice are among the most playful of all creatures and they devised endless games in the wheel—sometimes a tug-of-war in which contending parties tried to turn it in opposite directions, sometimes a cooperative enterprise with one clinging to the wire while the other rode him round and round. When the apparatus was full, would-be riders often queued up to wait their turn.

Besides being extraordinarily playful, mice are also extraordinarily devoted parents. Fathers will curl up with the babies when the mother leaves them for a few minutes; other females will do the same if they happen to have no babies of their own at the moment, and in fact are not always able to resist the temptation to kidnap the young, whom they take to their own nest. When it seems for any reason desirable to move a family, the mouslings are carried by the skin of the neck exactly as a cat carries kittens, though I once saw a baby, grown too large to be transported that way, led firmly back into the nest by the ear when his mother disagreed with him in thinking that he was not yet old enough to be allowed out. Mice are also fanatically clean, washing themselves and their young with exactly the same gestures a cat uses.

The sign that a new family is about to be born is a sudden frenzy of activity on the part of the mother who begins frantically to tear paper into bits and to carry it, piece by piece, into the nest, where it is arranged into a ball with a small hole open in the side. Tame as my mice were, they wanted privacy at this moment, and if I tried to peer in at the opening, the mother would seize a bit of paper and deftly close the hole in my face with all the decisiveness of a ticket-seller in a French railway station when, suiting the action to the word, he announces joyously: *"Le guichet est fermé,"* and goes out to lunch.

1953

Don't Expect too Much
from a Frog

Whenever I feel that I would like to see a frog—and you would be surprised how often that is—I have only to open the door of my living room and take two or three steps to a small pool in the shade of a large spiraea.

Before the fox got my two pet ducks that wintry day a few years ago this pool was theirs. For a full decade they swam gravely about on its six-by-ten-foot surface, blissfully happy and apparently unaware that water ever comes in larger pieces. They also chased one another with dizzy playfulness around and around its narrow circumference, stood on their heads to search for the worms they never found on its concrete bottom, and splashed madly at least once a day for the shower baths they love. From those ducks in their time I got many lessons in gladness and much moral instruction: A little world, I learned, is as big as one thinks and makes it. To be a big duck in a small pond is not necessarily ignoble. One can have Lake Michigan in one's back yard if one wants to. Water is much the same everywhere. It is better to use what one has than to regret what one has not. Where ignorance is bliss . . . If we are unhappy it is less often because of something we lack than because we do not know how to use what we have. Ducks want but little here below.

When, after a long and happy life—one had become a mother for the first time at the age of twelve years—these ducks at last fed the fox, I decided to keep frogs. I refurbished the pool which had leaked and gone dry, and because I am, I fear, a man of too little faith even in nature, I planned vaguely to collect from some pond specimens which might be persuaded to settle down with me.

I should have known better. Two days after my pool had

been filled the first frog had discovered it and taken up permanent residence. Within a week there was at least one individual of the four usual species of this region: the two spotted kinds, Palustris and Pipiens, which most people don't bother to tell apart; Clamitans, the robust fellow with the green neck and head; and Catesbiana, the huge basso profundo who alone has a right to the name "bullfrog." Sometimes these frogs now hide in the herbage or under a stone. Nearly always, however, at least one or two sit on the rough, slab-topped rim of the pool—motionless, unblinking, sublimely confident that sooner or later, but always quite safely in time, some insect will pass by to be snatched up with a lightning tongue. Its unerring, flashing speed is proof enough that the frogs are not unaware of the external world as they sit, seemingly absorbed in meditation, hour after hour. Yet for all that, they are as exempt as the lily from the curse of Adam. They do not work for a living. They do not hunt for food. They do not even sing for their supper. They merely wait for it to pass by and sing afterward.

As the summer rolls along I hope that I may learn something from them as I did from their feathered predecessors. But whatever they may have to teach me will not be as easy to translate into human terms as the lesson of the ducks. Because these last were warm-blooded they were much closer to me in situation and philosophy. Gladness and pain were for us recognizably the same things. They could set me a real example when they rejoiced so unmistakably in the little pool which had to serve them in lieu of a lake. But the frogs are antediluvian. Like me, they are, to be sure, alive, and their protoplasm is much like mine. But they seem strangely cold-blooded in a figurative as well as a literal sense. No doubt they feel the difference between well-being and its reverse; their satisfactions may be, for all I know, as deep or deeper than mine. But their monumental placidity is something which I can hardly hope to achieve.

That is one of the reasons why I like to have them about, why I am so acutely aware of the strangeness of having almost at my doorstep these creatures who can demonstrate what to be alive must have meant millions of years ago when the Amphibia were the most progressive, the most adventurous, one is almost tempted to say the most warm-blooded and passionate, of living creatures.

I need do no more than notice the grasshopper just fallen into the pool to realize that, comparatively speaking, the frogs are more like me than I had supposed. At least neither their anatomy nor their ways are as remote from mine as are those of the insects whose tastes and habits sometimes shocked even Henri Fabre with their monstrousness. So far as remoteness of soul is concerned there is at least as much difference between the grasshopper and the frog as between the frog and the duck; perhaps indeed more than between the duck and me. The frog got to be what he is by moving in the direction which was to end—for the time being at least—in me. Even though land insects were newcomers when the frogs were already a well-established family they took long ago the direction which was to carry their descendants further and further away from the rest of us; further and further from the frog, the duck, and the man. When I realize that, I feel that Catesbiana and I are not so different, as differences go in this world, as I had thought.

At least one thing which I already knew the frogs have by now taught several visitors who consented to inspect them. Part-time countrymen though all these visitors were, several saw for the first time that the frog, like the toad, is not "ugly and venomous," but "interesting looking." And this I know is halfway to the truth that they are beautiful in their own fashion and ask only that we enlarge our conception of beauty to include one more of nature's many kinds. They are as triumphantly *what* they are as man has ever succeeded in being, and no human imagination could devise a new creature so completely "right" according to the laws of his own structure and being. They are the perfect embodiment of frogginess both outwardly and inwardly, so that nearly every individual achieves, as very few human beings do, what the Greeks would have called his entelechy—the complete realization of the possibilities which he suggests. Frogs are not shadows of an ideal but the ideal itself. There is scarcely one who is not either a froggy Belvedere or a froggy de Milo. To realize this one need only go to frogs as so many critics have told us we should go to works of art, asking first, "What is the intention?" and then, "How well has this intention been achieved?"

I do not know what human being was the first to say that reptiles are not "vile" and toads not "loathsome." I do know that these clichés lingered even in the literature of natural history almost down to our own time and that perhaps most people still pick their way foppishly about the world, rather proud of the distaste aroused by almost everything which shares the world with them and apparently convinced that nearly everything except themselves was a mistake on the part of the Creator. Even Linnaeus expressed a distaste for the Amphibia and the reptiles. Even Gilbert White, who certainly knew better and felt better, absent-mindedly falls into the literary convention of his day and once refers to the ancient tortoise in his garden as a "vile reptile." Most moderns are still far from catching up with Sir Thomas Browne who, three hundred years ago, wrote into his *Religio Medici* something for which I am very grateful: "I cannot tell by what logic we call a toad, a bear or an elephant ugly; they being created in those outward shapes and figures which best express the actions of their inward forms. . . . To speak yet more narrowly, there was never anything ugly or misshapen, but Chaos. . . . All things are artificial; for Nature is the Art of God."

One of my lady visitors after looking for a while at Catesbiana expressed the opinion that he was "cute," and I restrained myself because I recognized that she meant well, that this was even, for her, the first faint beginning of wisdom. I did not ask as I was about to ask if the prehistoric saurians were "cute," if the stretches of geologic time are "nice," and if the forests of the carboniferous age are "sweet." As my frog gazed at both of us with eyes which had seen the first mammalian dawn, lived through thousands of millennia before the first lowly primate appeared and so saw more of the world than all mankind put together, I asked him to forgive the impertinence of this latecomer. The Orientals say that God made the cat in order that man might have the pleasure of petting a tiger. By that logic He must have made frogs so that we can commune with prehistory.

During the two centuries just past more has been written about the attitude of man toward the animals than in the two millennia before. Very little has been said even yet about their attitude toward us, and I sometimes wonder if that is not a coming topic just as its converse was beginning to be when Alexander Pope wrote his *Essay on Man*—which is, as a matter of fact, almost as much about man's fellow creatures as it is about himself. At least until dogs and cats begin to write books there is bound to be a rather large element of speculation in any treatment of the subject, but we can imagine what some of the domestic animals might say, as Miss Sylvia Townsend Warner did when she made one disillusioned canine say to another: "The more I see of dogs the better I like people." That, I am afraid, is a bit anthropomorphic and so perhaps are the implications of my own frequent wish that I could hear the comments of, say, some wise, tolerant collie on the conclusions concerning human nature to be drawn from the juxtaposition of the statement that "the dog is man's best friend" with the familiar exclamation, "I wouldn't treat a dog that way."

It is not, however, in the spirit of either frivolity or cynicism that I wonder what my frogs think of me. They think something because they show some awareness of my existence and the nature of that awareness, like the nature of the other relations between us, shows again how much more remote they are than the ducks, how much less remote than certain other creatures who are, nevertheless, in some sense alive. It is hard to believe that the insects are aware that we exist at all except as an impersonal force. In some part that may be because, with one exception, they cannot turn their heads over their shoulders to look at us. The exception is the praying mantis and when he cocks his improbable head over his improbable shoulder, I have to remind myself that he is one of the most primitive insects and not, as this gesture might suggest, the most like one of us. But I doubt that he, or a grasshopper, or even a bee, takes me in as, in some realer sense, the frog quite obviously does when he considers whether or not he had better leap into the water at my approach and comes to do so less and less readily as he gets to know me better. The difference between his awareness and that of a cat or dog who can understand even some of our words is immense, but perhaps no more so than the difference between that of the frog and the apparently utter obliviousness of the insect who is shut off not merely because he is less intelligent but also because such intelligence as he has is so utterly different from ours. His standards of value, if I may put it that way, are too irreconcilable with mine, with the cat's and with the frog's.

On a terrarium by my window is a huge ten-inch salamander from Florida with whom I have had some relation for eight or nine years. At least when he is hungry he looks up if I happen to pass by and he will waddle toward me if I offer a worm. Already my bullfrog will take beef from the end of a string when I offer it, but he has given no sign that he connects me with the bounty, and if he comes at last to do so, I shall still not know whether it is more than a quasi-mechanical association of a sequence of events. My old housekeeper repeatedly assures me that the salamander "knows her," and though I think that this is probably a pretty large overinterpretation, I am not convinced that the animal mind is as nearly a mere set of reflexes as the behaviorists confidently assert.

I admit that in eight or nine years this salamander and I have got into no very intimate, two-sided relationship, and this makes me wonder how much the budding acquaintance between the frog and me will come to. On his side, I imagine, it will not come to very much; I will not mean much in his consciousness. He is nearer to me than a grasshopper would be but nearer only as the sun is nearer than Betelgeuse or Betelgeuse is nearer than the closest of the extragalactic nebulae. The distance is still vast as we measure things. We can look at one another as the insect and I probably cannot, but we look across a gap as wide as that which separates the frog's origin in impossibly remote time from mine only a few thousand years ago. Perhaps some physicist who likes to think of time in terms of arrows which may point in one direction while other time-arrows point in the opposite would say that the gap across which we look actually is a temporal one. I am looking back at him and he is looking forward toward me —across the interval which separates the ancient time when he was the latest model from this present time when I am.

Perhaps I am already beginning to be an unimportant part of his dim consciousness. But whatever intercourse may ultimately develop between us will be marked by considerable reserve on his part, and he will never want to climb into my lap as a certain goose used to do. A calm sort of mutual respect is the most I look forward to. Of one thing, however, I am sure from experience: whatever relationship we do achieve will be on the basis of reciprocal tolerance and good manners. The lower animals seldom bicker and at most usually suggest only that we should leave them alone. They may fight for self-protection if one insists, but they would prefer only to agree to differ. When my frog gets enough of my company he will show me a fine pair of hind legs, but he will hurl no insults and make no cutting remarks. He will say only, "I should prefer to be alone."

Perhaps this is partly because he can make a cleaner getaway than people can when someone bores them, but I have noticed also and in general that only the higher animals can be bad tempered. I have seen a seal deliberately squirt a stream of water into a spectator's face—in fact the New York Aquarium had, many years ago, a notorious member of that species who did this regularly to the great delight of those waiting spectators who were in the know. But that was only rough humor and I have never been deliberately insulted by any creature lower than a chimpanzee. That was when I set one such an example of bad manners by deliberately trying to stare him down as he looked from behind his bars. Presently, he turned his back to me with great deliberation, lowered his head until he was peering out from behind his buttocks, and then pursed his lips to give me what is commonly know as a Bronx Cheer, though the present use of it seemed to suggest that it had been invented long before the borough was founded. I have never seen any other subhuman primate do anything which seemed so completely human, and I never at any moment in my life had a more lively conviction that we and the anthropoids really do come of a common stock. My intercourse with the frogs will never be marked by any incidents like that. Indeed it will probably seldom provide what could be called an incident at all. But that is the price one must pay for escaping also the possibility of anything approaching a disturbing clash. His sang-froid is what the words mean literally: cold blood. My blood is too warm not to want, often, a more lively if more dangerous intercourse— with ducks, with cats, and even with creatures as exasperating as the members of my own species frequently are.

Much the same sort of thing I am compelled to admit in connection with the frog's vocal comments. The four species gathered around my pool—which of course they legitimately think of as theirs—are respectively soprano, tenor, contralto, and bass. But what they croak at their various pitches is the same thing, even though it sounds weightiest when Catesbiana gives it utterance. The whole philosophy of frogs, all the wisdom they have accumulated in millions of years of experience, is expressed in that *urrrr-unk* uttered with an air which seems to suggest that the speaker feels it to be completely adequate. The comment does not seem very passionate or very aspiring, but it is contented and not cynical. Frogs have considered life and found it, if not exactly ecstatic, at least quite pleasant and satisfactory. Buddha is said to have made a comment much like theirs after all those years of contemplating his navel, and though I do not wholly understand it I think I catch the drift.

It is not, I realize, quite enough for me whether it comes from the pond-side or from the Mysterious East. I cannot live by it all the time. Not infrequently I find myself responding instead to the more passionate observations of Shakespeare or Mozart. But in that eclecticism which serves me as a philosophy of life it has its place. It is basic and a last resort. I like to hear it preached from time to time and to think that it is something one might at least fall back upon.

1953

How Intelligent Are the Animals?

Let us first consider the fact that animals are judged by their ability to solve puzzles of the special sort man has found himself good at, and that, in a word, the very definition of intelligence is one which man has devised to favor himself. If the beaver (a stupid animal, so they say), the lynx, or, for that matter, the dog or the cat, were to set the definitions and make the tests, it might well turn out that man showed up pretty badly when attempting the things which the dog or the cat could do well. How good are you at following a rabbit's scent or finding your way home when lost? How sure are you that the ability to do those things has less to do with the abstraction called intelligence than the ability to thread an artificial maze?

Suppose that the mathematicians in our society somehow got the prestige and authority which would entitle them to maintain that the ability to solve mathematical problems was the real test of intelligence, or of whatever you want to call "the highest manifestations of the mind?" Suppose that you were then summoned before one of the mathematicians, promised a sugar plum or at least a pat on the head whenever you did well, and then presented with a series of problems beginning, let us say, with a pair of simultaneous quadratics and ending with a rather tough differential equation. Suppose on the basis of your possibly poor showing you were classified as quite appallingly stupid, and suppose the mathematical master went on to conclude, not merely that you were not in any way intelligent, but also that, for this reason, you were obviously little capable of deep feeling and that only "sentimentalists" would consider it very important whether or not you were given much consideration in the management of the society.

Under such circumstances you would certainly protest that

whatever the importance or beauty of mathematical reasoning might be, some of your best, dearest, most interesting, and most charming friends were so far from being able to solve a differential equation that they would probably find it impossible to understand what one is. You would further protest that the power to solve problems of this sort, like a talent for chess, is so far from being a reliable guide to intelligence of other kinds that one might well be intimately acquainted with an individual without having the slightest reason for supposing that he either was or was not gifted with the special kind of insight which enables some people to see at once just where it is worth while to pull at a tangled knot or a differential equation. To apply analogous tests and to draw from them the conclusions which have sometimes been drawn calls to mind a statement made by the late Will Cuppy: "Frogs will eat red-flannel worms fed to them by biologists. This proves a great deal about both parties concerned."

One thing seems certain. The animals may exhibit little intelligence and all of them, except the apes, may be incapable of logical processes. Their lives may be, if you want to put it this way, radically thoughtless. But there is nothing they are less like than a mentally defective person. Hebephrenia, that all pervasive, dull sluggishness which characterizes human unfortunates deficient in normal powers, is the exact opposite of the mental state they seem to exhibit. Many of them are vivacious as no man ever is. Watching them at work or play, one often feels that they are more vividly alive than we ever are.

Notoriously, their senses are alert to a degree hard for us to imagine, and such sensual alertness seems to imply some correspondingly tingling awareness. Common sense long ago rejected Descartes' monstrous and gratuitous insistence that an animal, being a machine without a soul, could not possibly, even when screaming in agony, be feeling anything at all. But unless one is prepared to accept that thesis, it is difficult to see how one can deny that the dog, apparently beside himself at the prospect of a walk with his master, is experiencing a joy the intensity of which it is beyond our power to imagine, much less to share. In the same way his dejection can at least appear to be no less bottomless. Perhaps the kind of thought of which we are capable dims both our sensual and our emotional lives at the same time that it makes us less victims of either. Was any man, one wonders, ever as dejected as a lost dog? Perhaps certain of the animals can be both more joyful and more utterly desolate than any man ever was.

"We look before and after and pine for what is not." That fact was thus phrased in order to claim for us the privilege of a uniquely agonizing unhappiness. But is the claim really justified, does the knowledge that a past was and that a future will be add to or detract from the importance of the moment? Is sorrow's crown of sorrows the remembrance of happier things or could it be rather the inability to remember that happiness ever was or could be? The animal's woe—no less truly, perhaps, the animal's happiness—is unqualified by either memory or anticipation. It is a fact which fills for him the whole universe. He knows nothing of the consolations of either religion or philosophy. He cannot even say, "This also will pass." Every moment is his eternity because he cannot know that it will not last forever. If, therefore, his joy is without shadow, perhaps his being in misery is without alleviation. And that, so some might say, is what hell would be like. What other creature has ever been so miserable as an animal who has never known anything except want and abuse, and who cannot know that such a thing as kindness or even comfort exists in the universe?

For a long time now one of the most popular magazines has been publishing a continuing series of anecdotes illustrating the intelligence and wisdom of animals, both wild and domestic. These anecdotes are contributed by readers; there is no evidence that any check is made upon either the competence or even the veracity of the observers, and a good many of the tales are tall indeed. The only thing, I am afraid, that they really prove is simply that even in this rather too scientific age a great many people want very much to believe what their primitive ancestors took for granted—namely, that the consciousness of the beast is not essentially different from our own.

This it seems to me is at least an amiable weakness and reveals a kind of generosity of spirit very different from the arrogance of most laboratory scientists, who seem bent on demonstrating their own high endowments by demonstrating the absence of these endowments in all creatures except themselves. And it is odd that the two tendencies should coexist, with the laboratory scientist often defeating his own purpose by the grotesque inappropriateness of his experiments, while a great public eagerly accepts on the scantiest of evidence what sometimes sounds like a mere modernized excerpt from one of the once popular beast epics. Perhaps there is no connection between the two phenomena, but it would be pleasant to believe that the second is a reaction against the solemn absurdity of some of the mental testers who have posed the most preposterous problems and come up with the most preposterous conclusions. To answer nonsense of one kind with nonsense of an opposite sort seems frequently to have been the best the human race could do in the way of redressing a balance.

1953

The Civilized Animal

"There are many arguments, none of them very good, for having a snake in the house." So Mr. Will Cuppy once wrote, though he was gracious (or is it cynical?) enough to add: "Considering what some do pet, I don't see why they should draw the line at snakes."

Nevertheless one of my friends and neighbors has kept reptiles since he was seven years old and at this moment he has in his house a whole roomful, including some of the largest and most venomous of our native species. I have seen him stopped suddenly during a casual evening walk in the desert by a faint whir, seen him drop to the ground with a flashlight and then rise after a few seconds with a three-foot rattler held firmly and triumphantly just behind the head.

But it is some of his other pets—not of the sort to which Mr. Cuppy rather seems to be alluding—which concern me at the moment. The doorknob on his snake room is placed too high to be reached by his three children, of whom the eldest is now five, but he has reared free in the house two Arizona wildcats which, until they got too big, the children lugged about as though they were unusually phlegmatic tabbies.

Despite the dire phophecies of neighbors, nothing untoward happened to the children; and as for the cats, they went the way of many a domestic Tom. They took to staying out all night; then to staying away for several days at a time; and finally they did not come home at all. The last time my friend saw one of them he was up a telephone pole about a mile from the house and the other came out of the brush to the call, "Puss, puss."

Their current successor is an eleven-pound, five-month-old male of the same species who is even more completely a member of the family. He is housebroken and most of his behavior is precisely that of a domestic cat. He is very playful and, like many house cats, he walks about the edge of the bathtub while the children are being bathed, apparently fascinated by the human being's strange lack of distaste for water. When he makes a playful leap from five feet away to land on your chest or lap, the impact is considerable; but in many ways he is gentler than a kitten, or, perhaps one should say, seems more aware that his teeth and claws are potentially dangerous. Unlike most kittens, he makes "velvet paws" the inviolable rule and when he kicks with his hind legs in response to being tickled on the belly he keeps the murderous claws of his hind feet carefully sheathed—as a house cat usually does not.

I am not suggesting that always and for everybody a wildcat is a safer pet than *Felis domestica*. It may very well be that the adults are undependable; that they may, as is often said, be capable of sudden flashes of savagery; or that at the best they are likely to have an inadequate idea of their strength and weight. But to play with so gentle a specimen of what is commonly thought one of the wildest of wild animals is to wonder just how much justification there is for loose talk about "natural ferocity."

What is the "true nature" of this beast? Or is the question as badly phrased as it is when you ask about the "true nature of man"? In both cases the only proper answer may be that both are capable of many different things and that to judge the potentialities of the wildcat by what he is like when truly wild is as misleading as it would be to judge the potentialities of man by studying only the behavior of an Australian bushman.

I have never agreed with those enthusiasts who maintain that a man is "nothing but" what his social environment has made him. But I most certainly do believe that such environment has a good deal to do with his behavior. And though the extent to which the same thing is true of animals is considerably less, the fact remains that you can't know what an animal is really like unless you have known him as different environments have influenced him.

Some scientists are very loath to accept any observations that pet owners have to offer. Not without justification they distrust in fond parents that overinterpretation which is almost as inevitable in the case of a beloved animal as it is in the case of a child. Either is always given the benefit of the doubt. Happy accidents are assumed to be the result of intelligent foresight and the dog lover is often as sure that he can understand the precise semantic significance of a bark as the fond parent of a first child is sure that "aaaa" means "I love Mama."

Despite all this it is still true that the honest observation of well-treated pets can provide data as scientifically valid as any other. What a wild animal is like in the wild can be learned only by observing him in that state; but what you learn is relevant to that state only. In a different environment he becomes something else as surely as a man, moved from one environment to another, changes somewhat as a result of the change.

For the study of anything other than the most mechanically invariable behavior patterns, a pet is certainly a far better subject than a mere laboratory animal. If the pet is, as is sometimes objected, "under artificial conditions," at least these conditions are no more artificial than those of the laboratory and are more likely than the laboratory to expand rather than to freeze latent potentialities. In some ways a pet is more than a wild animal; in a laboratory, any creature is less—as anyone who has ever looked at such a captive with a seeing eye could not have failed to observe. In their loveless imprisonment the more intelligent seem to question and to brood over their Kafka-esque doom. It has imprisoned them for a crime of which they are unaware and prepared for them some future they cannot imagine.

Many of even the animals not commonly made pets respond gladly to the kindlier conditions life with human beings provides. Even in zoos—which are at best little better than model prisons—they develop an awareness of and an interest in people of which we would never suppose them capable if we knew them only in the wild. And it is not by any means merely an interest in the food which human beings sometimes provide. Monkeys are notorious exhibitionists and gibbons, especially, will put on performances at intervals after a preliminary ballyhoo of howls to collect an audience. Less spectacular performances by simpler animals are even more interesting—as, for instance, that regularly indulged in by a group of small ground squirrels in an animal collection with which I happen to be familiar.

These creatures were born in the very glass case where they now live. While still babies they learned to climb up one side of the case, hang momentarily from the roof, and then drop from it to the floor. As time went on they made less and less contact with side or roof until presently they were turning back somersaults with only a kick against the roof at the height of the circle. This performance attracted much attention from the spectators. Now, one need only take up a position in front of the case to have one or more of the squirrels assume his stance and make several rapid flip-overs. Would one ever have suspected from observing these creatures in the wild that they were capable of enjoying the admiration of human beings? Does vainglory find a place in such tiny bosoms? For how many millions of years has the desire to show off existed?

The most objective observer—if he does actually observe —cannot help being struck by the change that comes over an animal who has been really accepted as a companion. Not only cats and dogs but much less likely animals seem to undergo a transformation analogous to that of human beings who are introduced to a more intellectual, more cultivated, more polished society than that in which they grew up.

It is not merely that they adapt themselves to new ways. Their very minds seem to develop and they become more aware of other creatures, including man, as members of a society, not merely as potentially dangerous or useful objects. The human voice, especially, seems to fascinate and delight them. Except, just possibly, for monkeys and dogs, it is doubtful that they ever understand a word as such. The symbolic nature of language seems to be beyond them. But the emotion with which words are spoken communicates directly, and they seem capable of distinguishing many shades of it.

Beyond question it is true at least that they like to be talked to and that talking to them is very important if they are to be drawn into close association with human beings. As I know from experience, this fact is particularly if somewhat unexpectedly conspicuous in the case of geese, though it is much less so in that of ducks. A goose, like a dog, gets a different expression about the eyes if he is accustomed to having some human being speak to him. Thoreau describes the hen wandering about the kitchen of an Irishman's shanty as "looking too humanized to roast well." "Humanized" is precisely the word, and it is astounding to what extent many animals can become, in that sense, humanized.

There are, of course, limits beyond which no animal can go and there is a great difference between what different species are capable of. The difference between the very slight extent to which my salamander was humanized and what a really intelligent ape is capable of is enormous. But in every case—and that is true of man also—there are limits. To each, nature seems to say: Thus far shalt thou go and no farther. But we never know just how far a man or a beast can go until he has been given a chance. In neither case do the underprivileged furnish a fair answer.

How true this is is well illustrated in the two recent books *King Solomon's Ring* and *Man Meets Dog* by the distinguished Austrian observer Konrad Lorenz. His orthodox training as a scientist warns him against those pitfalls of overinterpretation and anthropomorphism which behaviorists are so eager to expose. But instead of taking for granted that animal behavior is always explicable in either mechanistic or anthropomorphic terms, he tries to discriminate and to recognize the genuine difference between behavior which is merely mechanically conditioned and that which seems to suggest in the animal rudimentary powers analogous to the human.

Not a man to fear the ridicule of neighbors, he has been observed quacking encouragingly as he crawled through tall grass followed by a line of baby ducks who seemed to take him for their mother. In this instance he was demonstrating not that the ducklings have any evident awareness of the situation, but that they are the victims of what seems to be a merely mechanical conditioning. Like some other animals they are born with a mechanism which is ready to click when they open their eyes. The first moving object they see becomes the thing they are determined to follow. If that first moving object is a man, they will follow him in preference to the mother duck whom they may have seen a few moments later. If, on the other hand, they see her first, it has already become very difficult if not impossible to teach them to follow anything else. This does not mean that all newly born animals have this curious mechanism. Many which have not do nevertheless also operate like a machine, though like a machine differently set up. To account for their behavior or for that of the baby duck it is not necessary to assume any psychic process distinguishable from the mere mechanism of the conditioned reflex.

But Mr. Lorenz does not stop there. He has lived intimately with mature specimens of much more intelligent fowl —especially the highly intelligent raven. Though some of its behavior may be as mechanical as that of the duckling, other actions seem less obviously so. Still others, especially those relating to its intimate association with man and its development of personality, seem to suggest not mechanism but a genuine psychic activity. And it is this which has led Lorenz to invent the new word he uses to describe errors of interpretation which are the opposite of those against which we have so often been warned. "Mechanomorphism," or the stubborn determination to see everything in terms of the machine, may be a fallacy as serious as anthropomorphism.

There are, to be sure, some psychologists who still insist that neither man nor any other animal ever exhibits any behavior not either instinctive or conditioned. To them the final triumph of what they continue to call by the Greek word meaning "the science of the soul" is to have demonstrated that nothing remotely resembling a soul, not even reason or the power of choice, really exists at all. But unless one accepts this thesis the most interesting as well as the least understood branch of psychology is that which does attempt to investigate those actions and those mental states which cannot be shown to be the result of mechanically operating laws.

What makes such studies as those pursued by Lorenz so exceptionally impressive is the fact that he not only recognizes the existence of such phenomena in animals as well as man but also the fact that association with human beings seems to liberate in animals their psychic freedom very much as, so it seems, civilization liberates them in man. Perhaps the chief difference between human and animal psychology, as between the psychology of the lower and the higher animals also, is simply that in both cases what "higher" really means is "exhibiting a more extended range of phenomena which cannot be accounted for in terms of mere 'conditioning.' "

Even more striking in certain respects are two recent English books, Len Howard's *Birds As Individuals,* which describes the surprising and often highly individual behavior of wild birds (especially titmice) who had been left their liberty but invited into the house, and *Sold for a Farthing* by Clare Kipps, which recounts the life story of a tame sparrow. Both these observers are amateurs, but Julian Huxley has vouched for both so far as their reports on the actual behavior of their companions is concerned, and he is ready to grant that they seem to have demonstrated that birds are capable of what might be called "social adjustment" to a degree not hitherto suspected.

What seems to have surprised both Huxley and other commentators even more than the adaptability and apparent intelligence of creatures generally assumed to be less intelligent than many mammals is the extent to which the birds also exhibited individual variation and differences of temperament; the extent, in other words, to which members of the same species seemed to develop what we might as well call "an individual personality." Thus the experience of Miss Howard and Miss Kipps seemed to contradict not only laboratory experiments but also what has been observed of birds in freedom because both suggest that bird behavior is nearly always typical; that individuality hardly exists.

The distinguished American ornithologist Roger Tory Peterson has this to say:

> The point that Miss Howard emphasizes . . . is that birds are *individuals.* Their actions often seem to demonstrate some sort of bird intelligence and do not always fall into the oversimplified mechanical patterns which some of us have come to accept. . . . As Dr. Niko Tinbergen, the great behaviorist of Oxford University, comments in *Ibis,* "Miss Howard describes most amazing things, and critical zoologists and psychologists, if not familiar with the ways of birds in the wild, may tend to armchair incredulity. . . . I have no such doubts, however." No other bird book in years has been the subject of so much discussion in England as has Miss Howard's. Some critics may feel that she occasionally resorts to anthropomorphic expressions. . . . Others may differ with her interpretations, but these should in no way be confounded with her facts. Her observations are very careful and

her descriptions sensitive and honest. It is a most unusual story she has to tell.

Should we dismiss the new evidence or should we say that the professional observers of wild birds have been wrong?

What puzzled commentators seem to have overlooked is a third possibility. Perhaps Miss Howard's birds not only seemed to have more individuality than wild ones but actually did have it. And perhaps they had it simply because they had moved into a social situation where individuality was recognized and given an opportunity to develop. In Bernard Shaw's *Pygmalion* the flower girl who is taught how to pass herself off as a member of sophisticated society announces an important discovery which she has made, namely, that it is not the way you behave but *the way you are treated* which makes the difference between those who are "ladies" and those who are not. Is there any reason why the same should not be, to a lesser extent, true of birds? To reconcile observations made upon any wild animal in a wild environment with those on the same animal after it has become accustomed to treatment as a pet it is not necessary to assume that the original observations were in any way defective or incomplete. Perhaps the seeming conflict merely reveals the fact that animals have a potential capacity for both a degree of individuality and a comprehension of a situation which the circumstances of wild life do not provide an opportunity to develop.

Many modern theorists seem to me to overemphasize a good deal the extent to which men are what "nurture" rather than "nature" makes them. But perhaps in the case of animals we have rather underemphasized it. What it may all come down to is simply that animals, like men, are capable of being *civilized* and that a civilized man or a civilized animal reveals capacities and traits which one would never have suspected in the savage.

We are no longer as surprised as our grandfathers were that an African native who has gone to Oxford can become so typically an Oxford man. Neither by studying an African savage in his native state nor by taking him into a laboratory would we ever be led to suspect the potentialities which can make him an Oxford man. Why then should we find it hard to believe that an analogous change may occur when a wild animal is given an analogous opportunity?

A few years ago I had arranged to spend the night at one of the remote Hopi villages in the house of a young woman educated to be a teacher in a distant Indian school but accustomed to spend her vacations in her native town. When I insisted that for dinner I wanted only that stand-by of travelers not quite sure of a cuisine, namely ham and eggs, she protested: "After all, that is two proteins."

In my instinctive arrogance I had to restrain an impulse to say, "Look here, no Hopi is going to prescribe my diet." But the situation was actually a very minor and superficial example of the phenomena which have compelled us to revise our whole conception of the nature of the difference between civilized and "primitive" minds. So far as difference in mental capacity is concerned it is now generally agreed that there is none—or that the primitives are if anything somewhat our superiors.

If you trust mental tests they seem to demonstrate that the average I.Q. of the Hopi Indian children is higher than that of the white. Most anthropologists seem to agree that there is absolutely no evidence that the human mind, as such, has improved at all during the last five hundred thousand years. All that civilization has done is to elicit potentialities. Hence there is no reason why a savage, taken into a sophisticated environment, should not become, as he sometimes does, either very highly civilized or, for that matter, an aesthete and a decadent. Is there, then, any reason for doubting that Miss Howard's birds had become what no one who had observed them only in the wild would have supposed them capable of becoming?

That animals are less plastic than human beings is obvious, and so is the fact that the ultimate development they can reach in the direction of individuality is, absolutely, much more restricted. But their plasticity seems sufficient to make a civilized bird very different from a wild one. And that, of course, is the most striking aspect of the vertebrates' superiority over the superficially more advanced insect. The one has potentialities. The other is fixed and finished. Therefore we might put it this way: some of the limitations of the wild animal are, like those of the savage, merely cultural rather than inherent. Those of the insects are not.

Science recognizes as valid and important the distinction between wild animals and "domesticated" animals. The only other category which it admits, even parenthetically, is that which it labels "pets" and which it dismisses as hardly worthy of scientific consideration. What I am suggesting in all seriousness is that full recognition should be given to that other category which I call "civilized."

The pet may or may not fall within it, depending upon how it is treated. Many show animals, no matter how pampered they may be, are certainly not civilized and indeed hardly deserve even the name of pets. Many a mongrel dog or cat, as well as many another creature of some species only occasionally adopted into human companionship, is much more than a mere pet simply because it is treated with understanding and with love; because it is accepted, if not exactly as an equal, at least with some understanding of the fact that it is capable of responding to a kind of attention and consideration which many kindly people never think of according to even a cherished pet.

The merely domesticated animal, in contrast, is not only something less than a civilized one but something radically different. It has ceased to live the life of nature without being given the opportunity to live any other. Its instincts have faded and its alert senses have sunk into somnolence. Much has been taken away and nothing has been given in return. Such a merely domesticated animal has become a sort of parasite without even developing those special adaptations that make the true parasite interesting in some repulsive way. It is merely parasitic by habit, not by constitution, and of all the animals it is the least rewarding to study because there is almost nothing which can be learned about it. The human analogue is the degenerate remnant of some primitive race which lives upon the fringe of a somewhat more advanced society but has become incapable of leading its own life without having learned any other. Natural history should, on the other hand, no more neglect the civilized animal than anthropology should neglect the civilized man. Without some consideration of both we cannot possibly know what either man or any other animal is capable of.

One of the most important, one of the most fateful developments of thought during the last few centuries has been that which stresses the closer and closer identity of human with animal nature. And that has meant, on the whole, not a greater respect for animal traits and powers and potentialities, but less and less respect for man's. Those potentialities which had once been assumed to be exclusively human now came to be regarded as less and less substantially real. Man was thought of as "nothing but" an animal and the animal was held to be incapable of exhibiting anything except what had formerly been thought of as "our lower nature."

If we are ever to regain a respect for ourselves it may be that we shall regain it by the discovery that the animals themselves exhibit, in rudimentary form, some of the very characteristics and capacities whose existence in ourselves we had come to doubt because we had convinced ourselves that they did not exist in the creatures we assumed to be our ancestors. Even if man is no more than an animal, the animal may be more than we once thought him.

No doubt there are those to whom the concept of the "civilized" animal will seem fantastic and the suggestion that man may regain his self-respect by learning to understand better his animal ancestors even more absurd. To call an animal civilized rather than merely domesticated is, so they will say, to imply that he is to some extent capable of sharing in what are purely human prerogatives. But such an objection is most likely to be raised by the more dogmatic evolutionists, who are, as a matter of fact, those who have the least right to assume a qualitative rather than a merely quantitative difference between the inherent capacities of man and the other animals.

Either man is unique or he isn't. If he is unique, then he cannot possibly descend through an unbroken line from the lower animals. If he does descend, or ascend, through such an unbroken line, then each of his capacities must have at least its embryonic analogue in the simpler creatures who preceded him.

Evolution implies development, not the sudden appearance of something totally new. No such totally new capacity could have evolved at all, but would have had to have come suddenly into being. And one of the most important of man's capacities is that which enables him to do more than simply "adapt himself to changed conditions." It is the capacity to develop those unsuspected potentialities that make "civilized" mean something more than merely "adapted to group life in a technologically complex society." An essential part of that something more is the development of a more varied, more vivid psychic life. And this is precisely the something more which the civilized animal also unexpectedly manifests.

1956

The Vandal and the Sportsman

It would not be quite true to say that "some of my best friends are hunters." Nevertheless, I do number among my respected acquaintances some who not only kill for the sake of killing but count it among their keenest pleasures. I can think of no better illustration of the fact that men may be separated at some point by a fathomless abyss yet share elsewhere much common ground.

To me it is inconceivable how anyone should think an animal more interesting dead than alive. I can also easily prove to my own satisfaction that killing "for sport" is the perfect type of that pure evil for which metaphysicians have sometimes sought.

Most wicked deeds are done because the doer proposes some good to himself. The liar lies to gain some end; the swindler and thief want things which, if honestly got, might be good in themselves. Even the murderer may be removing an impediment to normal desires or gaining possession of something which his victim keeps from him. None of these usually does evil for evil's sake. They are selfish or unscrupulous, but their deeds are not gratuitously evil. The killer for sport has no such comprehensible motive. He prefers death to life, darkness to light. He gets nothing except the satisfaction of saying, "Something which wanted to live is dead. There is that much less vitality, consciousness, and, perhaps, joy in the universe. I am the Spirit that Denies." When a man wantonly destroys one of the works of man we call him Vandal. When he wantonly destroys one of the works of God we call him Sportsman.

The hunter-for-food may be as wicked and as misguided as vegetarians sometimes say; but he does not kill for the sake of killing. The rancher and the farmer who exterminate all living things not immediately profitable to them may some-

105

times be working against their own best interests; but whether they are or are not, they hope to achieve some supposed good by their exterminations. If to do evil not in the hope of gain but for evil's sake involves the deepest guilt by which man can be stained, then killing for killing's sake is a terrifying phenomenon and as strong a proof as we could have of that "reality of evil" with which present-day theologians are again concerned.

Despite all this I know that sportsmen are not necessarily monsters. Even if the logic of my position is unassailable, the fact still remains that men are not logical creatures; that most if not all are blind to much they might be expected to see and are habitually inconsistent; that both the blind spots and the inconsistencies vary from person to person.

To say as we all do: "Any man who would do A would do B," is to state a proposition mercifully proved false almost as often as it is stated. The murderer is not necessarily a liar any more than the liar is necessarily a murderer, and few men feel that if they break one commandment there is little use in keeping the others. Many have been known to say that they considered adultery worse than homicide but not all adulterers are potential murderers and there are even murderers to whom incontinence would be unthinkable. So the sportsman may exhibit any of the virtues—including compassion and respect for life—everywhere except in connection with his "sporting" activities. It may even be often enough true that, as "antisentimentalists" are fond of pointing out, those tenderest toward animals are not necessarily most philanthropic. They no more than sportsmen are always consistent.

When the Winchester gun company makes a propaganda movie concluding with a scene in which a "typical American boy" shoots a number of quail and when it then ends with the slogan "Go hunting with your boy and you'll never have to go hunting for him," I may suspect that the gun company is moved by a desire to sell more guns at least as much as by a determination to do what it can toward reducing the incidence of delinquency. I will certainly add also my belief that there are even better ways of diminishing the likelihood that a boy will grow up to do even worse things. Though it seems to me that he is being taught a pure evil I know that he will not necessarily cultivate a taste for all or, for that matter, any one of the innumerable other forms under which evil may be loved.

There is no doubt that contemporary civilization finds a place in the vaguely formulated code of ethics to which the majority gives at least formal assent for what it is most likely to call "kindness to animals." It is equally obvious that this degree of recognition is very recent. The Old Testament does say that the virtuous man is kind to his beasts. Thomas Aquinas did disapprove of cruelty to animals, though only on the ground that it would lead to cruelty to men. But there is very little evidence in Western culture before the eighteenth century that the torture (much less the killing) of animals for sport ordinarily revolted anyone. English law, though it was lagging as usual somewhat behind enlightened opinion, did not forbid even the most sadistic abuse of animals for pure pleasure until 1822 when Parliament passed the first law protecting any animal against cruelty per se. Even today when the grosser, more gratuitous forms of needlessly inflicted pain are generally recognized as evil, the difference in attitudes toward killing for sport range through a gamut that must be as wide as it ever was.

Examples of three different but typical ways of refusing to acknowledge that any defense of such killing is called for may be plucked out of recent popular periodicals.

In the spring of 1955 a magazine called *Sports Illustrated* distributed a questionnaire intended to determine the public attitude toward hunting. An answer received from a woman in Tampa, Florida, was as follows: "I am not the sloppy, sentimental type that thinks it's terrible to shoot birds or animals. What else are they good for?" And *The New Yorker,* which reprinted her reply, answered the question with an irony likely to be lost on the asker: "Bulls can be baited by fierce dogs, and horses sometimes pay money."

About a year before, *The New Yorker* had also, though without comment and merely in the course of a report on the personality of the new United Kingdom's Permanent Representative to the United Nations, quoted Sir Pierson Dixon as remarking genially, apropos of some articles on sport which he had written for English periodicals: "I like this shooting thing, stalking some relatively large animal or, even more enjoyable, shooting birds. It's like the pleasure of hitting a a ball."

A little later *Time* magazine ran an article about how duck hunters near Utah's Bear River Migratory Bird Refuge (sic) "could hardly shoot fast enough" to bring down the ducks they found there and it adorned the article with a quotation from Ernest Hemingway's "Fathers and Sons": "When you have shot one bird flying you have shot all birds flying, they are all different and they fly different ways but the sensation is the same and the last one is as good as the first."

Of these three attitudes the first may seem the simplest and the most elementary, but perhaps it is not. The blank assumption that the universe has no conceivable use or meaning except in relation to man may be instinctive; nevertheless, the lady from Tampa is speaking not merely from naïveté. She is also speaking for all those minds still tinctured by the thought of the medieval philosophers who consciously undertook to explain in detail the *raison d'être* of the curious world of nature by asking for what human use God had created each species of plant or animal. If any given creature seems good for nothing except "sport," then it must be for sport that it was created.

Hemingway's utterance, on the other hand, is the most sophisticated of the three and the only one that seems to make the pure pleasure of killing a consciously recognized factor. The mental processes of the Permanent Representative are neither so corrupt as those of Mr. Hemingway nor so intellectually complicated as those of the lady from Tampa. He is not, like the first, looking for madder music and stronger wine, nor, like the second, attempting to answer the philosophical question of what animals and birds "are for." Because of the dreadful uncomprehending innocence sometimes said to be found most frequently in the English gentleman it has simply never occurred to him that the creatures whom he pursues are alive at all—as his phrase "like the pleasure of hitting a ball" reveals. And it is in exactly the same light that those of his class have sometimes regarded the lesser breeds without the law, or even the nearly inanimate members of all the social classes below them.

For the attitude farthest removed from this, Albert Schweitzer is the best-known contemporary spokesman. But one can hardly have "reverence for life" without some vivid sense that life exists even in "the lower animals" and it is this vivid sense that is lacking in the vast majority of sportsmen and equally in, say, the abandoners of pets and, not infrequently, one kind of biological scientist. Often not one of them is so much as tinged with the sadism which Hemingway's opinions and activities seem to suggest. It is not that they do not care what the abandoned pet or the experimental animal suffers but that they do not really believe he suffers to any considerable degree. In the case of the hunter it is often not so much that he wants to kill as that he has no vivid sense that he is killing. For him, as for Sir Pierson, it is more or less like "hitting a ball."

The conviction that "man is an animal" is certainly very widely held today, and the further conviction that man is "nothing but an animal" only somewhat less so. One might expect that these convictions would lead to the feeling that no benevolence, philanthropy, humanitarianism, "good will," or even simple decency can logically stop short at the line which separates the highest animal from those next below him and that less scrupulosity in dealing with any creature is justifiable only in proportion to that creature's lesser degree of sensibility and aliveness. Between the human being assumed to be only a species of animal and any other species no qualitative rather than merely quantitative distinction can logically be assumed to exist, and the wanton killing of an animal differs from the wanton killing of a human being only in degree. The two murders are not equally wicked but they are not wholly different either. Such wanton killing of an animal out of no necessity and not even for the sake of a minor need is at least a small murder—not an innocent game.

If the popularization of the biological sciences has not done as much as might be expected to foster some such convictions, that is in part the result of the attitude these sciences themselves have often taken. One of the intentions seldom absent from the pages of this book has been the intention to suggest in as many different ways as possible that to call man "an animal" is to endow him with a heritage so rich that his potentialities seem hardly less than when he was called the son of God. Much biological science has on the contrary tended to draw diametrically opposite conclusions, and not only to deny man the divine origin once assumed to be his but to deprive the animal kingdom to which he is assumed to belong of the powers which, during most of human history, it had been assumed to share in some degree with humanity.

Cartesianism maintained that every animal other than man was a machine, though man was not. But when Cartesianism was rejected by science, science took more away from man than it restored to the lower animals. Increasingly, at least until very recent years, it minimized and often denied the effectiveness of reason or the significance of consciousness in man himself and not surprisingly denounced as absurd the attribution to animals of what it hardly admitted as real in man. We were urged to study both him and the other animals exclusively in terms of instincts, conditioned reflexes, and behavior patterns. Hence it is not surprising that the ultimate result was not the treatment of animals with some of the tenderness and consideration due to man but, in the totalitarian states where science was for the first time freed from all religious, philosophical, or merely literary restraints, to treat men with the brutality usually adopted toward animals.

When Thoreau allowed himself to be persuaded to send a turtle as a specimen to the zoologists at Harvard he felt that he had "a murderer's experience in a degree" and that however his specimen might serve science, he himself and his relation to nature would be the worse for what he had done. "I pray," he wrote, "that I may walk more innocently and serenely through nature. No reasoning whatever reconciles me to this act."

In general, however, professional students of living things are only somewhat more likely than the average man to feel strongly any "reverence for life." One of the most distinguished American students of birds told me that he saw no incompatibility whatever between his interest in birds and his love of "sport." Many, perhaps most professional students find no reason too trivial to "collect" a bird or animal, though their habitual use of this weasel word may suggest a defensive attitude. And I have often wondered that sportsmen who find themselves subject to many restrictions have not protested as unfair the "collector's licenses" rather freely granted and sometimes permitting the holder to shoot almost anything almost anywhere and at any time.

Audubon slaughtered birds in wholesale lots so large he once remarked that birds must be very scarce when he did not shoot more than a hundred a day. Even the more exuberant of today's collectors are more aware that species are exhaustible, but many private collectors, as well as museums, are proud of their trays containing thousands of bird skins. Whatever may be said in justification of science's need for study specimens, it is still worth noting that the more trivial the question being studied the more lives it is likely to cost —as when, for example, an earnest student shoots hundreds of birds or animals just to find out whether or not he can establish a regional variety by proving that the average size of some item in the pattern of plumage or pelt is a millimeter greater in one geographical area than in another. Moreover, the record comes to seem to many more important than the living thing recorded and it is an accepted principle among ornithologists that since "sight records" can always be disputed it is the bounden duty of every student to shoot immediately any species believed to be hitherto unreported in the region where it is observed.

The first new species known to have settled without human aid in the United States is the cattle egret first seen in Massachusetts in April, 1952—at which time it was dutifully shot by the first knowledgeable bird-lover to see it. Such was his way of saying "Welcome, Stranger." By now the species is said to be well established in Florida. Was the desire to demonstrate the identity of the first observed specimen worth the further hardening of the heart it cost? Thoreau would have thought not. What little science gained in this particular instance was just possibly not worth what a bird lost.

Obviously the problem raised by all this is not solvable in any clear-cut way. The degree of "reverence for life" which man or any other animal can exhibit is limited by the facts of a world he never made. When it was said that the lion and the lamb shall lie down together, the hope that they may someday do so carries with it the obvious implication that they cannot do so now. Even Albert Schweitzer's rule that no life shall be destroyed except in the service of some higher life will be differently interpreted almost from individual to individual.

Just how great must be the good that will accrue to the higher animal? Interpreted as strictly as possible, his law would permit killing only in the face of the most desperate and immediate necessity. Interpreted loosely enough, it might justify the slaughter of the twenty thousand birds of paradise, the forty thousand hummingbirds, and the thirty thousand birds of other species said to have been killed to supply the London feather market alone in the single year 1914. After all, even fashionable ladies are presumably "higher" than birds and they presumably took keen delight in the adornments which the birds were sacrificed to provide.

Some pragmatic solution of the rights of man versus the rights of other living creatures does nevertheless have to be made. Undoubtedly it changes from time to time and it is well that the existing solution should be reexamined periodically. Because the 1914 solution was reexamined, comparatively few birds are killed for their feathers and it is not demonstrable that the female population is any the worse for the fact.

In India members of the Jain sect sometimes live on liquid food sipped through a veil in order to avoid the possibility that they might inadvertently swallow a gnat. There are always "antisentimentalists" who protest against any cultivation of scruples on the ground that they can logically lead only to some such preposterous scrupulosity. But there are extremes at both ends. Those who have scruples are no more likely to end as Jains than those who reject all scruples are likely to end as Adolf Hitlers. The only possible absolutes are reverence for all life and contempt for all life and of these the first is certainly no more to be feared than the second. If there is any such thing as a wise compromise it is not likely to be reached by the refusal to think. However difficult it may be to draw lines, they have to be drawn and draw them most men do, either thoughtlessly or with thought.

One may conclude that mankind could not continue to exist without killing some living creatures, just as one may conclude that without a willingness to resort to war self-preservation for a nation is impossible. Killing is evil and war is hell. But it makes a tremendous difference whether or not one concludes from these facts that any concern with honor and mercy or any refusal to accept any methods or countenance all cruelty is foolish. It makes the same sort of difference whether you say that life in the world is impossible without some self-regarding worldliness and that therefore men can never be other than remorseless egotists anywhere, or whether you say that, despite the cruel dilemmas with which a contingent universe continually confronts us, we can still sometimes elude or mitigate them. Though the lion and the lamb may never lie down together, it may still be that the more we do elude or mitigate the implications of that fact the better it is for man and beast alike.

In his actual practice, civilized man has been more ruthlessly wasteful and grasping in his attitude toward the natural world than has served even his most material best interests. The more we learn about the interdependence of living things, the clearer it becomes that the practical utility of the land upon which we live has been diminished seriously by the determination to allow it to serve no purposes but our own. Many once prosperous lands have, like Spain, found poverty and famine stalking across their fields and pastures without knowing what has brought the calamity upon them. In the United States many ranchers and many farmers have been invoking the same specter despite full knowledge of what they were doing, and because they were determined merely to get theirs while the getting is good.

Possibly—as some hope—a mere enlightened selfishness will save them in time. Perhaps it will teach them to save their soil from direct exhaustion and furthermore leave uncut upon the mountains some of the trees without which the rushing torrents from mountain rains will ultimately wash their farms away. Possibly, even, it will teach them also that the fox or the coyote who occasionally eats one of their hens or their sheep eats more often the rodents they will have to struggle less successfully against when they have eliminated all the predators. In Deuteronomy the husbandman is forbidden to glean his cornfields where the scattered grain belongs by right to the poor. Surely, even when no direct utility is obvious, it is a sin to grudge the small fellow creatures our crumbs and grudge even the wild flower its few inches beside the farmer's fence or along our roadside.

If the earth is still livable and in many places still beautiful, that is chiefly because man's power to lay it waste has been limited. Up until now nature has been too large, too abundant, and too resistant to be conquered. As Havelock Ellis once wrote without exaggeration, "The sun, moon and stars would have disappeared long ago if they had happened to be within reach of predatory human hands."

Such predatory human hands have exterminated many kinds of living creatures and rendered many a flourishing acre barren—but not so many as they would have destroyed had the reach of the hands not been limited. Our numbers and our ingenuity have been growing at a prodigious rate. We may not have progressed as far in certain directions as we commonly suppose, but there is no doubt about the reality of Progress so far as the power to destroy is concerned. The day is fast approaching when nature's resilience will no longer protect us from ourselves. We are on the point of being able actually to do what for several centuries we have dreamed of doing—namely, "conquer nature." And we may be reminded too late that "to conquer" means to have at least the ability to destroy. If the mass of men continue to be what they have long been, that ability will be used.

Even if we should learn just in the nick of time not to destroy what is necessary for our own preservation, the mere determination to survive is not sufficient to save very much of the variety and the beauty of the natural world. They can be preserved only if man feels the necessity of sharing the earth with at least some of his fellow creatures to be a privilege rather than an irritation. And he is not likely to feel that without something more than the intellectual curiosity which is itself far from universal today. That something more you may call Love, fellow-feeling, or "reverence for life," though —as was recently pointed out in a letter to a philological journal—Schweitzer's own term *Ehrfurcht* carries a stronger sense of "awe" than the English word that has been weakened in use.

And whatever you call it, it is something against which both urban life and some of the intellectual tendencies of our times tend to militate. Increasing awareness of what the science of ecology teaches promises to have some effect upon the public's understanding of the practical necessity of paying some attention to the balance of nature. But without reverence or love it can come to be no more than a shrewder exploitation of what it would be better to admire, to enjoy, and to share in.

Unfortunately the scientific study of living creatures does not always promote either reverence or love, even when it is not wholly utilitarian in its emphasis. It was the seventeenth-century naturalist John Ray who first gave wide currency in England to the conviction that God made other living things not exclusively for the use of man but also for both his delight and for theirs.

Unfortunately that laboratory biology which has tended to become the most earnestly cultivated kind of scientific study is precisely the kind least likely to stimulate compassion, love, or reverence for the creatures it studies. Those who interested themselves in old-fashioned natural history were brought into intimate association with animals and plants. Its aims and its methods demanded an awareness of the living thing as a living thing and, at least until the rise of behaviorism, the suffering and the joy of the lesser creatures was a part of the naturalist's subject matter. But the laboratory scientist is not of necessity drawn into any emotional relationship with animals or plants and the experiments which of necessity he must perform are more likely to make him more rather than less callous than the ordinary man.

At best, compassion, reverence for life, and a sense of the community of living things are not an essential part of his business as they are of the more vaguely defined discipline of the naturalist. And for that reason it is a great pity that the most humane and liberal of the natural sciences should play so small a role in the liberal arts curriculum. While still under the influence of an older tradition, field botany and field zoology were quite commonly taught in American colleges even in the remoter parts of the United States. Today few liberal arts undergraduates know anything of such subjects and often would find no courses open to them if they did.

In Columbia College, with which I happen to be most familiar, there are elementary courses available in biology, but they are designed primarily to meet the needs of those headed for the medical and other professional schools. They introduce the student to the subject via the anatomy and physiology of the lower animals and are confined so closely to dissection and other laboratory operations that he is seldom if ever brought into contact with a living plant or an animal living a natural life. Undoubtedly these courses serve their purpose, but they have little to contribute to education in the humanities and those committed to such an education very rarely attend them. If such a student should feel, for example, that he ought not be as ignorant as most of his fellows concerning the plants, animals, and birds which figure so largely in both British and American literature, he would get little help from the curriculum. There are many courses in "The Nature Poets" in American colleges. But nature is usually left out of them.

Very recently I had occasion to spend a week on the campus of one of the oldest and most respected of the smaller liberal arts colleges of the eastern seaboard. It was one that prides itself on its exclusive concern with liberal rather than preprofessional education. A benefactor gave it some years ago a beautiful wooded tract adjoining the campus which is lavishly planted with native and exotic flowering trees and shrubs. When no student or teacher with whom I had been brought into contact could tell me the name of an especially striking tree, I sought out the head of the botany department, who was also its only member.

He smiled rather complacently and gave this reply to my question: "Haven't the least idea. I am a cytologist and I don't suppose I could recognize a dozen plants by sight." The secrets of the cell are a vastly complicated and important subject. But should they be the one and only thing connected with plant life which a student seeking a liberal education is given the opportunity to learn?

That a similar situation does not always prevail I know from observation, but when it does not that is usually simply because the teacher employed happens to have a broader interest, not because those in charge of the curriculum are convinced that some knowledge of the natural world is a part of a liberal education. Biology as commonly taught is not a humane subject; it is simply an elementary preparation for the trade of the specialist.

To proceed from the dissection of earthworms to the dissection of cats—both supplied to hundreds of schools and colleges by the large biological supply houses—is not necessary to learn reverence for life or to develop any of the various kinds of "feeling for nature" which many of the old naturalists believed to be the essential thing. To expect such courses to do anything of the sort is as sensible as it would be to expect an apprenticed embalmer to emerge with a greater love and respect for his fellow man. And an increased love or respect for living creatures is one of the last things many college courses in biology would propose to themselves.

"Nature study" is often relegated to the lower levels and sometimes thought of as being really appropriate only to the kindergarten. Even in the elementary grades the tendency to devote more attention to dead animals than to living ones sometimes makes its appearance. In a very "progressive" school I have seen teen-agers introduced to the old dreary business of dissecting earthworms; and there are worse things than that when bungling, pointless experiments upon living animals are encouraged. The catalogue of a leading biological supply house boasts of the wide increase in the use of "nutrition experiments" (grandly so-called) in schools. It offers eight different deficiency diets together with the living animals whose malnutrition, when they are fed any one of these diets, may be observed by the curious. Very recently the head of the National Cancer Institute urged high school teachers to teach their pupils how to produce cancer in mice by the transplantation of tumors and in chicks by the injection of enzymes.

Is it sentimental to ask whether anyone not preparing for the serious study of anatomy is likely to be any the better for the dissecting of a cat, or whether anyone, no matter what career he may be preparing himself for, is any the better for having starved a rat or induced cancer in a mouse? However completely experiments up to and including vivisection may have justified themselves, is there any possible excuse for repeating them merely by way of spectacle?

By now it is as well known that a rat will sicken and die without certain minerals and vitamins as it is that he will die if given no food at all. Would anyone learn anything by poking out eyes in order to prove that without them animals can't see? Or, for that matter, from undertaking to find out for himself whether or not it is really true that even Jews can bleed? Yet to deprive animals of protein is hardly more instructive. Taught by such methods, biology not only fails to promote reverence for life but encourages the tendency to blaspheme it. Instead of increasing empathy it destroys it. Instead of enlarging our sympathy it hardens the heart.

The grand question remains whether most people actually *want* hearts to be tenderer or harder. Do we want a civilization that will move toward some more intimate relation with the natural world, or do we want one that will continue to detach and isolate itself from both a dependence upon and a sympathy with that community of which we were originally a part? Do we want a physical environment more and more exclusively man-made and an intellectual, emotional, and aesthetic life which has renounced as completely as possible its interest in everything inherited from the long centuries during which we were, willy-nilly, dependent upon what the natural world supplied? Do we want cities completely sterilized and mechanized; do we want art that imitates exclusively the man-made rather than the natural?

There is a sizable minority which has asked itself these questions and answered them with an unqualified "Yes." There is another minority, perhaps almost as large, which answers them with an equally definite "No." But the large majority has never faced these questions in any general form, though it is nearly everywhere drifting without protest toward a pragmatic affirmative.

No doubt all societies not completely static exhibit many of what the Marxists call "inner contradictions." In our own, some of the less spectacular of these contradictions involve the questions just asked. We set aside wild areas and then "improve" them out of all wildness. We teach kindness to animals and even reverence for life, but we also believe that fathers should teach their sons to hunt or encourage them to dissect cats and watch rats starve. Moreover, these contradictions flourish even within organizations that seem at first sight ranged on one side or another, and the organizations are often supported by an uneasy united front composed of what are really antithetical parties.

What, for example, are the national and the various state conservation and wildlife departments for? Are they to preserve wildlife or to provide game for hunters to kill? If for the latter, then is the justification the beneficial effects of sport or is it the contribution to the general economic prosperity made by the arms industry? When there is a conflict, what comes first?

It would be difficult to get from many organizations a clear-cut statement and I have been told of at least one instance where an officer of a state commission protested hotly against the exhibition in a state park of a young deer which children were allowed to pet because, so he said, making pets of wild animals creates a prejudice against hunting. And to leave no doubt concerning the ultimate reason for his attitude he is said to have added, "After all, guns and ammunition are big business."

I have no doubt that many of his colleagues would violently disagree but I have also been told (though this is for me mere hearsay) that when Walt Disney issued the early animal film *Bambi* he received *protests* from many quarters. Somebody can make more money out of slaughtering animals than anyone can make out of loving them. The hard heart is more economically productive than the tender one. The sporting instinct pays off. Reverence for life does not.

Upon whatever basis all the inner contradictions are ultimately resolved, the consequences for the physical, intellectual, and emotional life of tomorrow's man will not be trivial. The sum of all the resolutions will help determine whether we have decided to go it completely alone and to depend no longer upon nature for food, health, joy, or beauty.

An obviously unfriendly reporter revealed not long ago that President Eisenhower had ordered removed from the White House lawn the squirrels which were interfering with his putting green, and even so trivial an incident is a straw in the wind. To hold golf obviously more important than squirrels indicates a tiny but significant decision. It points toward a coming world where there will be more golf courses and fewer wild plants as well as wild animals—hence to a world less interesting and less rich for those who would rather hunt a flower or watch the scamperings of a squirrel than chivy a rubber ball over a close-cropped grass plot.

The late David Fairchild, who was responsible for the introduction of so many useful and beautiful plants into the United States, tells the story of an army officer assigned to an office building in Miami during the First World War.

"I haven't got anything but human beings around me in that building where I spend my days. Aside from the floor and the ceiling, the doors and windows and desk and some chairs there isn't anything but people. The other evening when I was feeling particularly fed up with the monotony of the place, I went into the laboratory and as I was washing my hands a cockroach ran up the wall. 'Thank God for a cockroach!' I said to myself, 'I'm glad there is something alive besides human beings in this building.'"

It may well be with such small consolations that the nature lover of the not too distant future will be compelled to content himself. Cockroaches will not easily be exterminated.

1956

We Look Before and After

Outside my window on that spring morning, as on this, a bird sang. Outside a million windows, a million birds had sung as morning swept around the globe. Few men and few women were so glad that a new day had dawned as these birds seem to be.

Because my window looks out on a southern landscape, my bird is a cardinal, with feathers as bright as his half-whistled song. Farther north in the United States he would be a robin, more likely than not—less colorful and somewhat less melodious but seemingly no less pleased with the world and his place in it. Like us, robins have their problems but they seem better able to take them in their stride. We are likely to awake with an "Oh, dear!" on our lips; they with a "What fun!" in their beaks. Mr. Sandburg's peddler was remarkable because he seemed so terribly glad to be selling fish. Most robins seem terribly glad to be eating worms.

For some time I had been thinking that I wanted to write a book about the characteristics and activities of living things. During the week or two just before, I had been wondering with what activity or characteristics I should begin. Reproduction, growing up, and getting a living are all, so I said to myself, fundamental activities. Combativeness in the face of rivals, solicitude for the young, courage when danger must be met, patience when hardships must be endured, are all typical characteristics. But my cardinal proposed a different solution. Is any characteristic more striking than the joy of life itself?

No starting place is less usual or would have seemed less suitable to many biologists. Some would certainly prefer to begin with origins—with the simplest creatures now living or with the theoretically even simpler ones from which they evolved. Others might choose an abstraction, but the abstraction would probably be "the struggle for existence" or "the survival of the fittest." Pressed to name the most fundamental characteristic of life, they would probably reply: "The irritability of protoplasm."

With them on their own ground I certainly had no right to quarrel. The cardinal and the robin do have to engage in a struggle for existence. The protoplasm in the cells of their bodies is, like that in mine, "irritable." But when I hear the word "robin"—especially when I hear a particular robin singing on a bough—I do not think: "Irritable protoplasm so organized as to succeed in the struggle for existence." I think that no more than when I hear my own name I think: "Member of the American middle class, subdivision intellectual, caught in an economy where he is not very comfortable and developing opinions which are the product of his social situation." An equally significant sort of fact about both men and birds is that individuals are more or less happy, terribly glad or terribly sorry to be doing what they are doing, and capable of making more or less interesting comments on their situation.

With this fact science can hardly concern itself. Such facts are not measurable or susceptible of objective demonstration. But to men and to robins alike they are nevertheless very important and very real. If this were not so I do not think I should ever have taken much interest in either human or natural history. And if I consented in the end to begin this book more conventionally, it was with some misgiving.

Men have surrendered a good deal of their capacity for spontaneous happiness, and there may be compensations. In any event our situation is one for which there is probably no radical remedy. Yet even for us happiness is still important and it is, or at least once was, a fundamental characteristic of life. Nothing the lesser creatures can teach us is more worth learning than the lesson of gladness.

Of this lesson the robin is an especially effective teacher, for the same reason that certain men and women are. He has, I mean, the gift of language. Even the happiest human poets may be no happier than some of their less articulate fellows but they are better equipped to communicate. Perhaps your robin and my cardinal are not more terribly glad that a new day has dawned than the field mouse was when the sun sank and the moon rose. But they put their gladness into sounds which are almost words. And unlike many other animals who make sounds, they speak our language. Their song is one we might, if we could, sing in some unreasonably happy moment. And it is this fact that makes us aware of them in a special way.

Perhaps it is no more than an accident. In no other respect are birds so much more like us than any other animals are. But language is one of the strongest of bonds and long before the dawn of history men took an especially sympathetic interest in birds because they could understand what the birds were saying, and because it appeared, as in the case of so many beasts it did not, that they had a seemly, and an eloquent way of saying it.

Sometimes we resent the fact that in human society so much honor is paid to those who are unusually articulate; that we pretend at least to honor the poet more than any other citizen; that even the mere gift of gab can open the way to fame, wealth, and power. About birds we might feel in much the same way. They sang for one another millions of years before any man overheard them, but they have profited perhaps unfairly from the fact that their song does communicate to ears so different from their own.

Even today they are less persecuted than any other small creature. Fewer people who see a bird say of it—as they tend to say of any other small animal they happen upon—"Here is a little creature who is alive and wants to live. Therefore let us kill it at once." And it is a significant indication of how much the vocal powers of the bird are responsible for the special regard in which they are held that laws protect "song birds" even though many so protected are only unmelodious relatives of those who actually sing.

Certain penalties, also, the birds have sometimes paid for making sounds so pleasing to human beings. Just because these sounds are inherently agreeable they can tickle the ear of men so self-absorbed that their imagination never carries them to the glad or sad singer himself and they regard him as no more than a mechanical music box which it is necessary to confine in a cage. At times it has even been the custom to put out the songster's eyes in the belief, true or false, that blindness improves his song. This can only mean that, in some limited way, beauty may be enjoyed without sympathy for or even curiosity about the living thing which produces it. Similarly, oriental potentates confine beautiful women in harems so that they may be conveniently "loved." Similarly, Ivan the Terrible, so it is said, blinded his architect to make certain that he could never build a basilica for any rival. Similarly, for that matter, ladies used to admire so much the color and texture of birds that they put them on their hats.

But whatever delights such aesthetics as these may know, there are some of us who do not envy them. To us, hearing the song without communion with the singer is no better than listening to sounding brass and tinkling cymbals. When we listen it is less because our ears are tickled than because we rejoice to know that there is rejoicing in the world around us. We want to divine what the bird is saying to himself and to his fellows; to feel that some emotion, if not some thought, is communicated. We assume that in some general way bird language is translatable.

The language of music, even of the music addressed by men to their fellow men, is notoriously easy to misinterpret —especially when we try to hear in it not only the emotion itself but the specific occasion of that emotion and when we attempt, for instance, to distinguish between the joy of falling in love and the joy of spending a day in the country. That way lies the embarrassment of Mendelssohn's friend who congratulated him on having got the very spirit of the Highlands into his Scotch Symphony only to learn that what he had been listening to was the "Italian" instead.

Mistranslating the song of birds is at least as easy. Because most of them sing best at mating time we naturally assume that they are love poets almost exclusively. And Darwin, with his stress on "sexual selection," encouraged the interpretation. No doubt most present-day ornithologists are partly right when they insist that the cardinal or the robin we have been listening to is not singing primarily to charm his mate or to tell the world that love is sweet in springtime. In fact, so they say, what he really means is: "All other robins or cardinals take notice. I am already here. I have staked out a claim to a certain robin- or cardinal-sized territory large enough to supply food for me and my family. Trespassers will be prosecuted." But partly right is not wholly right and the joyful exuberance of the song, whatever its specific message, is as unmistakable as the fact that both the Scotch and the Italian Symphonies are cheerful pieces.

Yesterday, outside this same southern window beyond which the cardinal had been singing, I watched the antics of a mockingbird, who had been at these antics for many days. Perched at the top of a high tree he sang most of the day and through a large part of the night. Besides singing he leaped every few minutes a foot or two in the air, flapping his wings wildly and then settling back upon the same topmost twig. Probably even the most unromantic ornithologist would not deny that besides proclaiming his possession of a territory my bird was also trying to attract the attention of a female bird. Some of them might even adopt my fancy that, as the days have passed, there have been signs of a growing desperation and that the mocker seems to be saying to himself: "For goodness' sake, where are all the women? There are supposed to be enough to go around and I am certainly a pretty good specimen as mockingbirds go. I can sing long and loud. And I can jump as vigorously as anybody."

The most important thing is not the question whether the mocker's song is saying "I love you" or "This is my home and my land." The most important question is simply whether or not he is, as he sounds, confident and happy. And I am sure that he is. When a man tries to charm a woman by his conversation or when he describes the countryside in which he has settled down to live we assume that some emotions accompany his words. And whatever the bird is saying, it fills his universe with joy.

Those creatures who cannot sing, or who do not speak our musical language when they do, communicate their joy in less direct ways. And the most eloquent of these ways is play. In some respects it is the most convincing of all the evidences of animal happiness because it demonstrates an excess of energy over and above what is required for the business of keeping alive. Those who study animals only in cages and laboratories know little about it. In prisons one must not expect to find much joy, human or animal. But the notes of field naturalists are full of accounts of the moonlight revels of rabbits and hares, of otters sliding down their chute-the-chutes into the water, of the gambols of the vixen with her young.

Only a few days ago two ground squirrels, so small that they must have just left their subterranean nests, came face to face outside my window. They touched noses, leaped each a foot into the air, and then scampered away in opposite directions "as playful as kittens." It makes no difference if you say that play is only "a preparation for the serious business of life." So presumably it is in the case of human children. But it is joy, not a realization of the necessity for exercise, which inspires the antics. Does anyone seriously doubt that gamboling children are having fun or that those emotions which accompany their play and constitute its meaning in their own immediate experience have nothing to do with joy?

In the room with me as I write, but confined to a roomy glass cage, is one of these appealing little desert animals called a kangaroo rat. I do not intend to keep him indefinitely because I do not like to keep "pets" who are not obviously as glad to stay with me as I am to stay with them. Nevertheless, the kangaroo rat is a solitary animal who, I like to think, is not lonesome in captivity or very much distressed by it. He spends a good deal of time pushing the sand about to make piles near his sleeping box, in filling his cheek pockets with the abundant food I supply, and in practicing that complete abstention from drinking which is his chief claim to fame.

In his cage I put a little exercise wheel like that which accompanies the old-fashioned squirrel cage. It took him some two weeks to learn what it was good for. The fact that he now races in it fast and expertly seems to me a considerable tribute to his intelligence, because the whole contraption is unlike anything for which his inherited reflexes could have prepared him or his previous experience taught him anything. But the real question in my mind was this: Does he enjoy running in a wheel or does he use it *faute de mieux?* Is this a kind of game or is it merely a poor substitute for the exercise he needs and would have got in freedom?

Of course I don't know. But an anecdote told me by the naturalist-photographer Lewis Wayne Walker after I had begun to wonder about the matter suggests an answer. Entering his barn one night, he was startled to see that an unused exercise wheel stored there was revolving of its own accord. He hid to watch, and presently a brown rat came out, climbed into the wheel, had a fine run, and then went away again. This rat could run as far and in whatever direction he wanted to run. He was not suffering from any enforced lack of exercise. But like a child to whom the family automobile is no novelty but who nevertheless wants to ride round and round on a carrousel, the rat was pleased for a change to run fast without getting anywhere. It was fun and that is all there is to it.

Perhaps man, beast, or bird does not find this kind of fun so important or so satisfying as the sort which consists in finding joy in an activity which has another purpose also— as when a man and woman set up housekeeping or a robin sings to the world his happy awareness that he is in possession of the territory his wife and children have need of. Nevertheless, the ability to do something for fun, for nothing but fun, is a strong indication that this other kind of joy is also within the capacity of even a brown rat.

When I say all this I am not forgetting that many biologists would deny it almost *in toto*. Dogmatic "behaviorism" now has few adherents among those psychologists who are concerned chiefly with human beings, but it still dominates the thinking of many students of our fellow creatures. They may not go quite so far as Descartes and his disciples once did when they insisted that all animals other than man are mere machines incapable of even pleasure or pain because they are completely without consciousness. But they do cling to the contention that it is "not necessary" to assume any conscious concomitants of animal behavior and that since it is not "necessary" they will reject it.

Not many years ago one such naturalist was careful to explain to a popular audience that a bird singing on the bough must not be compared to man singing in the bathtub. The man, he said, sings because he is happy; the song of the bird has "absolutely nothing" to do with "the joy of life."

Now neither he nor I can remember ever having been a bird. For that matter, however, neither he nor I has ever been anyone except our individual selves when we sang in a bathtub. But the assumption that the bird is joyous is very little less reasonable than the assumption that a neighbor who engages in melodious ablutions feels happy. In both cases we accept an analogy. We have no other evidence that human beings not ourselves are conscious at all. But common sense has always accepted the analogy of the bird and the analogy of the man as sufficiently persuasive. The man, we think, must be feeling something very closely similar to what we ourselves feel when we behave that way; the bird who sings and the animal who plays are probably feeling something at least remotely similar.

At least it is most certainly true that if the song of the robin does not express some sort of robin's joy analogous to our own then nature has no human meaning and we can study it only as we might study physics—merely because we are curious about how the machine works and may possibly learn things which will increase the efficiency of our getting and spending. Unless there is some emotion outside our own in which we can participate or from which we may draw comfort and joy then there is no universe beyond our own to which we can in any sense belong.

The ornithologist who has convinced himself that bird song "has nothing to do" with joy has not taken anything away from the robin. Ornithology notwithstanding, the robin continues to pour forth his heart in profuse strains of unpremeditated art. But such an ornithologist has taken a good deal away from himself and from those who feel constrained to believe him. They have forced themselves to live in a world that has come to seem, not joyful, but joyless. Robins and cardinals know better.

The gift for happiness is not always in proportion to intelligence as we understand and measure it. Birds are not as "smart" as dogs and monkeys are. But it is difficult to believe that even in liberty a monkey is as joyous as a bird or that he has the bird's special gift for gladness. Professor N. J. Berrill has put it thus: "To be a bird is to be alive more intensely than any other living creature, man included. Birds have hotter blood, brighter colors, stronger emotions . . . They are not very intelligent . . . [but] they live in a world that is always the present, mostly full of joy." More specifically Julian Huxley, surely no mere irresponsible sentimentalist, wrote thus after watching on Avery Island in Louisiana the love play of herons, who with loud cries of ectasy twine their necks into a lover's knot: "Of this I can only say that it seemed to bring such a pitch of emotion that I could have wished to be a heron that I might experience it."

The question whether a monkey can ever be equally happy is one upon which it would be better not to speculate. Inevitably it would lead sooner or later to another: "Can a man be as happy as a monkey?" And that had better not be asked. Perhaps some capacity for joy has been, must be, and should be, sacrificed to other capacities. Perhaps the happiness and solace which some of us find in an awareness of nature and in love for her manifestations derives in part from our imaginative participation in forms of existence from which the sacrifice of some of the capacity for joy in the interest of a capacity to think and a capacity to feel for others has not been very insistently demanded.

As for those who have never found for themselves either joy or solace in the teeming busy life which still animates those portions of the earth man has not entirely pre-empted for his own use, they might best be advised to begin by looking not for the joy they can *get* but for the joy *that is there*. And perhaps when they have become aware of joy in other creatures they will *get* by sharing it.

For me, at least, a bird is spokesman for more than merely himself and his kind. Just as individual men are accepted as spokesmen for their race and nation—permitted to sing its songs of triumph and of love—so the bird may be allowed to speak for other creatures. When I hear my cardinal I am reminded not only of all birds but also of all the furry and the scaled as well. Many of them are completely voiceless or so nearly so that they can only chirp or squeak. Others are so timid that I see their games rarely and by accident if at all. But the cardinal reminds me that many of these others might discourse of a joy perhaps almost as great if only they had the cardinal's gift of expression.

Nothing of what I have said need involve any sentimental unawareness of what is—to us at least—the tragedy and the cruelty in that same world my cardinal looks at and finds good. On yesterday's walk I came across the disemboweled carcass of a fawn, whose belly a coyote had ripped open. I needed no such reminder that even within the little stretch of earth visible from my window there are among the smaller creatures many such tragedies which occur daily and, especially, nightly. I see the hawk circling to kill and the buzzard circling as it hunts for the remnants of another's kill. In this world I have been celebrating, the fawn and the coyote cannot, by the law which imposes the contingencies of the natural order upon them, lie down together. If they did not accept this fact they could not be as joyous as they are. If I did not to some extent reconcile myself to it I might go on from protest to protest, until at least I must abhor the robin's slaughter of the worm as much as I did the coyote's slaughter of the fawn and end by finding both the life of man and all life outside him predominantly horrible.

Certainly neither the bird's world nor the world of any other creature is all joy. But even the question whether or not they have reason to be joyous is irrelevant. The tremendous fact remains that joyous they are whether or not it seems to us that they should be. Before our eyes they act out their joyousness and demonstrate very conclusively how fundamental a characteristic of life this capacity for gladness must be.

Perhaps joy is not so old as pain. Perhaps physical pain and physical pleasure are the earliest forms of awareness. But if joy is not so old as either, it may very well be older than

sorrow because for sorrow we need a stronger sense of the past and a stronger sense of the future than most animals probably have. Sorrow is the child of Memory and of Anticipation, neither of which it is likely that my cardinal knows much about. Sometimes it is said that Eternity must be more like Now than like anything else we can imagine. If this is so, then perhaps birds live in a series of almost discontinuous eternities. And many of them seem to be eternities of Joy.

Many reasons have been given by those who believe it a mistake for men either to create for themselves a wholly artificial environment or to remain unaware of the natural environment in which they live. The out-of-doors is said to be healthful for the body and tranquilizing to the spirit. Nature's ways are described as one of the richest subjects for the exercise of intellectual curiosity; knowledge of them is called indispensable for survival. All these reasons are valid. But none of them seems to me so persuasive as the simple fact that the lives of creatures other than man remind us compellingly of the fact that joy is real and instinctive. We have learned much that the animals do not know and developed many capacities they do not have. But they know at least one thing which we seem progressively to be forgetting and they have one capacity which we seem to be allowing to atrophy. To them joy seems to be more important and more accessible than it is to us.

Pleasure, which we seek as a compensation for the joy we so seldom feel, is both worth less and harder to come by. It requires some positive occasion and adequate occasions become harder and harder to create. Pleasure sickens from what it feeds on; joy comes easier the more often one is joyous. We relapse into melancholy or discontent and boredom. We suffer one or the other if we find at the moment no occasion for a different emotion. But nature, so it seems, relapses in joy. Is any other art more worth learning?

1956

Desert Toad

For a week, perhaps, I watched thunderclouds gather and come to nothing; or saw, a few miles away, the lazy unraveling of some patch of nimbus as its moisture dropped slowly to earth. Then one day our time came. The lightning moved closer; the thunder roared in our very ears; and, finally, the huge drops beat down viciously, leaving little craters in the sand where they fell. That time there was not much; but five days later the promise was fulfilled and I understood for the first time why the spinner of the Ancient Mariner's tale took only one short, unadorned sentence to tell of the most important event to occur in the poem. "And when I woke it rained." This was the real thing. Here and there on the uneven ground little puddles collected and stayed there, despite the sun which soon returned in full force, for nearly forty-eight hours. And with almost unbelievable promptitude the desert responded.

The oddest thing was a tentative sound which I heard first after the first insignificant shower. It came to me from somewhere out of the darkness, plaintive and feebly strident. It could be only some kind of a frog or toad, though no frog I had ever heard offered up to whatever his gods may be a plea like that. I could not remember ever having heard about desert frogs. Snakes, lizards, and tortoises, of course; but frogs, no. How, in a land where it is almost always dry, could a frog possibly find opportunity to lead the double life signified by the name of the group to which he belongs: the Amphibia? No wonder, I thought, that his voice sounds plaintive. How else can a creature who, so far as I know him, is happy only when wet or at least damp be anything but plaintive if the great Mother Nature has perversely cast his lot in a sandy waste? No frog of my acquaintance would put up with it.

132

After the second rain—the real one—the whole desert was suddenly vocal. Frog voices were lifted on every side. One might have thought one was living in a marsh, not a desert; might indeed, except for the strange southern accent, have supposed oneself back in New England on some spring day. Yet the songs, though no longer tentative, were nevertheless not the pure jubilation of the peeper. There was still, I fancied, a plaintiveness in them, as from a lingering sense of wrong. "It's high time," they said, "and we oughtn't to have been compelled to wait so long."

I seized a flashlight and went out to investigate. Being, like all members of their tribe, ventriloquists, they were at first not easy to locate. A voice always retreated as I approached, seemed always to be under the cholla or the clump of mesquite just beyond. At last, however, I came upon a monster puddle perhaps ten feet across and several inches deep. And there they were—some sitting gravely, knee-deep around the margin, others swimming happily about, only their goggle eyes above water but their hind legs visible below the surface as they gave the frog's perfect demonstration of the most effective leg stroke. One old fellow, sitting on the dead, fallen trunk of a cholla just at the water's brim, suddenly inflated his white throat and released a happy cry with an enthusiasm which shook him from stem to stern. I have never heard anything more heartfelt. The plaintiveness was gone, past wrongs were forgotten. He was hailing the wetness as a cock hails the first light of dawn. The swimmers on the other hand were merely practical fellows. Their actions demonstrated that this was the world-as-it-ought-to-be and that they were willing to let it go at that. But the poet had to proclaim it to the world. "Praise God from whom all blessings flow— sooner or later."

The specific name of one of our common eastern frogs is *clamitans*. That, I suppose, is the reason why, in my mind, frogs and the psalmist are all mixed up together. *De profundis clamavi*. It is not, I hasten to add, that I think disrespectfully of the psalmist as an old frog. It is rather that I think of the frog as a psalmist. One calls out from the depths, the other from a puddle. But the God to whom eternity is as a moment may find a similar lack of distinction between what we call depths and what we call puddles. And if the particular frog at whom my flashlight was at the moment pointed was pouring forth thanks rather than appeals for mercy, what he was saying had all the fervor if not all the articulateness of David's "A merry heart doeth good like a medicine" or "He maketh me to lie down by still waters." The sluggard should go to the ant, but the ungrateful might learn more from a desert frog on a wet night.

No reader, I hope, will mistake my piety for blasphemy. More than one, to my vast amazement, has done so in the past when, for example, I called New England's Day of the Peepers a sort of universal Easter. The trouble is, I suppose, that the pantheist keeps forgetting that his God is not a jealous God and that since All are One, no part of the whole is offended when another part is praised. He believes in many voices, many prophets, many incarnations, even; and he is grateful for them all. But *revenons à nos grenouilles*.

By the next night all was quiet again. Not one single voice out of what had seemed like myriads was to be heard. It is true that most of the puddles had long since dried up, but not the superpuddle I had investigated. It had shrunk to a quarter of its size, yet it was still bigger than most of those available the previous night and indubitably was still large enough to rejoice half a dozen of the frogs. Nevertheless, not one was to be found. All had vanished as mysteriously as they had come. The desert was again as frogless as I had supposed it always to be.

But why on earth should the creatures have got enough so soon? Must I revise completely my ideas about their tastes and temperaments? Is it possible that they have become so accustomed to an unfroggy dryness that one evening in the water is enough to last them for a while and that they crawl contentedly back to some hole in the sand? How and when do they lay their eggs, and where does that tadpole with which every frog must begin pass his youth? I know, to be sure, that certain tropical toads have the strange habit of sinking the eggs into little pits on the mother's back where they hatch out in due time and where the tadpoles, never knowing any body of water larger than the few drops which these pits contain, grow up. But if the southwestern frogs (mine, I am beginning to suspect, are actually toads) had any such fantastic habit, I am pretty sure I should have heard of it. The explanation must be simpler.

Before long I shall make a trip to consult some books and perhaps even some expert at the university who will enlighten me. My neighbors, of course, know nothing about the matter. "Sure, in the summertime you always hear those frogs after a rain. Darn things keep me awake sometimes." But their knowledge and their curiosity stop there. So far as they know (or care), frogs may be generated out of the sand when it gets wet, as the Egyptians thought they were generated out of the mud when the Nile overflowed its banks.

Until I get, in time, to my books or my expert I am not too unhappy to leave things as they are. The pleasures of ignorance—at least when accompanied by curiosity—rival those of knowledge, and I get a certain pleasure in this new country by assuming that it is actually unexplored so that what I find has never been found before. It has been a pleasure to check off one by one the expected things—to see my first horned toad and my first jack rabbit. But it has been an equal pleasure to be surprised by some plant or animal as new to me as though it were new to science.

In the long run I should grow restless and uncomfortable. For a reason which I cannot explain, I like to know that somebody knows, or that at least some book has recorded, quite a bit about every creature I am likely to see. I am not sure that I am not a little troubled by the fact that at least in the remoter parts of the world there are thousands of species of insects not yet named or listed. We are a race of Adams and it is assuredly one of our first duties to give names to the creatures who share our Eden. But for the time being I have still a little wondering to do about those frogs.

Those toads who surprised me by coming from nowhere after our first big rain and who sang their hallelujah chorus on every side have surprised me again. They have disappeared as mysteriously as they came. The desert floor and the desert air are as toadless as ever. Obviously, they are creatures as moderate as all amphibia should be, and one night of revelry was enough.

The next evening I did, to be sure, hear a few scattered voices, like those of stubborn guests who won't go home when a party is over. But all the rest had lapsed into silence and retired into invisibility. More than a month has passed, and despite one more rain as heavy as that which summoned them forth, not one has made himself heard. Nevertheless, I have a very good way of knowing that I did not dream the night they took over.

Forty-eight hours afterward, the largest of my puddles was swarming with tadpoles quite unaware of the fact that fate had assigned them an impossible situation. One more day of hot sun and the puddle was only a damp spot in the sand, covered at its very center with a mass of what had once been potential toads. Obviously the tadpoles had drawn closer and closer together as the puddle shrank, much as a human community might have concentrated itself as the waters of some rising flood drove all its members to the last remaining area of high ground. And they had been overwhelmed at last by the suffocating air, as human beings might have been by relentless water.

But how on earth do any ever survive to carry on the population which is obviously in quite a flourishing state? This puddle was an unusually large one. So far as I know, there was no other larger (and there is certainly no permanent water) within a mile or two of its position. I took it for granted that the tadpoles of this particular species must turn into toads in a remarkably brief period. But however brief it might be, it was obviously not brief enough to be covered by my puddle's duration. These toads, it would appear, ought to have become extinct in this region long ago. Obviously, they haven't.

Before long, I found that my ignorance was ceasing to be a pleasure. The first thing I discovered was that I need not have determined—as originally I did—to preserve it for a while; it has turned out to be not easy to dispel. My confidence that of course someone could answer all my questions was faith misplaced. No one, it now appears, knows very much more about my toads than I do.

Fortunately, I captured one of the two-inch adults and I kept him prisoner until I could consult Wright and Wright's authoritative check list of American toads and frogs. It was easy enough to identify him as the Sonoran spadefoot (*Scaphiopus couchii*) who inhabits Arizona, Utah, Mexico, and parts of Texas. He has an eastern relative, not especially uncommon but seldom recognized by the layman. Like all the spadefoots, he is a great digger with his hind legs and he is conveniently distinguished from all the Bufos (the genus to which the common garden toad belongs) by the fact that the contracted pupil of his eye is vertical like a cat's, not round or horizontal like that of the Bufos.

There is, then, no trouble about naming him, but the available information does not go much beyond that. He is believed to mate only once a year and always after a summer rain. At other periods he has been accidentally dug up out of the earth. But in what sort of pool does he successfully raise his family? How much of the time does he remain buried? Does he come out to eat occasionally during the almost year-long period when he is rarely if ever seen? Finally, how does he like the extraordinary existence which he seems to lead? On these questions, the books cover their silence with the air of not having the space to go in for that sort of thing. Queried face to face, the authorities shrug their shoulders: "Wish I knew." What a life the Sonoran spadefoot's must be! What does he *do,* buried in the sand for perhaps four-fifths of his time, even allowing for the supposition that he does venture forth to eat?

Gilbert White made famous the ancient tortoise in his garden who spent in naps most of the time he was not officially sleeping his winter sleep. It was, White thought, an odd whim on the part of God to bestow so long a life on a creature who seemed to care so little for it. But the case of the Sonoran spadefoot seems at least as remarkable. Many creatures hibernate and not a few estivate; but he is the only one of my acquaintance who does both, and his condition calls to mind that of the hillbilly of legend who suffered from insomnia. "I sleep fine nights; I sleep pretty well mornings; but in the afternoon I gets kinda restless." Yet on that rainy night when he did wake up, the spadefoot seemed very wide awake indeed.

I sincerely hope that in his underground cell he suffers no touch of claustrophobia. Perhaps this is Hamlet's nutshell and perhaps my toad feels himself, as Hamlet thought he would feel, "king of infinite space." I hope that it is not for him only one long morning-after, spent in recovering from his one big night; and if he meditates, I hope it is not exclusively and liquorishly of some July eleventh, or twelfth, or thirteenth.

Few creatures, surely, have ever been assigned by nature to a life more suited to contemplation. Spadefoots can have little experience of the outside world and hence little material on which to base any conclusions concerning nature or society. But there are subjects for which no experience is necessary. Some think that music, at least in its purely formal as opposed to its expressive aspects, is one. Less disputably, mathematics requires no experience of the world. Presumably a prisoner brought up in solitary confinement all his life might have developed the Pythagorean theorem or even invented Cartesian geometry. If the spadefoots are as thoughtful as they look, they must be engaged with some great abstract question to the pondering of which solitude and immobility are conducive. Perhaps it is something like the possible reconciliation of fate with free will. Or perhaps it is the real significance of the square root of minus one.

I rather hope it is the last, for I have never been satisfied that the practical use of the symbol for it as a direction indicator is the real, or at least the only logical, meaning. Someday, after Ina has had a little more time to think, I am going to whisper suddenly in her ear, "Complex variable!" The experiment will be as sensible as some I have read about.

1952

III. SHAPES OF EARTH

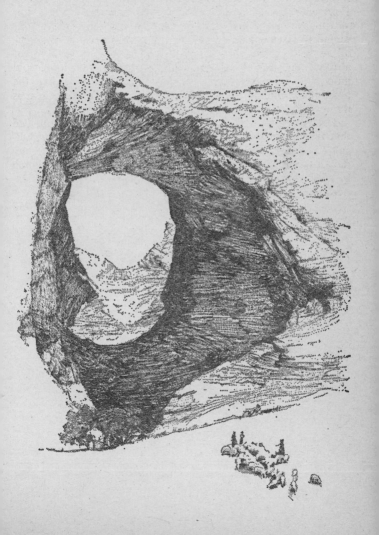

The finest workers in stone are not copper or
steel tools, but the gentle touches of air
and water working at their leisure with a
liberal allowance of time.

HENRY DAVID THOREAU

Coral Dunes

There are several different ways of enjoying scenery and the American Southwest is one of the best places to practice them.

If you are one of those to whom the beauty of a landscape means primarily form and color for their own sakes, then the bright colors and strange but fascinating forms found almost everywhere will be outstandingly rewarding.

Because vegetation is mostly sparse in the dry climate, the earth reveals its structure as it does not in regions where the shape of hills, mountains, and cliffs is smothered in green. Because so many of the formations are sandstone, they are multicolored in vivid reds, yellows and, occasionally, blues. Because they have been sculptured for centuries by wind-blown sand, they have assumed all sorts of fantastically beautiful shapes.

These great sandstone buttes are commonly called "monuments," and ancient as they are, there is something curiously modern in their style. They are not fussy and overly ornamented in the Victorian fashion. They are bold, stark, and angled, and a visit to, say, Monument Valley, which straddles the border between Arizona and Utah, is like visiting a gallery of hugely magnified modern sculpture. It is both strange and strangely beautiful.

There is another way of enjoying a landscape. It is to see it as not merely interesting shapes and interesting colors but as a record of our earth's history, a plain tale which tells those who know how to read it how and when these mountains, these valleys, these canyons, and these monuments came to be what they are.

Geology is the science of reading that record with a full understanding of all its details, and most of us are not geologists. But the main outlines of the story are readily understandable by anyone who takes the trouble to look at the large striking features of the landscape with that in mind.

Every year thousands of tourists pass through the little Utah town of Kanab, heading northward toward Zion and Bryce canyons or eastward toward the new Glen Canyon National Recreation Area. Most of them do not even notice a modest wooden arrow a few miles east of the town which points down a dirt road and is marked "Coral Dunes." Still fewer accept its invitation, and that is perhaps just as well, for the undisturbed beauty of the dunes (some dozen miles from the main road) is one of their charms. On an early June morning, my companions and I had them to ourselves in the cool of five thousand feet.

Much of northern Arizona and southern Utah is a land of towering sandstone mesas and buttes, some white, some pink, and some coral-red. They have been sculptured into fantastic shapes and are gradually being eroded away by water, frost, and especially by windblown sand. Some are half buried in their own detritus but still rise sheer above the semidesert plains. At the Coral Dunes, on the other hand, the prevailing wind has heaped and shaped sand into dunes as high as twenty-five feet, which, incidentally, recently furnished a perfect setting for a motion picture, whose action is supposed to take place in the Arabian Desert.

Nothing quite prepares one for the climactic view. The approach is across a semidesert, increasingly sandy but with the sand held in place by fairly abundant sage and juniper together with a few pines. All of them grow less and less abundant, and then one comes upon a true Sahara of drifting coral-colored dunes sloping gently upward on one side, dropping off abruptly on the other; sometimes rippled as though by waves of a seashore; sometimes almost unbelievably smooth and sleek.

At first, one is unaware of any living thing except, perhaps, for ravens calling derisively overhead. No animals are visible. But the most casual inspection reveals the fact that they are only unseen, not absent. There are tracks which can only be those of a bobcat and there are other curious little bipedal marks which proclaim the kangaroo rat. Most beautiful, and at first most puzzling, are long lines of the most delicate tracery, sketched across the smooth surface uphill and down. Each one is perfect despite its obvious fragility and all suggest some secret mysterious workman. What could have made them? Not a small lizard because there is no trailing tail mark. Certainly not a sidewinder rattlesnake, whose strange tracks are much broader and in other ways quite different.

It doesn't take much looking to find the answer. The tiny workmen are everywhere busy, often no more than a few yards from one another. They are little, shiny, quarter-inch, scarab-like beetles *(Sphaeriontis muricata)*. From the order to which they belong, it seems a pretty safe guess that their unresting progress uphill and down is motivated by nothing more spiritual than a search for the droppings of a jack rabbit. But it would not be difficult to imagine that they are artists, endlessly engaged in beautifying the dunes with the perfect but changeless pattern of lace which nature has ordained their six legs to make during many millenniums and which they will continue to make for untold millenniums hence—unless, as seems not improbable, man destroys their environment as he is destroying that of many more conspicuous creatures.

Most of the dunes are shifting, and they are often marching forward in the direction of the prevailing wind. Any sizable plant which manages to get established tends to anchor the sand around it, but more often than not it loses the struggle and is overwhelmed by the slowly advancing waves which may ultimately pass over it, leaving behind a shallower bed of sand in which a new generation of plants may be able to grow.

Evidence of that process is plainly visible in the Coral Dunes. One may see, for example, the skeleton of a pine killed sometime in the past by an advancing wave; beside it are younger pines or junipers which have grown since the crest of the wave passed by. On the leeward side of one of the highest dunes a single clump of sagebrush is visible. But it is doomed and half-buried already.

Many wild flowers, able to establish themselves and mature in much less time than the juniper or even the sagebrush, flourish in patches which here and there provide an arresting flash of color, standing vividly against the red of the dunes. Two are especially conspicuous—the large yellow member of the sunflower tribe *(Wyethia scabra)* sometimes called "mules-ears" and the lovely blue *Sophora stemophylla* which, from a short distance, might be mistaken for a lupine and which has no common name. Most surprising in the desert is a little mushroom, the desert puffball (*Tulostoma poculatum*).

All the larger plants must send down deep roots, and some of them may survive even an advancing wave of sand by raising their stems higher and higher as the roots go deeper and deeper. This is the method of a handsome yucca of limited distribution named *Yucca kanabensis* after the nearby town. A different solution to the problem is to spread out over a large area and send down two shallow roots every foot or two to snatch from the surface the water of the rare and usually limited showers. This is the method of another characteristic plant, the scurf-pea (*Psoralea lanceolata*), of which a single prostrate branch may be more than seventy feet long.

Dunes like these are both aesthetically pleasing and ecologically instructive. But they are equally interesting in another way. They occur less frequently than mountains or plains or valleys or canyons, but like all of these they are quite distinct and recognizable geomorphic features and, again like the others, they raise in any inquiring mind the question of how and why they came into being.

In terms of earth and atmospheric mechanics, the answer is always the same whether the material be the sands of a seashore, the gypsum grains of the great White Sands of New Mexico, the eroded sandstone of these Coral Dunes, or even the ice crystals of the snowdrift. And the forms assumed are so similar that a photograph of the White Sands might easily be mistaken for that of a New England snowbank.

Given a flat, open surface and hard grains of material too heavy to be blown away by the prevailing wind but not too heavy to be moved by it, the dunes are nearly inevitable. If the grains are too light, they blow away as dust; if they are too heavy (small pebbles, for example), they cannot be piled up by the winds. But if they are just right, you get the similar outlines of the same geomorphic feature. And there are minor variations in shapes, depending partly upon the character of the winds. But a dune is a dune is a dune.

Geographers tell us that the wind seldom lifts sand particles more than a foot or two, that the grains are usually simply rolled along, and that they come to rest when the wind's velocity decreases. Once started, a dune itself becomes an obstruction around which the winds swirl and deposit more sand. Because of the variations in wind velocity and sand supply there are different characteristic shapes in different regions, and those most characteristic of the Coral Dunes are what are called "barchans"—that is, hillocks with a sloping side up which the prevailing winds blow the sand and a steeper leeward side where the grains have come to their angle of repose.

Though the Coral Dunes of Utah are in many respects typical, there is one fact about them of additional interest: the material of which they are composed has been twice reduced to sand in the course of many millions of years.

The mesas and buttes which surround them are composed of Navajo sandstone formed during the Jurassic period (say 100 or 150 million years ago). But that sandstone was composed of the detritus from much more ancient mountains long before worn down. Now, this Navajo sandstone has itself been eroded away to make the sand which may (given more millions of years) again solidify into stone—either under water or, like the sandstones of nearby Zion, right on the desert itself, in which case they will still exhibit by their crossbedding the outlines of successive dunes, like those so clearly seen in Zion.

There are few more striking examples of the restlessness of our earth—always building up, tearing down, and then building up again as the result of the processes which will probably continue until a completely cooled earth can no longer raise mountains and its whole surface is reduced to a featureless plain.

Just before I arrived at the Coral Dunes, a local newspaper announced the coming invasion of a fleet of sand-buggies which proposed to race up and down over the dunes. Fortunately, wind will, in this case, probably erase their vandalism in a comparatively short time. But here is another example of the fallacy of "multiple use." You cannot use the Coral Dunes (now an undeveloped state park) for both sand-buggy racing and the quiet enjoyment of their aesthetic, ecological, and geological interest.

1966

Undiscovered Country

Resting some years ago at the summit of Navajo Mountain, which rises ten thousand feet just north of the Arizona border and up whose sides no road has ever been attempted, I looked down upon an area of stony, broken plateau which included, so I was told, an area as large as Connecticut but inhabited by no single man, white or Indian. For all I know, this may have been a slight exaggeration; for I have since learned from observation how persistently isolated settlers push themselves in from around the edges of uninhabited areas to take up lonely residence, sometimes in places fantastically inaccessible to the outside world. In any event, nevertheless, this is one of the few remaining "white spots" on the map of the United States, and much of it may fairly be called unexplored. Parties have traversed it from time to time, and there are a few recognized routes which follow tracks, sometimes passable to cars with four-wheel drives, sometimes not. It was through this area that in 1776 Father Escalante tried to make his way from Santa Fe to California and had such bad luck that few have since tried his route. One would have to travel far to find another area less well known or, for that matter, one which until now has offered fewer reasons other than aesthetic ones why anyone should want to know it.

In its own aloof, almost contemptuous, way it is nevertheless extraordinarily beautiful—nature's ultimate achievement in that Southwestern Style which surprisingly executes great monolithic forms, sometimes sculptural and sometimes architectural, in bright, multihued sandstone. About the style there is nothing to suggest the charm of the landscape which welcomes man; instead, there is only the grandeur of something powerfully alien, indifferent, and enduring, as though it had been made to please the eye and perhaps even to sooth the spirit of some creature older, as well as less transitory, than he. Ever since I got my Pisgah sight of it stretching away several thousand feet below the mountain, I have hoped some day to penetrate at least a little way into the almost unviolated fastnesses. And now I have done so.

One spectacular section was first "discovered" three or four years ago. The quotes I use for a reason to be presently apparent, but at least photographs were then first taken for publication and it became a region where one might with a minimum of effort become, if not a Balboa, then at least a pilgrim sufficiently early to feel that he had escaped the shame of being a mere vulgar sight-seer. There is nothing that a tourist despises more than another tourist, and Cathedral Valley, as it was promptly dubbed, is not yet on any tourist route.

The jumping-off place is Fremont, one of those surprising little communities due to the enterprise of the Mormons who industriously colonized every fertile spot. Fremont is only a few miles from a paved road; it has one telephone for the general use of the inhabitants and a power line connected with some hydroelectric plant far away. But it is also sixty miles from the nearest doctor or dentist, and from its eastern edge the great white area stretches away. I found there the descendant of an early settler who knew the country, was possessed of a jeep and readily persuadable to show me a region which he, unlike many natives of remote places, found absorbingly interesting. Within fifteen minutes after I had first laid eyes upon him we were off.

An ungraded road used by cattlemen leads up a mountain-side to a minor summit something over eight thousand feet high. From it one looks north toward a higher peak, which was still, in June, snow-clad at the top, its slopes clothed in aspens, some already in leaf, others, in the less-favored areas, not yet green. To the south, at one's feet, begins a panorama which seems totally unrelated to any other part of the landscape. The mountain falls precipitously away for several thousand feet and from its base there stretches, as far as the eye can reach, a desert floor shimmering in the hot sun. Here and there plateaus, miles long and miles broad, rise almost sheer from the flatlands. Between them, the floor is sprinkled with sandstone buttes, larger than any man built cathedral, which sometimes suggest Perpendicular Gothic, sometimes the Angkor Wat. Inevitably the impression is of an abandoned city, vaster than any city, ancient or modern, ever was. We negotiated the descent, and after a final plunge down a forty-five-degree angle, were upon the trackless floor itself, free to spend a long day circling the most impressive monuments, and in the process, gaining in respect for the capabilities of the jeep what we lost in that for the ability of the human body to absorb the bounces and the jerks incident to travel in a vehicle which—due allowance being made for its breadth— can go most places a horse can go.

In the course of that long day we saw no other human being, and had no reason to suppose that any other would come there within any particular period of time. It is thus truly a region uninhabited. But whether it is also "undiscovered" or even "recently discovered" is a different question, and others more competent than I have struggled with the attempt to define that much-abused term.

Vilhjalmur Stefansson's somewhat cynical formulation is perhaps as good as any. A country, he remarks, is generally said to be "discovered" when for the first time a white man —preferably an Englishman—happens to set foot upon it. After all, it was only in that sense that Columbus "discovered" America, and few places except the Poles have ever been discovered in any other. What we really mean by the word is usually "made known to that part of the world to which we happen to belong," and in that sense Cathedral Valley really was "discovered" only a few years ago. But our guide—a strict Mormon who refused tea and coffee, as well as tobacco—was also an honest man and he volunteered the information that for at least fifty years a rancher had been turning his cattle loose in the "undiscovered" valley for the winter and rounding them up again when the time came for their summer on the mountain.

Perhaps "unseen" would be a better word than "undiscovered." That term can be made to stick, for the guide told us also that when he showed the first photographs to the cowboys they expressed astonishment as well as interest. "Where on earth is that?" And when they were assured that they had been there a score of times, they admitted that, perhaps, they had. But cowboys are interested in the state of their cattle and the state of their range, not very much interested in scenery, no matter how sublime. Hence they had not "discovered" the valley, either for the rest of the world or even for themselves.

According to a theory at least as old as Immanuel Kant, a purely aesthetic experience is possible only in the presence of something which provokes no reaction other than contemplation. Thus a picture, no matter how realistic, differs from the object which it represents because the object invites us, as the picture does not, to act in connection with it. And though it seems unlikely that any of these cowboys had read the *Critique of Practical Reason,* they certainly confirmed Kant's theory. When they saw Cathedral Valley itself they performed the activities which it suggested. Only when they saw a picture did they discover the thing itself because, for the first time, they then engaged in that contemplation which alone can make us aware of things-in-themselves. Since I had no cattle to tend and not even a horse or a jeep to manage I was free to treat the valley as an object of contemplation and it was for that I had come.

In no country remotely resembling it have I ever settled down to live, even for a week or two at a time. Now that I have returned to a different desert, which was never so strange to me as the one I had just left, the incredible valley seems more than far away—rather as though it were part of some universe discontinuous with this one and as inaccessible as the fourth dimension. Having treated it as nothing but an object of contemplation, it has already lost all reality except that of a work of the artistic imagination, and I realize again that only a country which one has both lived in and contemplated can assume in the mind that special sort of solidity which no amount of mere sight-seeing can give it. Really to possess the Valley I should need both the cowboy's doing and my own looking—which is something no one, perhaps, has yet achieved for that particular region.

I am not by any means sure that I should like to try. The fact that I never have stayed long in any part of the monument country may be the consequence of a certain defensive reaction. There is a kind of beauty—and it is presumably the kind prevailing throughout most of the universe—of which man gets thrilling glimpses but which is fundamentally alien to him. It is well for him to glance occasionally at the stars or to think for a moment about eternity. But it is not well to be too continuously aware of such things, and we must take refuge from them with the small and the familiar. I am not among those who are said to have already hopefully registered their names as prospective passengers on the first experimental rocket which our military authorities send to the moon because I very much doubt that I should like to stay even long enough to prepare for the return trip. And there is a certain suggestion of the lunar in the regions I have been contemplating.

According to the geologists, the sandstones which compose them are quite young as rocks go—younger, for instance, than the uppermost layer of the Grand Canyon, below which the river has cut through successive strata to flow now over stone a billion years old. The limestone rim over which tourists peer was already formed while parts of Cathedral Valley were under water, and I myself have noticed, not far from it, a plain composed almost exclusively of shells which once belonged to quite up-to-date-looking mussels. Yet for all that, the monuments look older than anything else on earth—partly perhaps because their age and the effects of it come within the scope of the human imagination, to which a thousand years are something conceivable while millions are not. It is certainly in part because they seem so old and so unchanging, so finished yet so nearly indestructible, that they are overwhelming and awesome.

Wherever the earth is clothed with vegetation not too sparse to modify its essential outlines, it makes man feel to some extent at home because things which, like him, change and grow and die have asserted their importance. But wherever, as in this region of wind-eroded stone, living things are no longer common enough or conspicuous enough to seem more than trivial accidents, he feels something like terror. Despite the stunted junipers and the harsh little shrubs upon which cattle can support themselves if they have space enough over which to wander, this is a country where the inanimate dominates and in which not only man but the very plants themselves seem intruders. We may look at it as we look at the moon, but we feel rejected. It is neither for us nor for our kind.

Here indeed is "beauty bare," and whoever has looked upon it may claim to have shared the experience which Miss Millay once attributed to Euclid alone. Certain cultures have, to be sure, tried to imitate it in their own creations. It is in the spirit of the pyramids, both Egyptian and Mayan. But they are a symptom of something deliberately destructive of that which those of us who are children of the Renaissance call "human," a symptom, that is to say, of a determination to live with and to be like something in which we really have no part. As I climbed out of the vast emptiness up toward the heights where even snow and aspens seemed, by comparison, cozy and intimate, I tried to formulate in my own mind what it was that I had been most aware of as I stood in the shadow of one great block of sculptured stone to look across the clear air at another and another and another, towering in the distance. Perhaps what the landscape insisted upon was something which is only a little less obvious elsewhere. Perhaps it was only the platitude that man is small and that life is precarious.

But why should I say "only" a platitude? Art knows no triumph greater than that which consists in making a platitude valid again. Why should it be assumed that nature herself can accomplish more? It was worth going to Cathedral Valley really to appreciate for an instant facts so often cited and so seldom realized. Perhaps it was also worthwhile to leave it soon. Such truths are among those which no one should either totally forget or be too constantly aware of.

1952

Water Doesn't Run Uphill

Those who write about Grand Canyon generally begin by saying that it is indescribable; then they undertake to describe it. That error, at least, I shall attempt to avoid. Few have not seen some of the innumerable photographs which have been taken from hundreds of different points of view and, inadequate as they necessarily are, they give a better notion of the superficial features than direct word pictures can. They hardly suggest the vastness of the scale, but statistics also mean little because the imagination does not take them in.

You can say that the winding course of the Canyon is more than two hundred miles long, that it varies from four to eighteen miles in breadth, and that the walls of the inner gorge are, in most places, so steep that it is impossible to climb out—as various early adventurers discovered too late when their boats were wrecked and they left their skeletons in a prison from which they had not been able to escape. You can add that between Navajo Bridge, near the eastern entrance to the Canyon, and Lake Mead—which is two hundred miles by river to the west—the only place where it can be crossed by tourists is the little foot-and-mule bridge a vertical mile below the point where the two hotels face one another across a ten-mile gap. You can add that the shortest way to get across that ten-mile gap without making the arduous journey down one side and up the other is to make the more than two-hundred-mile journey which carries you around the eastern end of the Canyon and then west and south to the point just opposite the one you left.

Finally, if you like to go in for superlatives, you can say that no other valley (and a canyon is simply a narrow valley) is at once so deep and so narrow; that though there are narrower gorges and, in the Alps, for example, wider valleys lying farther below the summits of the mountains enclosing them, there is nowhere else on earth a valley or canyon at once so deep, so long, and so closely hemmed in by its walls. This last is the simplest and most obvious of the facts which make Grand Canyon seem unique even at first glance. But perhaps the wisest thing to say about it is what the distinguished German geologist, Hans Cloos, tells us: "I remembered, or tried to remember, that the Rhine Valley at Caub is only a few hundred yards wide and deep, and yet is also called a 'canyon.' "

Seen only from the rim and thought of only as a spectacle, the "view" has some of the insubstantiality of a cloudscape changing color and form almost from moment to moment. By noon the reds and whites and greens have been faded out to pastel shades, and the bold contours flattened almost to two dimensions. Then, as the sun moves westward and shadows begin to form, the strong colors begin to stand out again, the massive mesas and buttes which had been flattened against the opposite wall until they were almost unnoticed step boldly forth, and all the innumerable minor terraces, side canyons, and pointed projections emerge in sharp relief. In late afternoon the depths begin to fill with a haze which looks almost like sea fog but is actually blue sky, or at least the result of the same phenomena which make the sky seem blue—namely, sunlight scattered by innumerable tiny particles in a very dry and almost dust-free air. As the sun sets, its red light gives a fiery glow to the red sandstone and shale which form the eminences lifted out of the mist.

The tradition that has been followed in naming the various mesas and buttes "Shiva Temple," "Vishnu Temple," etc., is perhaps regrettable. It prettifies and trivializes what it might be better to leave without the distracting element of inadequate comparison. These "temples" are much larger and much more ancient than any historical names can suggest. Nevertheless, the tradition was begun in Major Powell's time and has at least the justification that if these great monuments are to be compared with anything man-made, it is the Oriental they suggest. They are not Gothic and they are even more obviously not Classic. But they do seem to suggest the riotous fancy of the East and have reminded many a spectator of the Angkor Wat—though neither any Oriental potentate nor even any Egyptian Pharaoh ever dared dream of construction on such a scale. By comparison, the largest pyramid is a pimple on the face of the earth.

Here we come face to face with one of the greatest paradoxes of the Canyon. It looks lawless, fantastic and whimsical. If it were on a lesser scale, one would be tempted to say "freakish." By comparison with the great simple outlines of most of nature's great works, by comparison with the Alps or the Himalayas or even Yosemite and Lake Louise, it seems deficient in rhyme or reason; a curiosity or mere anomaly; something dreamed rather than something illustrative of the grand principles in accordance with which our globe was formed.

Actually, however, once one has begun to grasp its meaning in structural terms, its rationale begins to emerge, and one begins to understand it, not as cloudscape, but as an astounding demonstration of what can happen when the same great forces that have elsewhere sculptured the earth in such varied but oft-repeated ways worked out their problem under a set of conditions never met elsewhere on any such scale.

Every feature expresses that logic which we have come to find indispensable in the human architecture we most admire. For every feature there is a why and a wherefore. And the plain answers to the why, the clearness of the logic, are the reasons for both its uniqueness and the sustained interest it can arouse. Nowhere else are landscape and geology more intimately related; the one more clearly an expression of the other. But the logic is not immediately apparent.

A tale often told in various versions concerns a cowboy (or a prospector or a scout) who found himself suddenly upon the rim, who gasped, and then exclaimed aloud: "Something has happened here!" Obviously something has—something stupendous and seemingly catastrophic. From the days of the Indians who wandered in and around it, through the days of the legendary cowboy and down to those of the real tourist, explanations ranging from the moderately ingenious to the howlingly absurd have been given.

Like so many peoples in so many different parts of the world, the Navajos have a flood story, and according to them a great inland sea at one time covered the whole area round about until finally it broke a passageway through the canyon

and then ran out. Since there was no Navajo Noah, all their
ancestors were turned into fish. For that reason no good
Navajo will eat fish—except, perhaps, out of a can of trader's
salmon from which the label has been removed. And before
you ask him how *he* happens to be here if all his forefathers
became fish, just pause to consider that he might, if he has
been to an Indian Agency school, ask you, in return, who
Cain's wife was. In religious discussions such questions are
bad manners.

More sophisticated answers offer a wide choice though
most of them will not stand up under even moderately
searching examination. Perhaps, so it has been said, the Canyon is a great crack which broke open when the earth cooled
—a simple theory very attractive to those who imagine that
we are living directly upon the cooled crust of a once molten
ball. But it is a theory hardly tenable in view of the fact that
thousands of fossils lie buried in the Canyon walls and could
not very well have been laid down there while the earth was
hot.

Still more fantastic was the suggestion that the Colorado
was once an underground river flowing through a cavern
whose ceiling fell in; somewhat more ingenious is the theory
that, since the promontories of the two rims could be more or
less exactly fitted into one another, they drifted apart, leaving the gap through which the river might flow. After all,
there is a respectable geological theory that Africa and South
America, which do look like adjacent parts of a jigsaw puzzle,
were once joined. And one of the projects of the Geophysical
Year was to attempt to determine whether or not any "conti-
nental drift" is now detectable.

The simplest, most inclusive, and at the same time vaguest
explanation is that which eighteenth-century geologists gave
when faced with any great disturbance of the earth's crust:
"cataclysm," or "catastrophe," they said. Or, in the cowboy's
words, "something happened"—something sudden, violent,
and too explosive to be reasoned about. That, in the day of
Cuvier and before Lyell founded modern geology, was the
answer to everything. From time to time, it was assumed, the
earth heaved, broke, and in the ensuing chaos every living
thing was destroyed so that, once things had quieted down
again, life had to start all over again, experimenting after
each catastrophe with new forms until, sometime after the

most recent, the Garden of Eden was planted and all the plants and animals now living (including, of course, man) were created. Hardly more than a century and a half ago that was what most people who had thought at all about such matters believed. The theory had, moreover, at least a secondary convenience. It accounted for the obviously very ancient fossils as vestiges of previous creations and made it possible to believe that man and all the still living animals were created on the sixth day of a recent new beginning.

If you listen long enough by the parapet in front of Bright Angel Lodge, you will hear all these theories expounded. But there is also a whole class of new ones which would never have occurred to the men of any age before ours and which reveal a fundamental change in man's sense of the relation between nature's powers and his: those explanations, I mean, which suggest human agency.

One park ranger insists that he was asked some years ago if the Canyon had been a WPA project. Perhaps the propounder of this question was only a satiric rogue. But suggestions almost as preposterous have been seriously made, and they are usually introduced with some such remark as, "You can't tell me it was made without human aid." Probably I should find it impossible to believe that any of the "human aid" theories were seriously advanced had I not myself once been stunned into silence by an educated woman who would hear no objection to her firm conviction that the vast sandstone buttes in Monument Valley were the remains of an ancient civilization.

Behind all such suggestions lies the unconscious assumption that man's works are by now the most imposing on earth and that his power now exceeds nature's. No age before ours would have made such an assumption. Man has always before thought of himself as puny by comparison with natural forces, and he was humble before them. But we have been so impressed by the achievements of technology that we are likely to think we can do more than nature herself. We dug the Panama Canal, didn't we? Why not the Grand Canyon? Actually we are suffering from delusions of grandeur, from a state of hubris which may bring about a tragic catastrophe in the end. And I cannot imagine how we may be cured of it if the only effect of coming face to face with the most impressive demonstrations of what nature can do and of the scale on which she operates is an intensification of the delusion that she has been conquered and outdone. When a man had accomplished some unusually impressive achievement it used to be said that he had "God's help." Nowadays we are more likely to assume that He needs ours.

But if nature, following her recognizable laws, made the Canyon "without human aid," then why did she do so many unusual things at this particular spot? Consider, to begin with, the most obvious anomaly. The mile-deep gash is cut through a high plateau seven to eight thousand feet above sea level and surrounded everywhere by lower-lying lands. To get to it one must climb up, no matter from what direction one approaches. Why did not the Colorado, like a normal river, flow around this obstruction as rivers nearly everywhere flow around even mere hillocks when they come to them?

Two hundred years ago anyone who had asked such a question would have been compelled to conclude that the river had just happened to come upon this strange channel through the plateau, though that answer would leave him with the equally puzzling question of how the channel came to be there. By the middle of the nineteenth century any reasonably instructed person would have known that rivers do not *find* channels but *make* them and that, improbable as it seems, the Colorado must have cut a gash a mile deep through the rock. But how did it get up there in the first place?

Now that the channel has been cut, the river flows normally—always from a higher level to a lower until it emerges from the Canyon and flows finally into the Gulf of California. Seemingly, it must once have run uphill—defying the laws of nature in order that it might someday flow normally again. An improbable story indeed! And why, even now, is it a paradox among rivers because it does not, at the Canyon, drain the country through which it flows? Most of the water which falls upon the surrounding region to the south runs downhill, away from the river, instead of draining into it.

Some two hundred miles northeast of Grand Canyon the San Juan River, one of the tributaries of the Colorado, cuts a canyon of its own. It is something more than twelve hundred feet deep instead of five thousand, and its length is only six miles. But it looks in many respects like a miniature version of its grandiose brother, and on any scale except that of Grand Canyon itself it is quite a spectacle. Geologists will tell you that the first of the surviving rock formations through which the river cut is slightly older than that at the rim of Grand Canyon, but to the lay eye the walls appear much the same and they have been eroded into terraces somewhat similar. Moreover, it is, in one respect, even more abnormal-looking. The river twists and turns in so extravagant and seemingly senseless a fashion (six miles to go one straight line mile) that it has earned the name "Goosenecks." Seven times it doubles back in such a way that it flows almost parallel with itself, and the stream runs now in one direction, now in the other, with only a narrow rock between two opposing currents.

One does not need to be trained to ask geological questions to be struck by the fact that this is not the way rivers swift enough to cut deep channels are accustomed to run. Swift rivers run straight; sluggish ones meander. Looking at the course taken by the now swift San Juan, one is likely to be reminded of some slow-moving brook lazing its way across a nearly flat meadow and running so feebly that the slightest impediments turn it aside as it follows the path of least resistance here and there across the flat surface. If such a meadow brook cut deeply enough, it would make its own "gooseneck" canyon. But of course it doesn't and it couldn't. It is not swift enough to cut much, and if it were swift, it would flow over the almost invisible little obstructions which now turn it this way and that. In fact, it meanders so irresolutely that it may vary its channel from time to time, leveling the meadow still further. But it will never cut a deep channel.

Obviously the San Juan at the Goosenecks must have been sometime a meandering stream. As a matter of fact, the Goosenecks form what geologists call "an entrenched meander." But what, one wonders, can have happened to turn this feeble little current into a torrent large enough and swift enough to cut through hundreds of feet of solid rock and yet not make the straight channel to be expected of a swift river?

Probably, one will think first of the possibility that the earth, in one of her periodic convulsions, suddenly raised or tilted the flat surface across which the stream meandered, thus making it swifter and for some other reason more abundant. But that won't do. Tilt the meadow with its brook, and the stream will simply leap over the sinuosities of its low banks to take a shorter cut from high ground to low. Under those conditions it might cut a channel but it would not be the channel of its old meander.

There is, however, an obvious explanation of the anomaly. The land must have risen, but risen so slowly that the stream was never dumped out of its channel; so slowly, indeed, that it deepened this channel as fast or faster than the land rose and thus preserved the same course it had taken when it was too feeble to do more than obey the demands of every minor variation in level.

The explanation would never have been accepted by, and would probably never have occurred to, anyone two centuries ago. Like all the explanations offered by geology today, it assumes vast stretches of time and assumes that the earth has existed for very much longer than anyone formerly dreamed that it had. The belief that its age was measured in a few thousands, not in many millions, of years was supported by the Biblical story. But even without that, the assumption was almost inevitable to a creature who instinctively measures things on a scale related to his own experience. It just didn't seem probable that anything had endured so much longer than man or the history he knew. Yet the existence of the Goosenecks and the Canyon—for which no credible explanation not involving millions of years is discoverable—is just one of the many kinds of things which gradually forced upon the human mind the intellectual conviction that the mountains, plains, and rivers among which man passes his brief life are old beyond his power to grasp, and make demands on his imagination that it can hardly compass.

Was Grand Canyon formed in precisely the same way as its small brother, the Goosenecks? Though many nineteenth-century geologists thought so, it is now generally believed that the explanation is not quite so simple. The Colorado also winds back and forth, but its meanderings are probably, in part at least, the result of rock structures encountered during its downward progress. It is not, in other words, merely the entrenchment of many meanders. But the essential fact that remains is this: The Colorado, like the San Juan, once flowed across flat country which lay at approximately the level of the present stream bed. It had climbed no mountains to get there, resisted no impulse to run steeply the shortest way downhill; and its height above sea level was not greater than it is now. The river, though it cut through rock now forming the rim, was never "up there."

Slowly, however, the earth began to rise under the river—never fast enough to dump it out of its channel, never so fast that it could not cut downward more rapidly than the earth rose. At the same time, the Colorado was becoming a mightier river. When the Rocky Mountains first rose, they had brought down more water and made or increased western rivers. Later, as each of the successive ice ages ended, melting snow and ice brought flooding waters and with them the sand and pebbles and stones with which the river cuts downward —not so much like the knife with which it is commonly compared, as like a file or a cutting disk well supplied with abrasive. Moreover, as geologists are fond of pointing out, the process was not like pushing a knife into a cake, but like raising the cake slowly upward against an immobile knife.

No one knows why the earth rises, falls, and sometimes buckles or breaks in its alarming way. But it has done just that many times in the past and is doing it now. A year or two ago one of the Galápagos Islands rose with such unusual suddenness that what had been a bay became a shore. The Himalayas are believed to be still in the making, and Mount Everest is said to be rising. Parts of the California coast are also rising; other parts of the United States sinking. Whether or not the rocks of the Canyon walls and floor are still moving upward, no one knows, though earthquakes in the region suggest that they may be, and there is plenty of cutting power still left in the Colorado. In recent times it has carried as much as 27,000,000 tons of sand and silt past Bright Angel Point in one day and probably averages more than half a million—another reminder that "human aid" couldn't approximate its work.

Mountains are still a great deal more massive than skyscrapers. The most awesome force that man-induced atomic fission has ever released is puny by comparison with that unleashed in a hurricane, to say nothing of that which lifted the Rockies and the Alps. If, as park naturalists often point out, the Empire State Building had been built on the river, its summit would be just barely visible from the rim as it peeped above the inner gorge some four thousand feet below.

That the Colorado dug out what our bulldozers could not is even more vividly suggested by a comparison with the work done on the Panama Canal.

That, I suppose, represents man's greatest attempt to rival nature as an earth mover. It involved the stupendous task of moving something like 450,000,000 cubic yards of dirt and stone. But the Colorado moves about 170,000,000 cubic yards *per year*—or more than a Panama Canal-full every three years. And it has been working—at various rates, of course—for several millions of years!

When did all this happen? When did the land begin to rise and the river to cut downward? How long have at least the beginnings of the Canyon been there?

No one knows exactly. Estimates have varied all the way from one to several million years. But on any scale except the human the discrepancy is not very great, and today the one-million-year estimate is generally regarded as untenable. A million or seven million years is a short time as geology goes and not so very long ago. In any case, the Canyon is what has been described as "a youthful geomorphic feature." In general valleys and canyons are likely to be the youngest grand features of any landscape except for those for which recent volcanic action is responsible.

Take even the discredited million-year estimate, and that would mean that the beginnings of the Canyon go back to about the time of the earliest half-man. Take the seven million, and it would already have been imposing by the time the first recognizable human existed anywhere. But in either case, the presence or absence of the nearly human would be the only really major difference so far as life on earth is concerned. Seven million years ago mammals were already becoming dominant, and flowering plants were already more successful than the fernlike and horsetail-like vegetation of earlier times. Seven million years ago there may have already been pony-sized horses on the American plains, though they were later to disappear and the horse was reintroduced by Europeans. A million years ago one of the great ice ages was about to begin and the woolly mammoth to flourish.

At whichever time the cutting may have begun, it was long after the last of the giant reptiles had perished and after his hardened footprints had already been buried beneath hundreds of feet of the shale and sandstone which had to be washed away before the footprints were again exposed. They can still be seen not many miles away. And as the river sawed slowly through the rising strata, its deepening walls exposed again to sight older and older formations going back more and more millions of years until, finally, they add up to more than a billion. Nowhere on the earth's surface (except possibly on the Canadian Shield) are to be seen rocks older than those which form the sides of the Canyon's inner gorge.

What has all this to do with the beauty of the Canyon or with the peace and quiet and solitude to be found on its rim? Some would answer "nothing," and for them that answer is perhaps correct. But it is not the only one. Spaciousness has a great deal to do with the sense of peace and quiet and solitude, and spaciousness can be temporal as well as dimensional. Seated at any point on the rim, I look up and down as well as east and west, and the vista is one of the most extensive ever vouchsafed to man. But I am also at a point in time as well as in space. The one vista is as grandiose as the other. I am small and alone in the middle of these great distances, vertical as well as horizontal. But the gulf of time over which I am poised is inconceivably more vast and much more dizzying to peer into.

There is also another, less intangible reason why even as a spectacle the Canyon is absorbing almost in direct proportion to one's understanding of its structure. The fantastic— and at first sight it seems *merely* fantastic—is only momentarily arresting. Nothing that is without rhyme or reason can hold the attention for long. Hence the Canyon takes a firmer and firmer grip as the logic behind the seemingly illogical begins to reveal itself. Why, one begins to ask, these varying colors, these oddly sculptured pinnacles, these walls, slopes, and terraces sometimes sloping steeply, sometimes lying almost flat in broad plateaus, and sometimes dropping vertically down?

The first few hundred feet below the rim are nearly vertical; next comes a gentle slope broken by towers and turrets; then, after another vertical cliff, a broad, almost level plateau; and finally, the sheer drop into the inner gorge, at the bottom of which the river races and foams over rapids and shallows.

And the most obvious questions are simply these: Why is

it so much wider at the top than at the bottom? Why is there
in some places an inner gorge into which the river fits snugly
and which is not very much wider at the top than at the
bottom? Surely the river was never ten miles wide and surely
it has not gone on shrinking progressively as it cut deeper and
deeper.

Of course not. All valleys widen as time goes on. In fact,
that is why most rivers make valleys, not canyons. But if most
rivers make valleys, then why did the Colorado make a canyon, and why has it obviously widened so much more at the
top than toward the bottom?

To the first of these questions, "Why a canyon and not a
valley?" the answer is that special conditions other than the
slowly rising land existed here. River courses usually become
valleys because, as the courses cut downward, water, frost,
and the other forces of erosion break down the sides so rapidly that the valley becomes wide faster than it grows deep
and, other things being equal, the less the cutting force of the
stream, the wider the valley will be in proportion to its depth.

To make imposing canyons you need a considerable river
carrying a large amount of abrasive material. But that river
must flow through an arid country where the breaking down
and widening of the sides will take place more slowly in
proportion to the downward cut than it does in regions of
normal rainfall. Because the rainfall in the West is so much
less than in most other parts of the United States, the West
is a country of canyons, great and small, as the East is a
country of valleys. And because all the conditions for canyon-
making were realized more extravagantly by the Colorado
River and the region through which it ran than anywhere
else on the globe, its canyon is the most triumphant example
of what a river can do. There was the rising land; the swift,
sand-filled river; and the arid country.

But why the deep, steep-sided V of the inner gorge in the
Bright Angel area and the sudden opening out at its rim, so
that the gorge makes almost a canyon within a canyon? Of
course, the inner gorge was more recently cut, but not much
more recently than the broad plateau which seems to separate
it from the higher, wider portions might suggest. The answer,
as we shall see when we get down there, is that the gorge is
cut in a different, much harder, much more resistant rock.
The plateau and all the successive strata above it are sedi-

mentary rocks laid down as sand, mud, and lime either underwater or on the surface of some ancient desert. But the rocks of the inner gorge are black, terribly hard, and so ancient that their earliest history is largely a matter of conjecture. Molten rock forced up through cracks from below has made great vertical seams of granite, but they are young by comparison with the older mass which goes back to that most ancient of all times, called the Archean. Undoubtedly, parts of it, too, were sediment in some past, a billion years ago, but it has been so heated and compressed and torn that its aboriginal character has been lost and it is very hard. The river must have cut very slowly through it, and weather has been able to affect very little its nearly vertical walls. Had all the rocks of the Canyon been equally hard, it might be now much less deep but much more narrow than it is.

Every cliff and terrace and pinnacle above the gorge is the result of differential weathering—the flats where some homogeneous stone has worn evenly away, the cliffs where something more resistant has stood boldly up, the pinnacles and mesas often the result of some cap of hard stone which has protected softer layers underneath, though they have been washed away everywhere else, thus leaving a pillar or a table still standing because protected from above. Or, if you prefer more technical language, a geologist will tell you that the plateaus are "geomorphically homogeneous" while "the stepped topography is due to the fortuitous alternation of beds having widely different resistance to erosion." He will add that drainage systems flowing down the sides have increased the variety with side canyons and amphitheaters; also that the varying colors which give to the exposed walls a sort of tuttifrutti appearance result from the equally fortuitous circumstance that there was "an alternation of light colored beds and dark colored beds, with the striking red beds in intermediate position."

When one has been talking in terms of millions of years, it is difficult to realize that the Canyon is not finished, that it is not made but in the making. Since the river still runs swift and still carries a tremendous load of cutting material, it must still be slowly wearing away the very hard Archean rock over which it runs—though unless the land is still rising (as it may be), it will cut more and more slowly as the gradient diminishes. On the other hand, the Canyon is getting wider much more rapidly than it is getting deeper, and the widening, unlike the deepening, is visually evident. Many of the large rock masses which form the promontories upon which visitors walk out for the best views into the depths are obviously separating from the rim by large cracks. The timid sometimes refuse for that reason to trust themselves to the rocks, though many will no doubt still be there hundreds of years hence. Other, smaller, boulders are more precariously attached, and looking over the rim one may see where still others broke loose, fell hundreds of feet down, rolled a hundred more along some slope, and finally came temporarily to rest— temporarily because it is inevitable that the new support will someday be washed away from under them.

Even more striking are the still fresh scars on the sides of the vertical cliffs where great slabs, many tons of weight, have sloughed off, crashed into fragments where they struck, and then poured into a stream of debris across terraces and down new cliffs. Inevitably, Bright Angel Lodge, if it stands long enough, will someday tumble into the chasm which now opens perhaps a hundred feet from its edge; the lodge on the north rim will fall even sooner, because it is closer to the disintegrating rim.

The cause of the widening, operative wherever any canyon or valley exists, is running or falling water, wind, the expanding roots of plants which get a foothold in crevasses and, where the weather is cold enough, the expansive force of freezing water which, like the roots, widens the cracks in which it gathers. The geologist, Edwin D. McKee, who has closely studied the process at Grand Canyon, thinks that the running and falling water is here very much the most important factor—especially the water which falls in the cloudbursts of summer and that which runs over the edge during the spring melting of the snow. At both such times sheets of water pour over the rim, remorselessly nibbling away limestone and sandstone, and shale, most of which were laid down under the same element that will reduce them ultimately to sand again.

How fast is this happening? No one, so far as I know, has attempted to measure or even to estimate the rate at which the average distance between the two rims is increasing. But at least it is not so very slow as earth changes are measured.

Major rockfalls, not to mention the minor ones, are relatively frequent. Some years ago, Emory Kolb, who had spent ten years on the rim, could report seven major falls within sight of his house, besides many others which could be heard. One, on the north rim just opposite Grand Canyon Village and plainly visible from there, was also audible across the ten airline miles between Village and opposite rim. During a thunderstorm in December, 1932, a great promontory just west of the Kolb studio dropped as a single mass and came to rest on the Supai formation more than a thousand feet below the rim. On a recent visit I noticed a huge fresh scar where a tremendous block which must have weighed many tons had broken off in 1954 from near the top of the Coconino sandstone (i.e., some five hundred feet below the rim). The major part of it lies now in fragments about three hundred feet lower, while a diminishing cascade of smaller and smaller fragments stream several hundred feet still farther down.

If the earth's crust in this region lies quiet for a time long enough, Grand Canyon will become a wide valley and finally, if time is still longer, a flat plain, all the successive layers of stone washed away, leaving the river to meander again as it once did—like an oversized brook across an oversized meadow.

Improbable? Already hundreds of feet of rock, laid down before the plateau was lifted to its present height, have disappeared completely, though they are still to be found on higher ground not far away. Time and time again in the earth's history "geomorphic features" more massive than the Grand Canyon have been leveled and obliterated only to have equally imposing features built again, either because the surface was forced up or because lava streams welled up from the earth's bowels.

As a matter of fact, this sort of thing has happened twice right where the Canyon now lies. To see the evidence of that we need to descend the mile below the rim and meet some of the oldest rocks face to face. But that journey had best be postponed for a while.

Meanwhile, a good way to dispel the human-aid delusion and the false sense of scale upon which it is founded is to probe the depth gingerly by strolling a mile and a half down the least used of the two principal trails which lead from the south rim to the bottom—remembering as you go that though you may stroll down to the bottom, you cannot stroll back up again. Such a mile and a half's probe will carry you only about eight hundred feet in vertical distance, but that is far enough to make the wall at one's back tower as high as all but the tallest skyscrapers, while the depths have not been brought detectably nearer. The broad Tonto Plateau, almost three thousand feet below the rim, looks just as far away as it ever did, and the bottom of the gorge is still usually invisible.

But though you seem to have made no progress toward plumbing the depths, you have already passed through quite a variety of changing scenes. For one thing, it is noticeably warmer, since to go eight hundred feet down is equivalent to going nearly five hundred miles southward, and the vegetation is noticeably different. So, too, are the color and the texture of the rocks and the shapes into which they have been sculptured. At first one zigzagged down two almost vertical walls, of grayish-white limestone separated by weak red sandstone. At about five hundred feet is sandstone of a slightly different color and so obviously different a texture that the line which marks the division between the two is clearly visible. This third layer is not quite so thick as the first two combined—something more than three hundred instead of something more than five hundred feet—and at just about the end of the mile-and-a-half walk it also suddenly ends where it rests upon a wall of red stone more startlingly different from either of the three previous walls than they are from one another.

The tops of the first mesas and buttes into which certain other rocks have been formed are mostly still below, and for some distance yet the steep wall down which one has been climbing is a wall and no more—sometimes almost perfectly vertical and everywhere cleanly rather than fantastically cut. Your walk will end near the top of this fourth layer, and on the exposed surface of a slab just by the side of the trail you will see very plainly impressed the neat double row of small footprints left by some four-footed creature when the rock was sand.

Any geologist will tell you that when you stood at the rim you were standing upon limestone laid down at the bottom of a shallow sea during the Permian period or, according to recently revised estimates, about 200,000,000 years ago; that your descent of some eight hundred feet had carried you back only a few million years farther without taking you beyond the limits of the Permian; and that these prints were made by some beast—perhaps reptilian, perhaps amphibian—who passed by there before the dinosaurs had got a start. They are real footprints in the sands of time; by comparison, the most enduring metaphorical ones left by the most ambitious and most successful of men are written in water.

Suppose there had been no geologist conveniently at our elbow. What could a reasonably observant person see for himself, what sort of notions could he form of the meaning of what he saw; what tentative theories advance of the how and the why?

This is the sort of question I have frequently asked of myself when faced with some natural phenomena I could glibly explain on the basis of what other men had learned. And the answer I am compelled to give is usually sufficiently humiliating to myself. I would not know much about the world I live in had I been compelled to depend upon my own observations. The only consolation is that most men would have to admit that, and even the best men have seldom advanced knowledge more than a short step.

Nevertheless, we may, I think, pay ourselves the compliment of assuming that our short walk would have taught us something. The grandness of the scale, which is obvious as soon as you get into the Canyon instead of merely looking at it, would have disposed of the notion that man had had anything to do with the formation, and I like to think that the theory of a great crack in the cooling surface of a molten earth would also have been disposed of by the obvious fact that the rock wall is not homogeneous and that the different kinds of stone are obviously in layers, one on top of the other.

In most places on earth exposed rock strata are exposed only to a shallow depth and are also so tilted, broken, or twisted that their character does not thrust itself upon the attention. But at Grand Canyon they have lain so quietly while they were sliced through like a layer cake that it seems almost as though they had been provided for the special purpose of demonstrating to an unobservant mankind that one great class of rocks are not the result of the cooling of a molten mass but that such rocks were, as the geologist says, "laid down," often one on top of the other. As the distinguished geologist, Charles Schuchert, once wrote on the Canyon, "Such a geological insight in the structure of the earth's outer shell is nowhere else to be had."

Just possibly I might have noticed for myself that embedded in the topmost layer are fragments which upon close examination are obviously bits of sea shell and of coral, and if I had noticed that, I would probably have wondered, as men wondered for so many years after fossils had become quite well known, how the devil they got there. But I doubt very seriously that I would have noticed a difference between the texture of the upper two and the third layers which are otherwise so similar—a difference obvious enough when pointed out and consisting in the fact that whereas the topmost formations are composed of thin layers separated by almost perfectly horizontal lines, similar lines in the layer below run in sloping curves which seem to outline subsequently buried humps—so that it is, as the geologists say, "cross-bedded." And even if I had noticed that, I am pretty sure the explanation, again convincing enough once it has been suggested, would not have occurred to me. The top two layers are solidified lime which fell quietly to the bottom of quiet seas and lay there undisturbed; the next layer is of windblown sand, the outline of whose dunes, later covered by more sand, is so clear that from their outline—steeper on one side than on the other—one can see even from which direction the prevailing winds once blew over that desert.

Would I have done any better, or done even so well, with the question raised earlier, not how the rocks got there, but how they had been slashed through? Looking through binoculars at the opposite wall, ten miles away, I could hardly have missed the fact that rock layers in the two walls match. Each conspicuous layer corresponds to a similar layer on the opposite side. The conclusion that they continue one another, or rather that they would if the great gash had not been cut, is irresistible. Would I have assumed some violent catastrophe which cut or broke it in a relatively brief time? Or would the fact, evident enough in the great masses of rock cracked off from the sides and waiting to fall, or the other great masses lying where they have fallen, have suggested that since the whole face of the region is certainly still slowly changing, then the grand features themselves might have resulted from slow change? If I had indeed concluded something of the sort, then would I have gone on to suppose that the river, glimpsed from some point on the rim, had done the job?

Give me the benefit of a large doubt and suppose that I would have. The largest difficulty would still remain. I would still have been faced with the problem of getting the river "up there" where, as a matter of fact, it never had been. Would I have solved that problem too? I very much doubt it. But it is some consolation to know that much simpler problems in geology did not suggest their obvious answers until a few generations ago, and that details concerning the Canyon are still being discussed as new facts come to light.

1958

Journey in Time

The Canyon has always had a great many European visitors. They are generally very appreciative, and rangers remark sadly that they are also much better informed, much better prepared to understand what they see, than the average American who frequently checks it off his list as he checks Notre Dame or St. Peter's in his guidebook. Sometimes, however, the European permits himself to remark that Grand Canyon, being American, is of course the *biggest* this, the *longest* that, and the *most* several other things in the world. And of course it really is.

In some ways the most significant of its "mosts" is this: nowhere else on the surface of the earth is so long a stretch of geological time exposed in such undisturbed, easily read layers. The distance of one vertical mile traces the history of something like a billion years, and they can be covered without hardship in a few hours' time. All this history is, to be sure, very ancient history. One must start the journey in time a good many million years ago during the Permian period. But that is not, comparatively speaking, so very long ago, after all, and when one gets to the bottom one will be walking on rocks already formed at a time further removed from the first identifiable fossil structures than the time of those fossils is removed from our own day.

The best way to make this stupendous journey is on the back of a mule which makes it scores of times a year without becoming any the wiser in geology and without developing an interest in the scenery. But he has become very wise indeed in all that is required to negotiate safely and with a minimum of trouble to himself the seven miles of narrow, twisting trail necessary for the mile of vertical descent. Of course, you can walk if you prefer, but most—especially those who have sauntered down a mile or two and then struggled back—prefer the mule. Like the descent to Avernus, the descent of the Canyon is easy; but the coming up again is hard. Somehow the trail has become much steeper as well as much longer than when one went down, and walkers who have heard that the earth is sometimes thrust up are often inclined to believe that the trail was tilted while they were at the bottom.

One of the oldest white man's trails to the river—no longer used except occasionally by walkers—is called the Hance, after that John Hance at whose tumbling cabin the lizards now keep their court. This Hance, who made or at least began it for his own use and that of other early hunters, was a somewhat mysterious character who responded to all questions about his past by declaring that he "did not like ancient history" and is believed to have come to the Canyon from somewhere in Texas about 1880, though probably not by the method he liked to describe to tenderfeet—i.e., on the back of one of a herd of buffalo upon which he dropped from a tree. Later he acted as guide to those few early tourists— including Theodore Roosevelt—who came before the park was established. Later still he declined into a professional "character" employed by the Fred Harvey Company after 1903 to furnish atmosphere—which he generated abundantly by telling very tall tales. But he had been a real character before he took it up as a profession and he was among the first to clamber down from the rim. As Buckey O'Neill, another old-time figure, said: "God made the Canyon, John Hance the trails. Without the other, neither would be complete."

The general course of Bright Angel Trail, the most used by tourists, had been followed for no one knows how many years by the Havasupai Indians, who then farmed the watered area on the Tonto Plateau which lies more than 2300 feet below the rim. About 1890 two miners reworked it and charged a toll to prospectors going back and forth to the mining claims which were later declared invalid. In 1928 it was acquired by the Park Service and since then it has been trod thousands of times by mules who seem to delight in terrifying their riders by facing meditatively outward toward the abysses it skirts before they turn daintily to face down the trail again.

Since this is to be a journey through climates as well as through time, it is just as well to choose carefully a good season of the year. The head of the trail, at seven thousand feet, is in a region where the sun is warm even in winter and the nights coolish even in summer. But the five-thousand-foot drop to the bottom is equivalent climatically to a journey of some three thousand miles southward. We start from an upper Sonoran zone where the dominant vegetation is the juniper and descend to a subtropical climate approximately equivalent to that of central coastal Mexico. Since that means intolerable heat in summer, we chose for this visit a day in early October. That means that even on the rim sunny days will be warm though the nights are chilly, while at the bottom —climatically three thousand miles farther south—the days will not be oppressively hot. At ten in the morning we mount our mules who appear to be perfectly aware of what is coming and mulishly resigned. But if one unneeded member of the string is left behind, he will bray dismally as his companions start off.

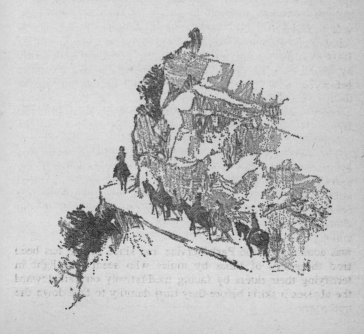

The entire journey down is through scenes indescribably grandiose, often between colorful hillocks and buttes but always austere and sometimes, especially within the inner gorge, somber almost to the point of gloominess. Vegetation is sparse and obviously just surviving; animal life extremely scanty. One is constantly reminded of terrific forces, vast stretches of time, and the death of whole races of once flourishing living creatures now reduced to a few mineralized skeletons or a few impressions in the hardened mud, and it is easy to realize how desolate and terrifying it all was to those earlier explorers who were completely alone in a forbidding, seemingly accursed land where nature was many things but certainly not kindly.

Here now at the bottom she smiles again. Water brings life, and wherever there is life, there is beauty and a sense of joy. Bright Angel Creek makes a kind of oasis. Birds again inhabit the trees; along the stream bank for miles scarlet monkey flowers and Cardinal flowers draw, even in mid-October, a curving red line. That sense of being almost perilously cut off from the rest of the world which one ought perhaps to feel is reduced to no more than an agreeable feeling of peaceful retirement. The little oasis one has come to rest in is snug and cozy, and though surrounded by buttes and cliffs, they so cut off the view in most places that had one been taken here blindfolded one would never guess how deep he was below all the surrounding country except the channel of the river.

If, however, the long journey down has soon begun to seem unreal, and if one would like to recover it, that is easy too. The corral where we dismounted is one of the few places from which the rim can be seen, and seen, actually, at almost exactly the place where the trail started. There the Kaibab limestone gleams white in the sun a mile above one's head. At night a light can be seen glimmering there like a star. It was from thence one came and it is back there one must somehow manage to get.

The journey down has given a perspective, a sense of the magnitude of the phenomena, one cannot possibly get from the rim. On the other hand, the coziness of Phantom Ranch is deceptive again, because it conveys an exaggerated sense of the extent to which the Canyon has been tamed. One dropped over the rim, one persisted for a few hours along a perfectly practicable trail, and one has arrived without incident or any great difficulty at the very bottom.

Actually, however, one has made merely a little foray along a carefully selected, long accustomed, and carefully engineered route to a single spot. But it is only along the rim and along the river that the Canyon is known with any thoroughness to anyone. Many of the buttes have never, so far as is known, been climbed; many of the walls, plateaus, and side canyons have, so far as the record goes, never been visited. All about are hundreds of square miles of terra incognita. Only a few years ago Arizona Senator Barry Goldwater discovered by helicopter a great natural bridge in the Redwall which had not only never been visited but whose very existence was unknown. And another single incident will suggest even better the wildness and the difficulty of the terrain.

In 1944 two army pilots bailed out of a failing plane at eighteen thousand feet above the lights of the village. Instead of landing there, they watched the lights disappear over their heads and came to earth on what turned out to be the Tonto Plateau. After three days they were spotted by rescuers who dropped food by parachute. But it was five days before organized parties could reach them. One party descended from the south rim but presently found itself cut off by an uncrossable side canyon. Finally a party on the north rim spotted a rockfall down the Redwall which promised the possibility of a descent, and they finally reached the victims. Stray only a little from the marked trail, and you may find yourself unable to get back onto it again.

On their first night below, some travelers still sway with their mules, dream of precipices, or begin in anticipation the slow climb back. I found myself instead half-meditating and half-dreaming about those long departed seas which had flowed in and then vanished; even more persistently of the great mountain ranges which rose slowly and then, infinitely more slowly, dissolved into sand and mud. How far from solid is the solid ground beneath one's feet, and how far from eternal are the eternal hills! Two Himalayas or Alps had risen and vanished on the site of the Canyon before life had got further than the protozoa and the jellyfish.

As soon as nature has made a mountain, she seems to

regret it and she begins to tear it down. Then, once she has torn it down, she makes another—perhaps, as here, precisely where the former mountain had once towered. Speed the action up as in those movies of an opening flower, and the landscape of the earth would seem as insubstantial and as phantasmagorial as the cloudscape of a thundery afternoon. "For a thousand years," said the psalmist, "in thy sight are but as yesterday." A thousand? Say rather a hundred million.

Rivers do the final work as they flow, more and more slowly, through the canyons they have cut down to a lesser and lesser gradient until they swing slowly back and forth in a shifting meander which gradually wears away even the minor hillocks and creates a featureless plain. This is to me one of the less dramatic but one of the most impressive of the geological processes, and I confess that I had never been able to visualize it clearly until I spent an hour or two looking out from an airplane flying at twelve thousand feet above a typical "old" landscape—a flat plain bounded by low hills fifty miles to the east and the west of the slow, ineffectual-looking river which wound peacefully along. How, one first wonders, could so insignificant a stream be responsible for a flat valley a hundred miles in width?

Look at its present behavior and you can see. Notice, for instance, that point where it now flows against the side of a low hummock. Then look at the sandbank just opposite. Obviously the stream flowed quite recently where the sand-bank now is. But as the channel silted up, the stream was thrown against the side of the hillock at whose base it now gnaws. Thus, in the course of a few thousand years, it swings in widening arcs back and forth until it flattens mile after mile of the broadening plain. "Peneplaining" is what the geologists call this process, and most of the wide, smiling vales of the earth have been thus made, though, at some still more distant day, some of them may again be lifted and broken into mountains just as that plain which had once been the Archean alps of the Grand Canyon region was lifted and broken anew to form the younger alps which had to be flattened in their turn before the Algonkian sediments could be deposited upon the plain they had again become.

How much longer will this cycle of mountain building and peneplaining go on? Will it repeat itself again here at the Canyon, which is so obviously already undergoing one of the first stages of transformation as water and ice are widening it? Will the river, still cutting deeper, tend to swing more widely as it slows down? Will it undermine the Canyon walls and, ultimately, wander slowly back and forth across a plain destined someday to become, perhaps, a sea and then, after the sea has deposited a new layer of limestone, to be tossed up into a mighty mountain range once more?

Something like this has happened more than once in the past, though of course no one can know whether or for how many times it will happen again. One set of forces is perpetually engaged somewhere in reducing the surface of the earth to the dead level of an almost featureless plain, and such a featureless plain is everywhere the final stage—unless it is heaved into mountains again or unless, as has frequently happened, volcanic eruptions spew lava upon it. But our earth is getting older. These successive levelings may be part of a sort of running-down process. Presumably, as the globe cools, the upheavals will become less frequent and less violent, though nobody knows for how many millions of years (certainly for more than a billion) they have been going on, for how long they will continue. And yet, presumably again, there will be an end to them when the heat pressures have finally reached an equilibrium.

Thus these phenomena, though local on our earth, constitute a kind of "increasing entropy" roughly analogous to the "running down" of the whole universe and its ultimate "heat death" which, a few years ago, was so confidently predicted as inevitable by Sir James Jeans and others. The sun cools, heat flows everywhere from hotter to cooler places, thus tending to equalize all temperatures until, ultimately, the temperature will be the same everywhere, and all energy will be in a stable equilibrium so that nothing can ever happen or change again. As one might put it too simply: Whatever goes up must come down, but it does not necessarily go up again.

Those who cannot anticipate with equanimity the death of the universe some billions of years hence may take heart from the fact that the most recent physical investigations have indicated that it is not running down as fast as was once thought. The sun is not merely burning; it is radioactive and not consuming itself nearly so fast as it would if it were no more than a ball of fire. The mysterious cosmic rays may be building energy up in unexpected places. The great clock of the universe may be at least partly self-winding or, in other words, there may be more life in the old boy than was once supposed. As the Cambridge cosmologist, E. A. Milne, wrote recently in more dignified language and with characteristic British calm when discussing large matters: "I am now convinced that an unconditional prediction of a heat-death for the universe is an over-statement."

Even the future leveling of the Grand Canyon may, then, be far from the end of the story. By the time some future geologist is studying the worn-down bases of the Rockies where they have been exposed by some canyon cut through thousands of feet of later sediments, the Archean rocks of the inner gorge of our Canyon may have been worn completely away or buried again deeper than they were buried when the Colorado first began to cut the strata which now overlay them.

In the bright sun of morning Phantom Ranch's rocky dell looks solid enough, and the clear, cold water of Bright Angel Creek seems to justify Tennyson's rash assumption that brooks go on forever. Life-giving water has made a cheerful spot, isolated and self-contained; and because the intimate little hills and crags shut it in nearly everywhere and thus close the view, one can easily forget that its position is so peculiar and so inaccessible. It might well be the Happy Valley prison of some western Prince Rasselas brought up ignorant of any other world.

1958

IV. NATURE AND HUMAN NATURE

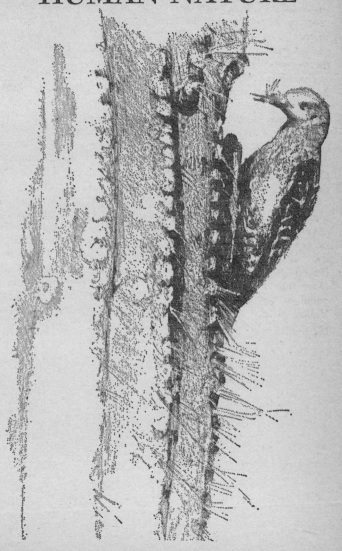

All things are artificial, for nature is the art of God.

SIR THOMAS BROWNE

Man's Place in Nature

What is "nature"? One standard reference devotes five columns to fifteen different and legitimate definitions of the word. But for the purposes of this article the meaning is simple. Nature is that part of the world which man did not make and which has not been fundamentally changed by him. It is the mountains, the woods, the rivers, the trees, the plants, and the animals which have continued to be very much what they would have been had he never existed.

In another sense man is, of course, himself a part of nature. But he is also in so many ways so unique that it is convenient to speak of man *and* nature, especially of man's relation to the rest of this nature of which he is also a part.

The relationship is something which he can never forget; but he responds to it in the most diverse ways. He regards nature sometimes as a friend and sometimes as an enemy. He loves it and he fears it. He uses it and destroys it. Nature is what he tries to get away from and then something he wishes to keep. He replaces it with his homes and factories, then wishes to return to it. He tries to impose on it human order and civilization, and then suddenly finds himself dreaming of a golden age when man and nature were one.

This paradox is as old as civilization itself. Though it is true that man never admired the more savage aspects of nature until life had become comparatively safe, it is equally true that he had scarcely built the first cities before he began to try to get away from them. In ancient Greece poets idealized the shepherd's life, and in imperial Rome the literary cult of the simple life had already reached the point where satirists ridiculed it. In our modern world the engineer, the industrialist, and the builder of skyscrapers moves his family to a country house in the suburbs. He plants trees and cultivates a garden. He acquires animals as pets, and perhaps he takes up bird watching—all of which reveals his unwillingness to let go of what, in theory at least, he has not valued.

Ancient as these paradoxes and conflicts are, there is today one supremely important respect in which they pose a problem that never existed in so acute a form before: now for the first time man can effectively act out his impulses and his decisions. He can, if he so desires, all but banish nature and the natural from the earth he has come to rule.

Until a few centuries ago man was not even a very numerous species. It has been an even shorter time since his technology became advanced to the point where he could upset seriously the ancient balances of the natural world. Formerly he might love nature or hate her, might attempt to preserve her or destroy her; but she was more powerful than he. Except for relatively small areas she remained in control. Now the balance has shifted. Man controls forces which at least rival and seem on the point of surpassing hers. He can decide as never before what part, if any, of the natural world will be permitted to exist. Thus the question "What is man's place in nature and what ought to be his relation to her?" is fateful as it never was before.

In its most abstract form this fundamental question was asked and opposing answers were given by the ancient religions. In the Hebraic tradition man was the child of God, and God was separate from, rather than a part of, nature. Greek paganism, on the other hand, worshiped gods who were themselves aspects of nature and it taught man to think of himself also as part of her. These gods were more at home in the woods and streams and mountains than in the temples built for them. Nature was the source of health, beauty, and joy, and to live in accord with nature's laws was wisdom. The Great God Pan, or nature god, was one of the most ancient and powerful of deities, so much so indeed that an early Christian tradition made the exclamation "Great Pan is dead" a cry of victory announcing the triumph for the new faith; and many centuries later, the neopagan poet Swinburne could turn it into a lament to Christ Himself: "Thou hast conquered, O pale Galilean; the world has grown grey from thy breath."

To Noah, unloading his animals after the flood, Jehovah said, "And the fear of you and the dread of you shall be upon every beast of the earth, and upon every fowl of the air, upon all that moveth upon the earth, and upon all the fishes of the sea; into your hand are they delivered." Throughout the Greek and Roman ascendancies and all through the Middle Ages the most admired aspects of nature were those which man has tamed, at least to a degree. It has often been said that the fourteenth-century Italian scholar Petrarch was the first man who ever confessed to climbing a mountain just for the sake of the view, and it is not so often added that, at the end of his description, he apologized for this eccentricity.

The conflicting attitudes which even today somehow relate "the natural" to "the divine" began to emerge some three centuries ago. The first great English biologist, the pious John Ray, in his enormously popular *The Wisdom of God Manifested in the Works of His Creation* (1691), maintained that God did not create the living world exclusively for man's use but that, on the contrary, He "takes pleasure that all His creatures enjoy themselves." And Ray urged that men should study nature as well as books because it was by such study that the greatness and goodness of God was most clearly revealed.

A bare generation later Alexander Pope, the most read English poet except Shakespeare, could put the same thing in epigrammatic couplets:

> Has God, thou fool! work'd solely for thy good,
> Thy joy, thy pastime, thy attire, thy food? . . .
> Is it for thee the lark ascends and sings?
> Joy tunes his voice, joy elevates his wings.
> Is it for thee the linnet pours his throat?
> Loves of his own and raptures swell
>   the note. . . .
>   Know, Nature's children all divide her care;
> The fur that warms a monarch, warm'd a bear.

Already we were halfway to Wordsworth's "the meanest flower that blows can give/Thoughts that do often lie too deep for tears" or Blake's "Kill not the moth nor butterfly/For the Last Judgment draweth nigh."

Out of such attitudes emerged the whole romantic glorification of nature which blossomed in the eighteenth century and continued almost unchecked to the middle of the nineteenth, when scientific objectivity began to struggle against it. By that time life had become comparatively secure and men increasingly were finding the somewhat terrifying spectacle of nature's savage grandeur thrillingly beautiful. Mountains, as modern scholarship has pointed out, were almost always called "sublime." The philosopher-statesman Edmund Burke devoted one of his earliest writings to distinguishing between "The Beautiful" (that which is soothing and reassuring) and "The Sublime" (that which strikes us with awe and with something almost like terror). Everywhere men were beginning to exclaim over thunderstorms, lashing seas, and icy peaks—over whatever suggested something grander and less comfortable than their own cities or, even, their own lawns and gardens.

In this period also grew the cult of nature as "the kind mother" or, in the words of Goethe, as "the living garment of God." This wildly unrealistic view attributed to nature below the human level a consistent kindliness and benevolence which man himself to this day has by no means achieved. Nature is not always a kind mother; she is as often a stern and sometimes a brutal one. Yet Burns spoke of "Man's inhumanity to man" and contrasted it with "Nature's social union" which, he said, man had so cruelly disturbed. Wordsworth's God had his dwelling in "the light of setting suns," and "Nature," he proclaimed, "never did betray the heart that loved her."

It was against such romantic idealism that the nineteenth century gradually rebelled until, just after the mid-century, Charles Darwin took a position at the opposite extreme and drew his picture of a natural world which assumed its form through the operation of mechanical processes, and which was devoid of anything which could be called moral values.

If few today doubt that Darwin's theory of "natural selection through the struggle for survival" explains much, there are many who insist that it does not explain everything. Some of the most primitive organisms have survived for many millions of years—far longer than other more advanced organisms and possibly longer than man himself will prevail. If only "the fittest survive," then the sea squirt is fitter than any mammal—including, perhaps, man. And "natural selection" cannot account for the intensification of man's consciousness or the value which he puts upon such ideals as justice, fair play, and benevolence. It cannot account for them inasmuch as creatures in which these traits are not conspicuous are at least as successful in the "struggle for survival" as he is.

If nature herself has exhibited a tendency, if she seems to "want" anything, it is not merely to survive. She has tended to realize more and more completely the potentialities of protoplasm, and these include much that has no demonstrable "survival value." Evolution itself has spread before us the story of a striving toward "the higher," not merely toward that which enables an organism to survive.

If the romantic view of nature was mere wishful thinking, merely the projection upon nature of our own fully developed desires and ideals, then Darwinism generated a romanticism in reverse in which all is conflict, violence, and blood. But the fact is that animals do not spend all their time fighting for survival, though for the sake of excitement anti-romantic popular books and films do strive to give that impression. Animals also give tender love to their offspring as well as, sometimes, to their mates and the fellow members of their group. Those theories of human society which propose ruthless, devil-take-the-hindermost political and social systems sometimes claim that they are in accord with the laws of nature, but they are not.

There was a time not too long ago when orthodox science talked only of instincts, behavior patterns, chemical drives, and the like, while any tendency to see in the animal even faint analogies to the conscious processes, the intelligence, or the emotions of man was ridiculed as sentimental and "anthropomorphic"—i.e., stated in terms appropriate to man only. But the tide has turned. So notable a student of animal behavior as Konrad Lorenz has protested against what he named "mechanomorphism"—the interpretation of animal behavior exclusively in terms of the mechanical—which he calls an error no less grave than anthropomorphism. Animals are not men, but neither are they machines. If they cannot think as man does in terms of abstract concepts, neither are they controlled entirely by push-button reflexes. To some extent they exhibit the beginnings of "the human." They can sometimes take in a situation and modify their behavior in the light of circumstances. They have individuality also; one does not behave exactly like another. Even insects, once thought to be the most automatic and invariable of creatures, seem to be able sometimes to change purposely the pattern of their conduct.

As a matter of fact, the life of the senses in some of the higher animals is possibly more vivid than ours, and in some of them the emotions may be more powerful also. As Sir Julian Huxley, one of the greatest living authorities on evolution, has said of the birds he has observed with scientific exactitude: "Their lives are often emotional, and their emotions are richly and finely expressed. . . . In birds the advance on the intellectual side has been less, on the emotional side greater: so that we can study in them a part of the single stream of life where emotion, untrammeled by much reason, has the upper hand."

Thus all the strange powers and potentialities of the living thing are diffused throughout animate nature—which remains mysterious, and our relation to it no less so. The universe is not the mere machine which early Darwinians tended to make it. The man who thinks of his dog as another human being is wrong, but no more so perhaps than his opposite who refuses to acknowledge any kinship. Yet an appreciation of this truth still leaves unanswered the question of man's own position. To what extent is he unique; to what extent is he not only "higher" than any other animal, but also radically different from, and discontinuous with, that great chain which connects by close links the humblest one-celled animal with the most intelligent of the apes?

The traditional answer, given by some philosophers and theologians, is that man is an animal to which something (a soul, if you like) has been added and that this something distinguishes him absolutely from all other living creatures. This answer is at least logically tenable, whether you accept it or not. If, on the other hand, you say, as some old-fashioned biologists did, that though man has "evolved" by purely natural process, he is nevertheless endowed with capacities of which not a trace is to be found in any other animal, that is not logically tenable. "Evolution" implies the growing complexity of things previously existing in simpler form. Hence man's consciousness, thought, and sense of purpose must either have been added to his natural endowment by something outside nature, or they must have truly evolved from something in the "lower" forms of life.

William Morton Wheeler, the late great student of the social insects, once wrote that we can only guess why animals are as they are and can never know except very imperfectly how they came to be what they are. Nevertheless, he added, "[the fact] that organisms are as they are, that apart from members of our own species they are our only companions in an infinite and unsympathetic waste of electrons, planets, nebulae and stars, is a perennial joy and consolation." It is upon this "perennial joy and consolation" that the deepest and most rewarding "love of nature" must rest.

Even to say that we can and should know this joy and consolation is not to answer all the questions. How far should we not only enjoy nature but also follow her; to what extent should we take our cue, as it were, from the natural world? We are something more than merely part of it. However we came to be where we are, our position is, as an eighteenth-century poet put it, "on the isthmus of a middle state." We face back toward our primitive ancestors, perhaps even to the ape; but we also look forward to we know not what.

To what extent then should man, to what extent dare he, renounce nature; take over the management of the earth he lives on; and use it exclusively for what he sometimes regards as his higher purposes?

Extremists give and have always given extreme answers. Let us, say some, "return to nature," lead the simple life, try to become again that figment of the romantic imagination, "the noble savage." Henry David Thoreau, the greatest of American "nature lovers," is sometimes accused of having advocated just that. But he did not do so; he advocated only that we should live more simply and more aware of the earth which, he said with characteristic exaggeration, "is more wonderful than it is convenient; more beautiful than it is useful; it is more to be admired and enjoyed than used."

Others suggest a different extreme. They talk about "the biosphere" (loosely, that which has been here defined as the natural world) as contrasted with "the noosphere" (translated as that portion of the earth upon which man has imposed his own will so successfully that whatever conditions prevail there do so because of his will). It appears that civilization, according to this notion, is to be completed only when the noosphere is the whole earth and the biosphere is completely subordinated to the human will.

Within the last one hundred years we have approached faster and closer to that condition than in all the preceding centuries of civilization. But would man, whose roots go so deep into nature, be happy should he achieve such a situation?

Certainly he would become a creature very different from what he is, and the experience of living would be equally different from what it has always been. He would, indeed, have justified his boast that he can "conquer nature," but he would also have destroyed it. He would have used every spot of earth for homes, factories, and farms, or perhaps got rid of farms entirely, because by then he could synthesize food in the laboratory. But he would have no different companions in the adventures of living. The emotions which have inspired much of all poetry, music, and art would no longer be comprehensible. He would have all his dealings with things he alone has made. Would we then be, as some would imagine, men like gods? Or would we be only men like ants?

That we would not be satisfied with such a world is sufficiently evidenced by the fact that, to date at least, few do not want their country house, their country vacation, their camping or their fishing trip—even their seat in the park and their visit to the zoo. We need some contact with the things we spring from. We need nature at least as a part of the context of our lives. Though we are not satisfied with nature, neither are we happy without her. Without cities we cannot be civilized. Without nature, without wilderness even, we are compelled to renounce an important part of our heritage.

The late Aldo Leopold, who spent his life in forestry and conservation, once wrote: "For us of the minority, the opportunity to see geese is more important than television, and the chance to see a pasqueflower is a right as inalienable as free speech."

Many of us who share this conviction came to it only gradually. On some summer vacation or some country weekend we realize that what we are experiencing is more than merely a relief from the pressures of city life; that we have not merely escaped *from* something but also *into* something; that we have joined the greatest of all communities, which is not that of men alone but of everything which shares with us the great adventure of being alive.

This sense, mystical though it may seem, is no delusion. Throughout history some have felt it and many have found an explanation of it in their conviction that it arises out of the fact that all things owe their gift of life to God. But there is no reason why the most rationalistic of evolutionists should not find it equally inevitable. If man is only the most recent and the most complex of nature's children, then he must feel his kinship with them. If even his highest powers of consciousness, intellect, and conscience were evolved from simpler forms of the same realities, then his kinship with those who took the earlier steps is real and compelling. If nature produced him, and if she may someday produce something far less imperfect, then he may well hesitate to declare that she has done all she can for him and that henceforth he will renounce her to direct his own destiny.

In some ways man may seem wiser than she is, but it is not certain that he is wiser in all ways. He dare not trust her blindly, but neither does he dare turn his back upon her. He is in danger of relying too exclusively upon his own thoughts, to the entire neglect of her instincts; upon the dead machine he creates, while disregarding the living things of whose adventure he is a part.

We have heard much about "our natural resources" and of the necessity for conserving them, but these "resources" are not merely materially useful. They are also a great reservoir of the life from which we evolved, and they have both consolation to offer and lessons to teach which are not alone those the biologist strives to learn. In their presence many of us experience a lifting of the heart for which mere fresh air and sunshine is not sufficient to account. We feel surging up in us the exuberant, vital urge which has kept evolution going but which tends to falter amid the complexities of a too civilized life. In our rise to the human state we have lost something, despite all we have gained.

Is it merely a sentimental delusion, a "pathetic fallacy," to think that one sees in the animal a capacity for joy which man himself is tending to lose? We have invented exercise, recreation, pleasure, amusement, and the rest. To "have fun" is a desire often expressed by those who live in this age of anxiety and most of us have at times actually "had fun." But recreation, pleasure, amusement, fun, and all the rest are poor substitutes for joy; and joy, I am convinced, has its roots in something from which civilization tends to cut us off.

Are at least some animals capable of teaching us this lesson of joy? Some biologists—but by no means all and by no means the best—deny categorically that animals feel it. The gift for real happiness and joy is not always proportionate to intelligence, as we understand it, even among the animals. As Professor N. J. Berrill has put it, "To be a bird is to be alive more intensively than any other living creature. . . . [Birds] live in a world that is always the present, mostly full of joy." Similarly Sir Julian Huxley, no mere sentimental nature lover, wrote after watching the love play of herons: "I can only say that it seemed to bring such a pitch of emotion that I could have wished to be a heron that I might experience it."

This does not mean that Sir Julian would desire, any more than you or I, to be permanently a bird. Perhaps some capacity for joy has been, must be, and should be sacrificed to other capacities. But some awareness of the world outside of man must exist if one is to experience the happiness and solace which some of us find in an awareness of nature and in our love for her manifestations.

Those who have never found either joy or solace in nature might begin by looking not for the *joy they can get,* but for the *joy that is there* amid those portions of the earth man has not yet entirely pre-empted for his own use. And perhaps when they have become aware of joy in other creatures they will achieve joy themselves, by sharing in it.

1961

On Being an Amateur Naturalist

This is an age of specialists and I am by nature as well as habit an amateur. That is a dangerous thing to confess because specialists are likely to turn up their noses. "What you really mean is," they say, "a dilettante—a sort of playboy of the arts and sciences." You may have a smattering of this or that but you can't be a real authority on anything at all, and I'm afraid they are at least partly right. Not long ago my publisher asked me for a sentence or two to put on a book jacket, which would explain what he called "my claim to fame." And the best I could come up with was this: "I think I know more about plant life than any other drama critic and more about the theater than any botanist."

That sort of thing was once quite respectable. You could, like Francis Bacon, take all knowledge for your province. But there is just too much of it today. One has to choose between knowing more and more about less and less or doing what the specialist contemptuously calls "spreading yourself thin."

Now I could put up some sort of solemn defense of the fellow who chooses to interest himself in a lot of things and gets a general view of the world he lives in. After all, "amateur" means literally "lover" and an amateur of, say, natural history, very often loves the wonderful world of nature in a way that the specialist in, say, the classification of garter snakes, probably did when he was young, but long ago forgot all about while dissecting specimens preserved in formaldehyde. Plato and Aristotle called themselves, not sophists or wise men, but philosophers and lovers of wisdom. The important thing is that the amateur is a lover of whatever he is an amateur of.

At least that is the excuse I give to myself. I think what I have wanted most out of life is to find living itself rewarding.

I'm sure that I have wanted that more than I wanted wealth or fame. As Thoreau said, I don't want to feel when I come to die that I have never lived. Like Thoreau again, I am inclined to say that I came into this world not primarily to make it a better place to live in, but to live in it be it good or bad. And that is part of the amateur spirit. I haven't always been happy—who has—but I have usually been interested.

Another of the advantages of being an amateur in natural history or anything else is that there are certain unconvincing poses you don't have to take. Consider, for example, the case of the professional who has wrangled a place on an expedition to Timbuktu or the Solomon Islands. Convention demands that he tell everyone that he is making a sacrifice to that stern master called Science. When he writes the nearly inevitable book he will stress the discomforts and dangers of his exploits: the terrible heat (or cold), the dreadful roads, the nauseating food, the exhaustion, and the narrow escape from wild beasts or wilder men. Still, he is glad to have suffered all this because it has enabled him to Make His Small Contribution to the Sum of Human Knowledge. What he may possibly not know but what all his readers do know is that nine times out of ten this is pure eye-wash. What he really wanted was the somewhat masochistic pleasure of going to the Solomons or some other outlandish place, while the benefits to that abstraction called Science are just a *good* reason, not the *real* reason, for going.

Your unashamed amateur, on the other hand, is not obliged to practice any of this hypocrisy. When he gets a chance to go somewhere he is perfectly free to tell the truth. My *excuse*, he can say, is to add a new bird to my life list or to photograph a something-or-other in its native habitat.

Practically in my back yard are some of the most beautiful as well as some of the strangest of plants and flowers. There are also enough mysteries unsolved by science to keep an investigator busy through a whole life without having to go anywhere, as Henri Fabre kept busy studying the insects found on an acre or two in southern France.

Yet instead of staying in my back yard I have, during the last four years, made some fourteen or fifteen expeditions in the company of respectable scientists to the astonishingly primitive area of Mexico known as Baja California, which is not as far away as Timbuktu or the Solomons, but is, I imagine, almost as strange and remote from what we call the comforts of civilizaion. My *excuse* was, among other things, to see in its only home a certain giant treelike monstrosity so grotesque that only a botanist could love it. The Mexicans call it a *cirio,* the professionals give it the resounding name *Idria columnaris,* but a generation ago when the first American botanist saw it in its native land, he opened his eyes in a wild surmise and exclaimed: "There ain't no such animal. It's a Boojum!"—and that name, borrowed from the author of *Alice in Wonderland,* has stuck.

This I say was my excuse. The real reason for going was that I expected to enjoy myself; and I did.

Traveling with assorted specialists, I have come to realize that some—and by no means the least competent—are specialists in one thing and amateurs in all the others. But some, on the other hand, are profoundly uninterested in everything except their specialty—like one I knew who attended nothing except water beetles and, since there isn't much water in Baja California, this was the next best thing to being a specialist on the snakes of Ireland.

Your amateur, on the other hand, is delightfully, if perhaps almost sinfully, free of responsibility and can spread himself as thin as he likes over the vast field of nature. There are few places not covered with concrete or trod into dust where he does not find something to look at. Best of all, perhaps, is the fact that he feels no pressing obligation to "add something to the sum of human knowledge." He is quite satisfied when he adds something to his knowledge. And if he keeps his field wide enough he will remain so ignorant that he may do exactly that at intervals very gratifyingly short. A professional field botanist, for instance, has done very well if in the course of a lifetime he adds a dozen new species to the flora of the region he is studying. Even a hitherto unrecognized variety is enough to make a red-letter day. But to the amateur, any flower he has never seen before is a new species so far as he is concerned and on a short trip into a new area he can easily find a dozen "new species."

Of course he is well and somewhat guiltily aware that he could not have all this fun if the more responsible specialists had not provided him with the treatises and the handbooks which answer his questions and reduce what he has seen to some sort of order. More relevant is the further fact that if the specialist did not go on field trips, the amateur would never be fortunate enough to be allowed to go along with him.

Another advantage of accepting an amateur standing— and it's the last I am going to mention—is this: It permits one to speculate freely and to get "further out" than a specialist fearful of his responsibility dares to go. And it sometimes happens that a free speculation will suggest to the specialists an attempt to put props under it. That is what happened in the case of evolution. Several early amateurs indulged in the wild surmise that man and the ape might be ralated. It's quite possible that the idea would never have occurred to Darwin if they hadn't. After all, one of the speculators was his own grandfather.

Now let me give an example from my own experience: Not very long ago I had the privilege of accompanying a group of biologists who were dredging up marine organisms in Mexico's Gulf of California. Every now and then a haul would include a small bag of rather leathery jelly whose only conspicuous feature was two open tubes communicating with the water around it. Even I did not have to be told that this was a sea squirt, famous in biology as one of the two most primitive surviving organisms which possess that ancestor of the vertebrate column known as a notochord. What makes it even more remarkable than Amphioxus, the other primitive possessor of this fateful gadget, is this: in the case of the sea squirt, the notochord is present only during the creature's embryonic stage and it disappears as the sea squirt grows up. This must mean, so the biologists say, that sometime, many millions of years ago, it abandoned instead of following up the possibilities which the notochord opened to the living organism. It rejected Progress. Instead of evolving, it devolved. The fruit of my observation of the sea squirt is a very short fable.

Once upon a time an unusually bright little sea squirt invented for itself a notochord. "This," it muttered, "will make me more fit to survive and, as even a sea squirt knows, only the fittest do." Unfortunately his thinking did not stop there. "In some millions of years," he said, "I will become a true vertebrate—first a fish, then an amphibian, then a reptile, then a small mammal, then an anthropoid, and ultimately Man Himself. Having reached that exalted state, I will be able to take evolution into my own hands, I will invent the wheel, the steam engine, the dynamo, and even the hydrogen bomb. . . . I will . . . but shucks, do I really want to do all that? Maybe it would be wiser, maybe I would survive longer (and survival is the only objectively demonstrable good), if I just went back to being an old-fashioned instead of a new-fashioned sea squirt." Thanks to that decision, he has survived longer than most of the organic forms which succeed him and may quite possibly survive all those now alive, including Man himself.

I am still not sure whether to call this little fable "The Road Not Taken" (with apologies to Robert Frost) or, more colloquially, "The Little Squirt Who Wouldn't."

At any rate, I think there is a moral somewhere.

1962

Wilderness As More Than a Tonic

In 1962 the Sierra Club of California published a magnificent book of seventy-two large color photographs by Eliot Porter. Though I wrote a brief introduction for it, this is not a plug. As a matter of fact, my subject did not begin to worry me until the introduction was in type and I learned for the first time that the title of the book was to be *In Wildness Is the Preservation of the World*.

"Oh dear," I said to myself, "that is a foolish title." Nature lover though I am, this is going too far. "Wilderness is a tonic and a refreshment. I think we are losing something as it disappears from our environment. But to call it 'the preservation of the world' is pretty farfetched." True, I doubt that we can be saved by increased production or by trips to the moon. In fact, I sometimes doubt that we can be saved at all. But wildness! Now really!

Another shock came when I learned that the phrase is a quotation from Henry David Thoreau. Henry, I know, confessed his love of exaggeration and once said his only fear was the fear he might not be extravagant enough. But he rarely said anything really foolish. I thought I had better look up the context. And not to keep the reader in suspense (if I may flatter myself that I have generated any) I must confess that I have come to the conclusion that what Henry said is neither foolish nor an exaggeration. It is a truth almost as obvious as "the mass of men lead lives of quiet desperation."

Here is the context: "The West of which I speak is but another name for the Wild, and what I have been preparing to say is, that in Wildness is the preservation of the World. Every tree sends its fibers forth in search of the Wild. The cities import it at any price. Men plow and sail for it. From the forests and wilderness come the tonics and barks which brace mankind."

What is this wildness Thoreau is talking about? It is not D. H. Lawrence's Dark Gods and neither is it the mindless anarchy of some current anti-intellectuals. Those are destructive forces. Thoreau's wildness is, on the other hand, something more nearly akin to Bernard Shaw's Life Force—it is that something prehuman which generated humanity. From it came a magnificent complex of living things long, long before we were here to be aware of them, and still longer before we, in our arrogance, began to boast that we were now ready to take over completely; that henceforth we in our greater wisdom would plan and manage everything, even, as we sometimes say, direct the course of evolution itself. Yet if—as seems not unlikely—we should manage or mismanage to the point of self-destruction, wildness alone will survive to make a new world.

Like so much that Thoreau wrote, this appeal to wildness as the ultimate hope for survival is more relevant and comprehensible in the context of our world than it was in his. A few of his contemporaries—Melville and Hawthorne, for instance—may have already begun to question the success of the human enterprise and the inevitability of progress. But life as it is managed by man was becoming increasingly comfortable and seemingly secure. Men were often anxious (or as Thoreau said "desperate") concerning their individual lives. But few doubted that mankind *as a whole* was on the right track. Theirs was not yet an age of public, over-all anxiety. That mankind might plan itself into suicide occurred to nobody. Yet, though few today put such hopes as they have managed to maintain in anything except the completer dependence upon human institutions and inventions, the possibility that we have too little faith in "wildness" is not quite so preposterous a suspicion as it seemed then.

In a world which sits, not on a powder keg, but on a hydrogen bomb, one begins to suspect that the technician who rules our world is not the master magician he thinks he is but only a sorcerer's apprentice who does not know how to turn off what he turned on—or even how to avoid blowing himself up.

Should that be what he at last succeeds in doing, it would be a relatively small disaster compared with the possibility that he might destroy at the same time all that "wildness" which generated him and might generate in time something better. Perhaps there is life (or shall we call it "wildness") on other planets, but I hope it will remain on ours also. "Pile up your books, the records of sadness, your saws and your laws. Nature is glad outside, and her merry worms will ere long topple them down."

This wildness may often be red in tooth and claw. It may be shockingly careful of the type but careless of the single life. In this and in many other respects we are unwilling to submit to it. But somehow it did, in the end, create the very creatures who now criticize and reject it. Nor can we be so certain as we once were that we can successfully substitute entirely our competence for nature's. Nature is, after all, the great reservoir of energy, of confidence, of endless hope, and of that joy not wholly subdued by the pale cast of thought but which seems to be disappearing from our human world. Rough and brutal though she sometimes seems in her far from simple plan, it did work, and it is not certain that our own plans will.

A very popular concept today is embodied in the magic word cybernetic—or self-regulating. "Feedback" is the secret of our most astonishing machines. But the famous balance of nature is the most extraordinary of all cybernetic systems. Left to itself, it is always self-regulated. The society we have created is not, on the other hand, cybernetic at all. The wisest and most benevolent of our plannings requires constant attention. We must pass this or that law or regulation, then we must redress this balance of production and distribution, taking care that encouraging one thing does not discourage something else. The society we have created puts us in constant danger lest we ultimately find ourselves unable to direct the more and more complicated apparatus we have devised.

A really healthy society, so Thoreau once wrote, would be like a healthy body which functions perfectly without our being aware of it. We, on the other hand, are coming more and more to assume that the healthiest society is one in which all citizens devote so much of their time to arguing, weighing, investigating, voting, propagandizing, and signing protests in a constant effort to keep a valetudinarian body politic functioning in some sort of pseudo-health that they have none of that margin for mere living which Thoreau thought important. It's no wonder that such a situation generated beatniks by way of a reaction.

Many will no doubt reply that Thoreau's ideal sounds too close to that of the classical economists who trusted the cybernetic free competition of Herbert Spencer *et al.* and that it just doesn't work. But is it certain that our own contrary system is working very well when it produces, on the one hand, a more or less successful welfare state and, on the other, an international situation which threatens not only welfare but human existence itself?

Should the human being turn out to be the failure some began a generation or more ago to call him, then all is not necessarily lost. Unless life itself is extinguished nature may begin where she began so long ago and struggle upward again. When we dream of a possible superman we almost invariably think of him as a direct descendant of ourselves. But he might be the flower and the fruit of some branch of the tree of life now represented only by one of the "lower" (and not necessarily anthropoid) animals.

When I recommend that we have a little more faith in the ultimate wisdom of nature, I am not suggesting that national parks, camping trips, and better bird-watching are the last best hope of mankind. But I do believe them useful reminders that we did not make the world we live in and that its beauty and joy, as well as its enormous potentialities, do not depend entirely on us. "Communion with nature" is not merely an empty phrase. It is the best corrective for that hubris from which the race of men increasingly suffers. Gerard Manley Hopkins, unwavering Catholic Christian though he was, could write:

> What would the world be, once bereft
> Of wet and wildness? Let them be left,
> O let them be left, wildness and wet;
> Long live the weeds and the wilderness yet.

The modern intellectual feels very superior when he contemplates the cosmology unquestioningly accepted by his ancestors. Their view of the universe was always so quaintly homocentric. Everything must find its ultimate explanation in man's needs. There was only God's Will on the one hand and the natural world which He created for man's convenience on the other. But we have only exchanged one kind of homocentric cosmology for another. For God's Will we have, to be sure, substituted the mindless mechanism of Darwinian evolution and assumed that a mere accident put us in a position to take advantage of what chance created. But in at least one respect we have only arrived by a different route at the same conclusion as our benighted ancestors: Only we count. Only we have minds. Only we can escape from absurdity. Only we, lifting ourselves by our own bootstraps, can save ourselves.

Pure Darwinism insists that we were elevated to what we regard as our exalted state by sheer accident followed by ineluctable necessity and that if nature seems to have been wise that is sheer illusion. But perhaps there was some wisdom as well as blank necessity in her processes. Man needs a context for his life larger than himself; he needs it so desperately that all modern despairs go back to the fact that he has rejected the only context which the loss of his traditional gods has left accessible. If there is any "somehow good," it must reside in nature herself. Yet the first item of our creed is a rejection of just that possibility.

"Nature books" generally get kindly reviews even from those who regard them as no more than the eccentric outpourings of harmless hobbyists. For that reason it was a salutary shock to come across in the admirable but not sufficiently well-known magazine *Landscape* an excoriation of the whole tribe of nature writers in a review by Professor Joseph Slate of a book to which I had contributed a chapter. Its author calls us for the most part mere triflers in the genteel tradition, too devoted to the gentler pages of Thoreau and Muir, too little aware of the Dark Gods.

He has, to put it mildly, a point. We do not dig deep enough. We slip too easily into a spinsterish concern with the pretty instead of the beautiful. We tend to get only just far enough away from the "cute" to think of the natural world as primarily a gentle consolation instead of a great force, and we are content to experience it only superficially. He is also quite right when he accuses us of quoting too seldom those passages of Thoreau which face, as we hesitate to face, things dark enough in one way if not exactly in the way which D. H. Lawrence celebrated.

Consider, for example, the passage from *Walden* which begins: "We can never have enough of nature." Stop there and you might conclude that he was about to embark upon just the kind of discourse Professor Slate finds so objectionable. But read on and you will come in the next sentence to wildness at its most wild:

We can never have enough of nature. We must be refreshed by the sight of inexhaustible vigor, vast and titanic features, the sea coast with its wrecks, the wilderness with its living and its decayed trees, the thunder cloud, and the rain which lasts three weeks and produces freshets. We need to witness our own limits transgressed, and some life pasturing freely where we never wander. . . . I love to see that nature is so rife with life that myriads can be afforded to be sacrificed and suffered to prey on one another; that tender organizations can be so serenely squashed out of existence like pulp, —tadpoles which herons gobble up, and tortoises and toads run over in the road; and that sometimes it has rained flesh and blood! . . . Poison is not poisonous after all, nor are any wounds fatal.

This is not the world we made and it is not the world we hope for. Neither is it the one where Thoreau himself most often felt at home. But it is at least an all but inexhaustible potentiality. Powerful as our weapons are, vast as is the destruction we are capable of, there is in part the least amiable but also the oldest and most enduring aspect of what Thoreau called "wildness" and it may survive when we have destroyed the better order we tried to make. To remind ourselves of its existence is only one (but not the least important) of the rewards for those who "in the love of Nature hold communion with her visible forms."

Thoreau was not a pessimist. He had faith in man's potentialities though little respect for the small extent to which man had realized them. He did not believe, as some do today, that man was a failure beyond redemption—he believed only that his contemporaries were failures because the true way had been lost a long time ago and primitive man (still a savage even if a noble one) had taken the wrong road toward what he mistakenly believed to be wisdom and happiness. Thoreau's return to nature was a return to the fatal fork, to a road not taken, along which he hoped that he and others after him might proceed to a better future.

Please note that he called "wildness" merely the "preservation," not the "redemption" or the "salvation," of the world. It may well be that its redemption may depend upon aspects of nature almost exclusively human. But man of the present day is more and more inclined to feel that mere survival or preservation is all he can hope for in the immediate future. If he is indeed granted a second chance to discover a genuinely good life, it may require him to go far back to that point where the road not taken branched off from the dubious road we have been following for so long and which we more and more stubbornly insist is the only right one because it takes us further and further away from the nature out of which we arose.

How far back would we have to go to find that road not taken? Could we, even supposing that we wanted to find it, reverse the direction in which our civilization is moving; or are the Marxians right and man is not a free agent but inevitably the captive of evolving technology that carries him along with it willy-nilly?

Thoreau thought he had an answer: "Simplify!" We get what we want and if things are in the saddle it is because we have put them there. And I have no doubt that he would say, "If you have hydrogen bombs that you are beginning to suspect you don't really want, it is because you have for too long believed that power was the greatest of goods and did not realize soon enough that it would become, as it now has, a nemesis."

Perhaps he was right and perhaps if we don't have a change of heart, if we don't voluntarily simplify, we and our civilization will be simplified for us in a grand catastrophe. That would take us a good deal further back than is necessary to find the road not taken.

1963

The Delights of Unnatural History

"Do not all charms fly at the touch of cold philosophy?" Keats answered his own rhetorical question by saying that they did—taking the rainbow out of the sky and clipping the angels' wings.

For this opinion he has been scolded, off and on, ever since. Truth is stranger than fiction, and the wonders of science, as he has been sternly reminded, are more wonderful than any others. The rainbow is still there—not, to be sure, as evidence of God's promise to Noah—but as an even more interesting demonstration of the laws of dispersion. The universe is wider than our notions of it ever were and a treatise on biology, we have often been reminded, is more amazing than any medieval bestiary.

Perhaps. Yet the two most celebrated animals that ever lived, never lived—the phoenix and the unicorn. There must be some reason other than perversity for this fact. To this day the simple—and that includes many poets—prefer them (along with such slightly less famous creatures as the kind pelican and the toad who bears a precious jewel in his head) to the lungfish or the platypus.

The average man, though no poet, is more likely to believe that an elephant never forgets or that the hoopsnake rolls merrily along with his tail in his mouth than he is to know (or care) whether or not the 'possum is a marsupial. When the Emperor Franz Josef happened to see an eagle that one of his huntsmen had shot, he is said to have inquired wonderingly what had become of its other head. The Amazon may not be the only river named after women, but it is the only one which comes to my mind and it was so called because these warlike ladies were moved to South America when the original African homeland had become sufficiently well known to make it pretty evident that they were not to be found there. The imagination just couldn't bear to give them up, and if the Himalayas are ever thoroughly explored, the Abominable Snowman is sure to turn up somewhere else.

Though I have read a good deal about real animals and how they behave, though I have even written something about them in my amateurish way, I am at least as much fascinated by what is sometimes called unnatural history as I am by the natural. Nothing could be more amazing than Von Frisch on the most recently discovered wonders of the bee, but for sheer delight I would rather take to bed with me that credulous Roman, Pliny the Elder; the better- (but not too well-) informed Edward Topsel in whom the actual and the picturesque era are charmingly blended; or, best of all, the medieval bestiary so admiredly and sympathetically translated by the late T. H. White.

Truth may be stranger than fiction but it is strange in a different way. That, I think, is the key to the mystery. As a naturalist I am always shocked at the thought of extinction. Like Theodore Roosevelt, "when I hear of the destruction of a species I feel as if all the works of some great writer had perished." But who misses the passenger pigeon or the dodo as he would miss the phoenix and the unicorn if they disappeared from the imagination? God made the first two; man made the second. And for that reason he has an especial affection for them. Since fiction is what we make up, it is inevitably what we would like to be true. Too much of what we find out, even when it isn't (as it all too often is) disconcerting, strikes no responsive chord in our nature. Unlike fancy, it is not the world we would have made had we had the making of it.

When a medieval monk explains to me that the peacock shrieks so hideously because he is vain, but has such ugly feet that he cries in rage every time he happens to see them, I feel that this is precisely what ought to be true. It is a pseudo-fact I shall remember long after I have forgot the latest experiment to demonstrate that 'possums "play dead," not because they hope to deceive me, but because fear has so over-stimulated their adrenal glands as to paralyze the muscles.

How, until I have forgot that fact or alleged fact, can I ever again accuse anyone of playing 'possum? Like too many other scientific facts, it just isn't humanly usable. A 'possum playing dead would certainly be more interesting if he knew what he was doing. So would a bird practicing the broken-wing trick—so much more interesting indeed that I am going to believe that it does know, until the mechanists get even better negative evidence than they have now. After all, none of them have ever been 'possums or birds.

Myth and unnatural history overlap. Each, no doubt, feeds the other. But they are not the same thing. Even those myths which were part of a living religion were not believed in the same way that pseudo-scientific facts were believed because, as that believer Samuel Johnson himself pointed out, the credence we give to "the truths of religion" is always different from that accorded to "the facts of ordinary life"—which latter is what unnatural history was supposed to be.

On the other hand, unnatural history, though distinguishable from myth, is also in part the product of similar tendencies and the needs of the human mind. Ignorance, misconception, and credulity contribute to it. But it is not merely any or all of these things. It is also a creation of the human imagination and therefore, like the myth, a wish fulfillment which reveals something about human nature, however misleading its picture of external nature may be. Men believed in unicorns and believed that they had seen them not so much because they were inaccurate observers as because such a beast would be a highly desirable addition to our fauna. Since he did not exist, it behooved man to invent him, and invent him he did. Indeed, he did much more than that. He invented a theory to justify the invention, not only of the unicorn, but also of any other possible beast which nature had, as we now know, unfortunately forgot to create.

This nature, as we all learned in school, was formerly believed to "abhor a vacuum" and we were probably told that Galileo took a great step into the modern world when he announced, after experimenting with a suction pump for water (and presumably with a touch of irony), that "nature does not abhor a vacuum below thirty-four feet"—which happens to be the height of a column of water which atmospheric pressure is sufficient to sustain. But perhaps there are some, even among readers of the *American Scholar*, who do not know (and I apologize in advance to those who do) that the premise "nature abhors a vacuum" once covered much more than the physical. It meant that the universe is a *plenum*. The perfection of God implies that everything possible is also actual; and since a unicorn *could* exist it certainly *must* exist —somewhere, if not in any conveniently observable place. To say that it didn't was a blasphemous denial of the perfection of God and the consequent perfection of the universe He had created.

Here, for example, is what was said on that subject in a thesis proving the existence of the unicorn and published in 1661 by a certain George Caspard Kirchmayer who apparently stole it from a contemporary though he himself was a professor at Hamlet's alma mater in Wittenburg and a member of both the English and the Viennese Royal Academies:

> Who cares any longer to be of such simplicity as not to hesitate to oppose his own view to many proofs both divine and human, for the existence of the unicorn. . . . If, says the acute Scaliger, anything were missing, a vacuum would be created in the forms of animal life. This would be a far greater fault in nature than a vacuum in space without substance.

This same Professor Kirchmayer was, however, equally convinced that the phoenix was a mere fable and convinced for a similarly sound reason. All accounts of this bird agree that there is never more than one phoenix alive at a time. God would certainly not permit any creature to get away with so plain a defiance of his universally applicable injunction: Increase and multiply.

But where did all the delightful nonsense which the medieval mind was to elaborate so exuberantly come from? It must be very old since there are in the Old Testament various oblique references to some of the most familiar tales (like the refusal of the raven to feed its young until they show black) which seem to imply general familiarity with them. Yet there is not much of it in the surviving Greek literature of the Golden Age because that age, though obsessed by myth, was already developing too strong a sense of fact to write first-rate unnatural history.

Even Herodotus was cagey about the phoenix. "They have also another sacred bird . . . called the phoenix, which I myself have never seen except in pictures." (That would have been enough to convince any bestiary writer.) Aristotle, the master of those who know, knew quite a bit that isn't so, but he was a scientist who would never have permitted himself to believe anything just because it would be agreeable to do so; and when he goes astray for any cause other than the simple inadequacy of his data (a phenomenon not unknown in the most modern of sciences), it is not because he indulged his fancy but because he had rather too much confidence in pure reason—like the German in the familiar anecdote who evolved the elephant out of his inner consciousness.

For thousands of years date growers had been tying flowers of the male tree to the branches of the female in order to fertilize them, but Aristotle could demonstrate by logic absolute that plants must be without sex and he proved it so convincingly that the scientific demonstrations of the eighteenth century had a good deal of difficulty in making headway against his authority. He could also explain why snakes have no legs: No animal with a backbone ever has more than four (which is true enough) and a snake is so long that four wouldn't do him any good (which is a bit farfetched).

It was the Romans, and especially Pliny, who passed on to the medieval masters in this field most of the hints which they elaborated. Because no age since has accepted a cosmology so completely homocentric, the medieval masters took it for granted that anything that would illustrate God's detailed provisions for the convenience or the instruction of man must necessarily be true. And since the universe was a metaphor, the metaphorical interpretation of any fact or imagined fact must be the most significant one.

The future Cardinal Newman had, for a time, great difficulty in accepting the claim of the Roman Church to infallible authority in matters of faith and morals. But the difficulty vanished when it occurred to him that such an authority would be very helpful to man, that God always provided what man needed, and that therefore he must have provided this convenience. This is precisely the line of reasoning which the monkish compiler of unnatural history followed out, even when dealing with the most specific details. Your modern who wants to find instructive morals in nature is often inconvenienced by the necessity of getting his facts reasonably straight; but the monk had no hesitation in finding the moral first, and he took it for granted that nature would necessarily illustrate it somewhere. He did not find it difficult to believe that the widowed turtledove never consented to a second marriage because that would set a good example to the human female and, if he had heard that the newborn lion cub lay dead for three days until his father breathed upon him, that was so pat an allegory of the resurrection that one need inquire no further.

On the other hand, even Pliny, when recounting a wonder, often cites specific instances of the testimony of a supposed eyewitness. In his account of the elephant, for instance, he tells us that Mutianus (who was three times Consul and therefore presumably a responsible fellow) "states that he himself was witness to the fact that when some elephants were being landed at Puteoli and were compelled to leave the ship, being terrified at the length of the platform which extended from the vessel to the shore, they walked backwards in order to deceive themselves by forming a false estimate of the distance."

But just because the medieval writer had such complete faith in the *a priori* and almost as much in "the authorities" (i.e., anyone who had ever told a tall story before the writer's own time) he rarely felt it worthwhile to limit himself to what we should regard as acceptable testimony. That the medieval zoologist should have been ignorant does not surprise us much. Considering the circumstances under which he lived, it is, as a matter of fact, astonishing how much genuine information is mixed up with the extravagant nonsense in the better bestiaries. The compiler was a long way from either Africa or India and from an elephant. It is extremely unlikely that he had ever seen one or even known anybody who had. Yet he tells us, for example, that their period of gestation is two years—which is almost precisely accurate. Then he goes on to repeat the oft-repeated tale that elephants cannot lie down because they have no joints in their legs and are compelled to lean against trees when they wish to sleep.

What does surprise us is the medieval zoologist's calm confidence that this is the best of all possible worlds; that God's ways are not mysterious but plainly evident to anyone who will observe them; and that there is nothing in nature which does not either supply a need or at least present a useful moral. Being a monk, as he usually was, he had renounced the wicked world of men but he had no doubt that here was nothing wrong with the universe except man's wickedness. One could not possibly get further than this from existentialism or radical alienation. To the monk the physical world was an allegory of the moral and the spiritual. To him, it seemed therefore perfectly obvious that the soundest scientific method was simply to ask of every observed phenomenon, "What purpose does it serve?" or "What lesson does it teach?" If the only answer he could come up with was one that must have seemed rather farfetched even to him, he accepted it for the same reason that the modern physicist accepts the paradoxes of his science: "What other explanation is possible?"

To us it seems that no "scientific method" could be more completely unscientific than the usual medieval one. "Teleological" has become the dirtiest word in the vocabulary of the modern interpreter of natural phenomenon. But the medieval scientist was not merely silly. Given his premise that the universe embodies a purpose and that this purpose is human welfare, his methods followed as naturally as the method of our science follows from the premise that man is merely an accident in a universe which knows nothing of his peculiar desires, needs, and standards of value which he has somehow or other most improbably acquired.

One assumption leads naturally to another. We think "the doctrine of signatures" extraordinarily silly, but if you take it for granted that God created the various members of the plant kingdom to serve human purposes, then what is more likely than that He would give a key to the various uses so that, for instance, the liver-shaped leaves of the liverwort inform us that it is good for diseases of the liver; and the habit of certain saxifrages to grow in the disintegrating fissures of rock indicates that it will similarly disintegrate kidney and gall-bladder stones?

The only cause for astonishment is how long such beliefs lingered into the age of science. A mid-seventeenth-century herbalist writes of the herb commonly known as horse tongue: "The little leaf-like tongue, growing upon the greater, is no light argument that this plant is effectual for sores in the mouth and throat." Though John Ray, the first great English biologist and a true scientist in our understanding of the term, rejected the doctrine of signatures as unsupported by convincing evidence, he was still sufficiently inclined to teleology to write:

> One observation I shall add relating to the virtues of plants, in which I think there is something of truth, that is, that there are, by the wise disposition of Providence, such species of plants produced in every country as are most proper and convenient for the meat and medicine of the men and animals that breathe and inhabit there. Insomuch that Solenander writes, that from the frequency of the plants that spring up naturally in any region he could easily gather what endemical diseases the inhabitants thereof were subject to: So in Denmark, Friesland, and Holland, where the scurvy usually reigns, the proper remedy thereof, scurvygrass, doth plentifully grow.

The more we have learned, or think we have learned, about the universe, the less tenable such assumptions have come to seem. In fact, the intellectual history of Western man is often summed up as consisting of the various stages of his disillusion with the assumption that the world was made for him; that he is the most important thing in it; that it has a humanly understandable meaning, and purpose; that "all evil is good not understood." Copernicus and Darwin are conventionally, and no doubt correctly, regarded as the key figures because they mark such clear and such radical steps toward a new concept of man's place in the universe. They are angels with flaming swords who stand guard at the gates of the fool's paradise from which we have been expelled.

If any reader has begun to suspect that I suffer from so much nostalgia for this Paradise Lost that I plan to defy the guardians of the gate and reenter it, I hasten to assure them that I neither believe that possible nor wish that it were. I have more faith in the doctor with his syringe full of antibiotics than in any herbalist, however skilled he may be in reading plant signatures. Preparing recently for a trip around the world that would include some unusually unhealthy regions, I had myself inoculated against nine different maladies instead of planning to cull along the road those symbols which, if I believed Ray and his authority, the learned Solenander, would surely be growing where any of the nine diseases were especially prevalent. But I do have one more comment to make.

In quite properly rejecting the assumption that a theory must be true if it is comforting or consoling we have acquired, it seems to me, a tendency to lean over backward in the opposite direction. The more any sociological or physiological or psychological theory offends our dignity, or seems to deprive us of the power either to control our destiny or even to understand our own aims and motives, the more likely it seems to us to embody the truth. If Darwin tells us that we are the product of blind chance; Marx-Leninism that our ideals and ideas are mere ineffectual "ideologies"; Freud that we don't know what is going on in our own minds, and sociology that we are what our own society makes us rather than what we choose to be, the very fact that all these theories are rather dispiriting makes us inclined to accept them. Sometimes I find myself suspecting that if we really did understand the universe and our place in it, this universe might not be as completely alien as we have come to assume. After all, we too are a product of it.

The late Will Cuppy kept several *bêtes noires* in his mental zoo, and he frequently trotted them out in such delightful works of more-or-less-natural history as *How to Become Extinct* and *How to Tell Your Friends from the Apes*. A favorite target was Aristotle, although why he chose him rather than that amiable, industrious, and boundlessly uncritical gossip, Pliny the Elder, I was never able to understand.

After all, Aristotle did know a lot and he took his responsibilities seriously. He did not, to be sure, realize (as we do) that most biology is highly improbable and that it is, therefore, very dangerous to put any faith in *a priori* logic because the facts usually turn out to be what no sane man would ever be inclined to suppose. Nevertheless, and aside from this tendency to believe that an absent fact could be supplied by reason, Aristotle did very well indeed, even by the standards of this factual age. When he undertakes to explain why snakes don't have legs, his explanation may sound rather like one of Kipling's *Just So Stories*, but that is not his general tone.

Pliny, on the other hand, is something else again. Whenever he abandons summaries of other writers to enter upon speculations of his own, he gives a certain amiable imbecility full range, and becomes a delightfully foolish companion. For one thing, his complete abandonment to the most farfetched of teleological explanations is a not unwelcome relief from modern science, which so firmly represses any reassuring assumption that the universe is in any way adapted to our needs and wishes, or has ever had any idea whither it was headed. Those of us who have been rebuked (as I have) for teleology or anthropomorphism, just because of some such figure of speech as "the cactus is a tropical plant which learned how to live in the desert," and have been sternly told to say instead, "has become adapted to desert conditions," are tempted actually to applaud when Pliny comes up with something like his comment on the cork oak: "When this tree is debarked, it does not die as other trees do because Nature, like a farsighted mother, dressed it in a double bark, knowing well that it would be frequently debarked." This is an example of cart-before-horse almost as entertaining as the observation said to have been made by a Mohammedan theologian in the Middle Ages, when he cited as one of the most striking examples of God's kindly concern for the welfare of His children the fact that He never sent rain to the desert where it would be wasted, but only to the fertile valleys where it would do some good.

In both of these cases, the interpreter was at least interpreting an actual fact. Pliny, at his best, thinks up an absurdity in order to explain something that isn't true to begin with. For example, he tells us that snakes have such an aversion to the ash tree that they will go through fire rather than touch its leaves or branches and that it is, therefore, "a wonderful courtesy of Nature that the Ash has flowered before serpents come out of hibernation and does not cast its leaves until they have gone again."

As for me, I have never been quite sure that there is not something immanent in nature which inspires it with a sort of purpose and I think it is possible to imagine that without recourse to any crude teleological interpretation of nature's phenomena. Moreover, I do find something at least intriguing in the fact that the very sciences that reject such notions have been compelled to reveal correspondences between the needs of human beings and the conditions of our physical world that would have impressed believers in design far more than Pliny's ash tree or cork oak—although the correspondences I have in mind also are, no doubt, carts rather than horses.

It is a commonplace, for instance, that the higher manifestations of life as we know them seem to require a set of conditions so special that none of the other planets in our system comes anywhere near providing them and that, therefore, those who believe that these manifestations exist elsewhere in the universe are forced to fall back upon the probability that, among the billions of planets outside our own system, some may be very much like our earth.

And while I am willing to grant that life may have begun as the result of a "fortunate accident," which has never during our earth's megabillion years' history happened again, that accident would seem a lot easier to take for granted if we still believed, as our ancestors did, that the miracle was repeated thousands of times a day when insects, reptiles, and other forms of life were created out of mud or "corruption."

Consider also the fact, not only that water is necessary, but that it must also exhibit a peculiar property. It must get heavier as it grows colder but, oddly enough, reverses this process at about 39° Fahrenheit and begins to get lighter again. Because it does behave in just this odd way, the bottom of the lake is warmer in winter than the top; ice begins to form at the surface rather than on the bottom; and by thus providing an insulator it limits the depth of ice. If water got heavier and heavier as it got colder and colder, the ice would start forming at the bottom and in all but the warmer regions lakes would freeze so solid that they would hardly melt by the end of summer. Hence most of our surface water would be locked up in ice. Not long ago I asked a distinguished geologist what would have happened if water had not had this peculiar property. He replied, "Well, we would probably all be dead; or more probably still, none of the higher forms of life would ever have evolved."

Now all this is more or less commonplace, and I do not cite it in any effort to revive teleology or to suggest that it represents more than another of the many happy accidents that explain our universe. But I do like to consider things curiously and the other day a curious fact, which I do not remember to have seen commented upon before, happened to occur to me. It led to some reflections which I am going to call "Seeds and Civilization."

The seed is, of course, a rather recent invention, as recent goes in the time scale of the earth. Plants reproduced without seed for a much longer time than has passed since seeds were invented, and flowering plants did not become dominant until a mere sixty or seventy million years ago. Yet, as I shall attempt to demonstrate, if seeds had not been invented in what might be called the nick of time, civilization could never have developed, and we might still be hunters and food-gatherers instead of masters of a technology which, unfortunately, may be about to turn the tables.

Anthropologists still use the old terms Paleolithic and Neolithic to distinguish between the men who came before and those who came after a sudden leap forward. But they now know that it was not polished stone weapons that made the difference. Men were able to make better implements because they had invented agriculture. Thus the seed of our civilization was literally a seed. And before man could discover how to use the seed, nature had first to invent it. And it took nature herself millions of years to invent step by step this wonderful device. The plant kingdom could get along very well without them, but human civilization would be impossible.

Green plants, something like the scum that grows on ponds, may be a billion years old, but neither they nor many later vegetative types produced seeds. They reproduced themselves in a variety of complicated ways of which the most advanced was the formation of spores like those upon which the ferns still depend. This almost microscopic spore has to lie on the moist earth until a single tiny cell divides repeatedly to form a flat thallus; the thallus develops male and female organs; the ovules produced in the female organ are fertilized by a kind of sperm; and from the fertilized ovum what we recognize as a fern develops.

It is possible, of course, deliberately to raise a fern from a spore, but it is vastly more difficult than raising a plant from seed. Moreover, the processes are so difficult to oberve that even as late as the eighteenth century they were not understood. A seed, on the other hand, is a wonderfully convenient device. It is a kind of egg that differs from the ordinary animal egg in one important particular. It is an egg that starts to hatch, then arrests the process and enters upon a dormant period in which it may remain alive but unchanging for many years, or even—in at least one known case—for centuries. The advantages of this arrangement for man, as well as for the plant, are obvious. And the most obvious of all is the fact that a seed, unlike an egg, can be kept until a convenient or suitable time has come for it to make itself into a plant again.

The fresh egg of a chicken contains nothing that suggests what it will produce. And it won't keep. Only if it is warmed for a time, while still fresh, does even the outline sketch of the primitive fowl begin to develop. But the seed, before it had ripened, had already formed a miniature plant or embryo, which anyone who has ever broken open a bean or a peanut has seen nestled down between the two halves of the seed proper which contain a food supply. Upon this food supply the germinating plant will depend while the roots and leaves of the embryo plant are developing to the point where they can draw nourishment from the soil and the air. In the embryo itself are enzymes so powerful when aroused into action that peanut butter would not keep fresh if the embryo had not been removed from the nut before it was crushed.

I am not going to arouse the ire of science by suggesting that when nature invented the seed she did so with the intention of making civilization possible. We may grant that it was only another happy accident. But nature did invent the convenient seed and took, as I said before, a very long time to perfect it. Essentially, and enormously simplified, what happened was this: Spores, like those of the fern, became pollen and the plant "got into the habit" of going through an abbreviated form of the thallus stage of the fern on the parent plant itself, and it thus created a seed with an embryo. Our confidence in the astonishing fact that if you plant a pea you get a pea and if you plant a petunia you get a petunia is sublime. Any fool knows that—now. But our primitive ancestors did not know and they were so far from being fools that, as so many anthropologists maintain, the Cro-Magnon caveman had as much native intelligence as we do. Yet he and his forebears had been on the earth many hundreds of thousands of years before it was discovered—quite recently, indeed— that one can plant the seed of a plant in the ground and get another plant just like it.

Anthropologists say, also, that before man knew how to grow things he was compelled to be an aimless wanderer following game animals and wild crops wherever they could be found. Once he had grasped the secret meaning of the seed, he could have a dependable food supply that didn't have to be searched for. He could settle down, have a home, form a community, become a sort of domesticated animal instead of a wild one, and then rapidly develop, one after another, the characteristics of civilization. For several hundred thousand years his advance had been at less than a snail's pace and his numbers so few that he was an unimportant, barely surviving species. Within only a few thousand years after agriculture had begun, he was to become lord of the earth with a written word, religion, philosophy, literature, and a hundred material possessions to contribute to security and comfort. When those of us who like to consider things curiously buy (perhaps in a dime store) a package labeled peas or petunias, we are not likely to realize that we hold a miracle in our hand—something that took nature hundreds of millions of years to invent and man several hundred thousand to find out his use for. We could still be civilized men without steam or electricity or telephones or automobiles—many men before us were highly civilized without them—but we could not be much more than very clever animals with little use for our intelligence if nature had not invented the seed; and if some genius, forgotten thousands of years ago, had not been seized by one of the most prodigious notions ever to visit the human brain.

1965

The Moth and the Candle

The moth who singes his wings has pointed many a moral but he does not "desire" the flame, not even in the dim way that the first scorpion to leave the water may have "desired" to succeed in his dangerous adventure. The moth accomplishes no purpose of his own and none appropriate to nature at large. He is merely the victim of a situation which can seldom have arisen before man put in his appearance long after moths and many other insects had developed a tropism which was usually harmless during millions of years.

A moth's wings beat faster when light falls upon his eyes, and when it falls more strongly on one eye than on the other, the wings on one side beat faster than those on the other. Irresistibly his flight curves toward the source and if he reaches it, he dies—a victim of one of the mistakes which nature sometimes makes because even she cannot foresee every eventuality.

But in the case of a certain moth which lives in the desert and of a certain candle which grows there the situation is different.

Almost anywhere in the Southwest you will find as a conspicuous feature of the landscape one or another of the yuccas with their large bundle of stiff, sword-sharp leaves and, in early summer, an incredibly tall spire of innumerable creamy white blossoms held high on a great spike which shot up suddenly from the middle of the sword cluster. Pass by again in the fall and the spire will be bearing handsome pods which split open as they dry and scatter innumerable shiny black seeds on the sand. Though a bit difficult to gather, the pods make a fine addition to a winter bouquet and those who gather them often notice that each is perforated by at least one hole from which some insect has obviously emerged.

217

Sometimes the collector will search for a "perfect" specimen, but perfect ones are not to be found. The "infestation"
was necessary. Either the ovary from which the pod developed was "infested" or it didn't mature. Thereby hangs a tale
as strange as any the desert has to tell and in certain important respects the most difficult to explain of all the strange
tales which are told of the interdependence of insects and
flowers. The hole was made by the larva of a moth, and just
to make the question we are about to ask as neat as possible,
it happens that certain species of yucca are still commonly
called by the name which the Spaniards gave them: Our
Lord's Candle.

Does *Pronuba yuccasella,* the moth in question, "desire"
this particular candle? Please wait until you have heard the
whole story before you answer.

Everybody—or at least everybody old enough to have been
a child before directer methods of sex instruction came into
fashion—knows about the bees and the flowers. If he did not
lose all interest in the subject as he began to realize its remoter personal implications, he probably now knows at least
in a very general way that many plants depend upon many
insects and some, even, upon certain birds, to help them in
what the eighteenth century liked to call "their nuptial rites."
Orchard growers tend bees principally to increase their yield
of apples and plums and pears; Darwin wrote a classic on the
pollination of orchids; the Smyrna fig would not fruit in
California until the particular wasp which acts as marriage
broker for it in the Near East was imported to perform his
function here, etc., etc.

But in every known case except that of the moth and the
candle it is a somewhat one-sided affair with all the "intention" being on the part of the flower. Though the insect may
be lured by a scent which it likes—even by the stench of
rotten meat in the case of certain tropical blossoms pollinated
by flesh-eating flies—and though he may be rewarded with
nectar or with edible pollen, he does not do anything directly
calculated to fertilize the flower. Sometimes the flower is so
constructed that, for instance, the insect cannot get at the
nectar without brushing against the pollen-bearing anthers
and then against a stigma which will ultimately conduct the
gene-bearing protoplasm of the pollen down to the ovules

below. But he does not deliberately fertilize the plant and it would not affect his chances of passing on the torch to his posterity if the flower were not fertilized. The plant uses the insect but there is no active cooperation on the insect's part.

Consider, on the other hand, what happens in the unique case of the yucca and its attendant moth. In the first place, though there are many species of yuccas, only a single one of them—and it does not grow in this region—appears to be capable of getting along without the moth upon which all the rest depend. Moreover, the moths, in their turn, are no less completely dependent upon the yuccas because their larva cannot feed upon anything except its maturing seeds. But this situation, which is odd without being unique, is not all. What *is* unique is the fact that the moth goes through a series of purposeful actions which have no other function except to fertilize a flower which could not be fertilized in any other way. If we naïvely interpreted its actions, we should find ourselves compelled to say that it "knows what it is doing."

The classic observation was made seventy-five years ago by the remarkable Missouri entomologist, Charles V. Riley, though the subject has been much studied and written about since Riley himself fully described the crucial, incredible event as he observed it on a cultivated species grown in the neighborhood of St. Louis. Several different insects frequent the flowers to eat the nectar or the pollen but perform no service in return. Meanwhile the female of the indispensable moth rests quietly in the half-closed blossoms.

When evening comes she goes in turn to several of the flowers just opening for their one night of perfect bloom. While the male, who has already done his duty, flutters uselessly about, she collects from the anthers a ball of the pollen which is surrounded by a sticky gum to prevent its accidental dispersal. After she has collected under her chin a mass somewhat larger than her head, she climbs the pistil of a different flower and into it she inserts her egg tube about a third of the way down from the top and injects several eggs. However, she "knows" that if she left it at that her larva would have nothing to feed on. Accordingly, she mounts the rest of the way up the pistil, deposits the pollen ball on the stigma, and moves her head back and forth to rub the pollen well in. She eats neither nectar nor pollen. She gets no immediate benefit from her action. It has no purpose other than to fertilize the flower.

The insect which does these remarkable things is nothing much to look at—a little inch-long moth, silvery white in color and, so far as anyone knows, quite conventional in behavior except during the one great moment when it is impelled to act as though it knew a great deal about the physiology of plants as well as about the life history of its own species.

Most of what happens after the fertilization of the flower follows a familiar pattern. The flowers wither and a few days later the wormlike larva can be found. In time it will bore its way out of the maturing pod, drop to the ground, spin a cocoon a few inches below the surface, and there transform itself into an adult completely equipped to repeat, next year, the whole complicated process. Since there are commonly not more than two larvae per pod, they eat only a few of the perhaps two hundred seeds which the pod produces. From the standpoint of the yucca it is a very good arrangement since the sacrifice of a few seeds is a small price to pay for a very efficient job of fertilization. The staggering question for anyone who has committed himself to "explaining" nature is simply this: How on earth was such a system of mutual cooperation for individual ends ever worked out?

Evidently the yucca and the yucca moth came to their mutual understanding a long time ago—certainly before the plant genus had evolved the many species now flourishing— because, with the one exception previously mentioned, they all seem to be signatories to the agreement; certainly, also, long enough ago for the Pronuba moth to have itself evolved into at least several distinguishable species, because those which visit certain yuccas are slightly different from those which visit others. On the other hand, moth and yucca have not always worked together, because the flower continues to secrete a nectar which now merely attracts useless insects of various sorts and presumably it learned to do that at a time before Pronuba got into the habit of paying a visit on business of her own for which no honeyed inducement is necessary.

Apparently, sometime during the millenniums when the two were engaged in a late phase of their evolution and separating themselves into the different species of moth and yucca, they must themselves have kept together. "Wherever thou goest I go," said the moth, because, again with the one single exception, where a yucca is native, so is a Pronuba. Attempt to grow the former outside its range and it may flower very nicely. But "no moth, no seed" seems to be the absolute rule.

William Trelease, student and monographer of the yucca genus, calls attention to the fact that "the mutual dependence seems absolute" and he then permits himself a cautious, scientific understatement when he remarks that the fact is "no doubt of the greatest suggestiveness," though "its meaning has escaped both botanists and zoologists."

Now the relatively simple one-sided arrangement which is so prevalent in the plant world is difficult enough to understand. Geology seems to demonstrate that the earliest flowering plants depended, as the conifers do today, upon the chance that some of their abundant pollen would be carried by the wind to the waiting ovaries. Then, since all organic matter is potentially edible by something, it is assumed that certain insects got into the habit of eating pollen, accidentally got some of it entangled in the hair on their bodies as many still do, and accidentally rubbed some of it off on the stigmas of the other flowers they visited. Since, for the plant, this was more effective than wind pollination and involved less waste of vital material, those plants which were most attractive to insects got along best. And as the degree of attractiveness accidentally varied, "natural selection" favored those which were most attractive, until gradually all the devices by which plants lure insects or birds—bright colored petals, nectar which serves the plant in no direct way, and perfume which leads the insect to the blossom; even the "guide lines" which sometimes mark the route to the nectar glands—were mechanically and necessarily developed.

Gardeners usually hate "bugs," but if the evolutionists are right, there never would have been any flowers if it had not been for these same bugs. The flowers never waste their sweetness on the desert air or, for that matter, on the jungle air. In fact, they waste it only when nobody except a human being is there to smell it. It is for the bugs and for a few birds, not for men, that they dye their petals or waft their scents. And it is lucky for us that we either happen to like or have become "conditioned" to liking the colors and the odors which most insects and some birds like also. What a calamity for us if insects had been color blind, as all mammals below the primates are! Or if, worse yet, we had had our present taste in smells while all the insects preferred, as a few of them do, that odor of rotten meat which certain flowers dependent upon them abundantly provide. Would we ever have been able to discover thoughts too deep for tears in a gray flower which exhaled a terrific stench? Or would we have learned by now to consider it exquisite?

The whole story, as it is usually told, of how flowers developed is thus a rather tall tale, as indeed the whole story of evolution is. But it does fall just short of the completely incredible even though we are likely to feel an additional strain when we begin to bring in the more remarkable features and find ourselves compelled to believe in the gradual blind development of the more intricate devices by which a flower is often adapted to some particular insect or bird and the exact correspondence between, say, the length of a given flower's tube and the length of the moth's proboscis or the hummingbird's bill which is going to reach down into it. But when we come to Pronuba and the yucca we get something more staggering still. That two different organisms should have simultaneously adapted themselves one to another is, if I understand the laws of probability, at least four times as improbable as that one should have adapted itself to the other. I am not saying I don't believe it did. On the whole I think I do, at least with one reservation. But sometimes I can't help saying to myself, "A man who will believe that will believe anything."

Since Darwin's day the fact that evolution did, somehow or other, take place has been made overwhelmingly clear. Because that fact could not really be doubted, most students felt compelled to accept what seemed to be the best available explanation of "how" it could possibly have happened. Yet the fact remains that a great many students have been just a little unhappy about that "how" and that a good deal of the work which has been done since Darwin's day has been concerned with an attempt to make the whole thing seem a little more credible.

Nearly everybody came to feel that Darwin's summary

reliance on minute, accidental variation and natural selection was a bit too casual. The discovery that organisms were capable of sudden big-step "mutations" as well as minute variations helped. All sorts of experiments were designed to prove that some slight accidental advantage like the lighter color of a mouse living on sand really did increase significantly its chances of survival. The mathematically minded got into the game, notably Sir Ronald Aylmer Fisher who recently summarized in formidable equations his contention that chance is not chance when statistically studied and that the "progress" made in the course of evolution was no more merely fortuitous than the profits of the proprietor of a roulette wheel are. Given time enough, he is bound to win. The "laws of probability" take the chanciness out of chance.

All of this helps. But one might as well admit also that the work done since Darwin constitutes a tacit admission on the part of the investigators that they would feel a bit more comfortable about the whole business if it could be made less hard to swallow, that quite possibly there is some factor operating which has not been taken proper account of. And when we come to the case of Pronuba and its elaborate working arrangement with the yucca we have an especially hard nut to crack. Accident, mutation, selection, statistical probability, etc., all seem to leave it a little mysterious still. Even granted a very long time for the thing to work itself out, we seem to be approaching the limits of credibility. It has been argued, to take the most extravagant case, that if a hundred apes were to bang away at a hundred typewriters for a long enough time, then, sooner or later, one of them would have to compose accidentally *Paradise Lost,* complete and exact to the last comma. But do we believe that he ever would?

Many would admit that most of the difficulties could be made to vanish if only we might assume the intrusion of some factor not wholly accidental and mechanical. If there were only some intelligence, however feeble; some intention, however dim; some power of choice, however weak, which the evolving organism could have used to take advantage of the opportunities which chance provided. If only, in other words, the whole process of evolving life were not assumed to be so lifeless.

Nevertheless, most of the scientists who would even admit the convenience of such an assumption are aghast at the suggestion that it might be made. They throw up their hands in horror crying, "Teleology," "Vitalism," "Lamarckian nonsense," and the rest. There is no evidence, they say. And if you go beyond evidence you open the way to the most baseless speculations. The whole enterprise of science might just as well be given up. "No, no, no. Hard as it may be to swallow the official version of how either the Pronuba moth or Homo sapiens came to be what he is, you must not ask us to admit the possibility that there is purpose at work in the universe at large or even that the scorpion who came to land and the moth which joined up with the yucca had the dimmest conception of what he was doing."

We would be particularly happy, they say, to argue the whole question out in connection with your moth because, of all the highly evolved creatures, the insects are notoriously the most completely in the grip of their reflexes and their instinctive patterns of behavior. On the one hand, their life histories are extraordinarily complex. The spider's web, the wasp's wise provision of living but paralyzed prey for its young, and the complicated organization of ant society are unparalleled in their intricate effectiveness by the procedures of any other creature except man. Entomology is one long tale of marvels. Yet, on the other hand, no other creatures are demonstrably so incapable of varying the set pattern of their behavior, so demonstrably unaware of what they are doing, or of why they do it. Thus the very class of animals which appears superficially to be the most purposeful is the very one in which not only purpose but even the possibility of consciousness seems most obviously absent. They are capable of behavior a thousand times more impressive than any a dog could ever rise to, yet a dog is far more intelligent. Not mentality of any kind but the reflexes established by chance are what produce the greatest wonders and those "evidences of design" which seem, at first sight, so convincing.

This makes a strong case against the simple assumption that purpose in the universe at large or intelligent planning in an individual animal species furnishes a sufficient explanation for what has happened in the course of evolution. Probably most of the mechanisms which science has so painstakingly explored really have operated effectively. But does this really demonstrate that something besides mechanism, say merely some very dim awareness and purpose, has never, to return to the word chosen a moment ago, "intervened" to tip the balance in one direction or another, to make the successful working out of some such arrangement as that of the moth with the yucca easier to understand than it is on the basis of a purely mechanical process? And are there not, after all, some observable phenomena which hint at powers present in even a modern insect which make such intervention not unthinkable?

We must grant that the insects as we know them today really do seem to come close to being those mere mechanisms which Descartes and the Cartesians insisted that all animals really are. Perhaps nobody—not even the most extreme mechanist—would today maintain, as Descartes did, that when a dog howls with pain he only *seems* to be suffering because he merely "operates like a watch by springs" and cannot feel anything; or that, as one of Descartes' disciples put it, all animals "eat without pleasure, they cry without pain, they grow without knowing it; they desire nothing, they fear nothing, they know nothing." But much of the time many insects really do seem to be almost purely mechanical.

Nevertheless, "much of the time" is not the same thing as "always." As a matter of fact, one single incontrovertible instance of an insect which did not behave mechanically, which exhibited desire, or will, or the power to choose a preferable alternative, would be enough to make it not only possible but probable that he had powers which might intervene in the course of evolution even now. Those powers would suggest that his primitive ancestors may have been able to intervene more effectively before they came—as they may have—to rely more and more on the instincts into which acquired habits gradually hardened. In man, "conditioned reflexes" are usually something which do not precede but succeed acts directed by consciousness. Why may not the conditioned reflexes of the insect have arisen in the same way out of habits of behavior first acquired with the help of his dim consciousness?

But can an "incontrovertible instance" of purposeful behavior in insects be cited? That would seem to be the crucial question and the answer to it is that quite a number of instances can be cited which are at least not usually controverted even though they are often brushed aside.

Take for example a few recently cited by Evelyn Cheesman,

a recognized authority who was for many years Curator of Insects for the Zoological Society of London. Most of her most recent book, *Insects: Their Secret World,* is concerned with describing what appear to be the fixed, invariable, perhaps almost completely unconscious, behavior patterns of insects, including even the highest. But there is a last chapter called "Individual Actions" in which she cautiously describes observed cases where instinctive behavior seems to have been momentarily superseded by a purposeful action designed to meet an unusual situation. I shall choose only one, partly because it is both simple and comic.

The individual which exhibited this instance of what must amount to genius in an insect was a solitary wasp of the New Hebrides. It had got into the habit of visiting Miss Cheesman's breakfast table for sweets and she had got into the habit of performing little experiments upon it. When it had retired to its tiny burrow for the day and stood just within the entrance on guard against intruders who might steal its larder of insect food, the experimenter would tap threateningly with a pair of forceps and the wasp would emerge to do battle, leaping upon the forceps and trying to bite into the steel.

". . . When the forceps remained still she seemed satisfied that the enemy was slain and would return to the burrow, rushing in head foremost as was her habit. Directly she turned her back to do this I would give her a little tap. Now what is interesting is that such habits are hereditary. That particular species always enters her burrow head first . . . but that particular wasp after several times having a tap from the forceps wouldn't turn her back again. She lowered herself very cautiously backwards into the burrow, keeping a bright look-out for this treacherous enemy which pretended to be dead and then came to life again when she was not looking. It is an interesting point, because it proves once more that some insects are not completely hide-bound by their instincts, but that individuals can change a hereditary habit on occasions."

Why should Miss Cheesman and I after her make such a fuss about so small an event? Simply because upon its interpretation some very important implications depend. If this particular wasp could change its behavior to meet intelligently a new situation, then it was not a machine "wound up like a watch." It was not merely something to which things happen. It was also capable of playing an active, not merely a passive, role in "adjusting to circumstances." And if Pronuba, admittedly now a creature far less bright than a wasp, has or ever did have any similar capacities, then her working agreement with the yucca need not have been wholly the result of chance. She may have taken advantage of a situation which presented itself and, however feebly, played her part as an individual in the course of evolution.

To admit that is to make a thousand times less incredible the fact that every spring thousands of moths perform the actions without which neither the yucca nor the moth could produce another generation. But that is not all. It relieves us from the necessity of assuming that the universe has been, at least up to the appearance of man, as will-less, as purposeless, as meaningless—one must almost say as dead—as the orthodox view tends to assume.

Some of the reasons why this commonly *is* assumed are sound enough, at least as far as they go, but some of them are merely the result of a human weakness which scientists share with the rest of mankind. Mechanisms are much easier to study than intelligence or purpose is. A great deal of progress has been made during the last hundred years in understanding them and the scientists are probably right in saying that such progress would not have been made if they had permitted their determination to discover these mechanisms to be weakened by too ready a willingness to say, when faced with a problem, merely "intelligence," "purpose," etc. If we may be permitted the military terms with which recent years have made us all too familiar, their procedure was *tactically* sound because it served the immediate purpose. But it may be proving to be *strategically* unfortunate because it has resulted in a dogged adherence to a "nothing but" hypothesis which some believe is already being exposed as untenable.

A merely human weakness accounts for the fact that many scientists, like many laymen, hold onto a hypothesis both because they are stubborn and because the hypothesis implies something which they *want* to believe; because, to put it more brutally, it confirms a prejudice. And it is an amusing fact that the wholly mechanistic theory of insect behavior can be made to serve the interests of either of two diametrically opposed prejudices.

On the one hand, it is commonly upheld by atheists so fanatical that they are afraid to admit the reality of purpose or intelligence or will lest the admission lead somehow to a belief in God. On the other hand, one of the most fanatical insisters upon the dogma that never, under any circumstances, does an insect contribute anything to the seeming "wisdom" of its behavior was that sincere and orthodox Roman Catholic, Henri Fabre.

Probably he had never heard of the yucca moth. At least I remember no mention of it in the ten volumes of his *Souvenirs Entomologiques*. But it would have delighted him as a notable addition to his imposing collection of the elaborately effective procedures followed by creatures without intelligence. Every one of them was, he insisted, proof of the existence of a God who, in his wisdom, had contrived the little machines which unconsciously do precisely what they need to do if they are to live their often outrageous lives.

Face to face with such phenomena as the cruel shrewdness or seeming shrewdness of many parasites, he spoke of *le savant brigandage de la vie*—the expert criminality of life. And he never faced the problem which seems to arise when one places the responsibility for such a villainous system of exploitation directly upon a personal God. But he never wavered. The wonders of instinct confirmed his Catholic theology as conclusively as they confirm the atheism of many mechanists.

Somewhere along the line of this argument, the less trusting of my readers may have wanted to raise doubts not so much concerning the argument itself as concerning the alleged facts upon which it is based. Does Pronuba really do any of these things it is said to?

After all, entomologists are always coming up with wonders about ants, bees, and what not. Laymen seldom see them with their own eyes and if by any chance they take an hour off to look, they are more likely than not to see nothing remarkable. Insects take their time. For long periods they behave in what seems like a completely witless fashion—as Mark Twain discovered when he convinced himself that the ant and his extraordinary reputation for sagacity was a complete fraud.

The Mr. Riley who first told the world about Pronuba was

a distinguished entomologist. He had the confidence of his
professional brethren and textbook after textbook has repeated
his tale. But is it just possible that he was over-enthusiastic?
How many other people have watched the performance and
can vouch for it from their own experience?

Well, I confess that the shadow of such doubts crossed my
own mind. Of the various references to Pronuba with which
I was familiar, only one after Riley's own seemed on internal
evidence to be indubitably firsthand. The most learned entomologist of this region where yucca flourishes confessed
that he had never seen the performance and didn't know
anybody who had. Not too willingly—since I knew the difficulties, which include, besides the dilatoriness of the insect,
darkness, a limited blooming season, and flowers lifted high
above one's head—I decided to try to see for myself. And not
to sustain any suspense which any reader may feel, I did.
Three times Pronuba demonstrated before my eyes how she
performed the crucial act, mounting the pistil of the recently
opened flower and with prolonged purposefulness rubbing
the pistil vigorously to get the pollen well in.

Partly to avoid the possibility that some amateur alienist
might telephone a mental hospital that for several evenings
a maniac had been seen standing for two hours and more
peering at yucca flowers with a flashlight, I decided to make
my observations well out into the desert and some twenty
miles from town. And for poetic if not for strictly scientific
reasons it was a good idea. It is one thing to read about what
Pronuba does. It would be quite another to see her at work
in a neighbor's back yard. But the performance belongs properly among the mysteries which one can only appreciate
fully when the context is remote from the human and as
exclusively as possible in that of almost timeless nature.

The moonless night was brilliant with stars. In the distance
a coyote pack obligingly set up its chorus which is as wild a
sound as one is likely to hear anywhere. And then, presently,
there was Pronuba, even more insignificant looking than I
had expected her to be, performing her delicate operation
precisely, no doubt, as her ancestors had performed it millions of times during millions of springs. On the horizon the
lights of town were just visible. In all that town few knew
about, perhaps none had ever seen, the strange actions of this
silent moth without whom the tall spires of flowers would

never conceive their seeds and without whom, therefore, the whole race of yuccas would gradually die out. It was for the almost invisible moth, not for you or me or any aesthetically appreciative human spectator, that the great masses of flowers were lifted high.

As little Pronuba moved her head back and forth I remembered the question once asked by the American essayist Charles D. Stewart after he had described what looked like a remarkably purposeful action on the part of a spider who suddenly cut the main cable of his web and thereby sent flying an intruder of another species with designs upon an insect caught in the owner's web. "Is it God who is doing these things," Stewart asked, "or is it a spider?"

Fabre would have answered without hesitation, "God." Most biologists would reply with equal assurance, "Neither." But few are willing to admit what seems to me not wholly improbable—namely that the spider himself had something to do with it.

1955

What Are Flowers For?

There are those who are indifferent to the sea or oppressed by the mountains, who find forests gloomy and animals repulsive. There are even those who say that they hate the country. But no one ever hated flowers, and no other beauty—not even woman—has been more often celebrated.

There is nothing to which poets have referred more frequently, and the poetry of everyday speech pays its own tribute in a score of familiar phrases: the flower of youth; the flower of chivalry; the flower of civilization. Nothing else, either natural or man-made, seems to embody so completely or to symbolize so adequately that perfect beauty which, if the expression be permissible, flowers in the flower.

Grass and leaves are grateful to the eye. No other color is so restful as green. But how monotonous the earth would be if this green were not shattered again and again by the joyous exclamation of the flower! It seems to add just that touch of something more than the merely utilitarian which human beings need if they are to find life fully satisfactory. Flowers seem like a luxury that nature has grown prosperous enough to afford.

The stern scientist will, of course, dismiss this last statement as an absurd fantasy. Flowers, he will insist, are strictly utilitarian—except, of course, in the case of those which man himself has perverted in cultivation. Flowers are the plants' organs of generation and their purpose is not to be beautiful, but to produce seeds with a maximum of efficiency. Yet even the stern scientist will admit that nature invented many remarkable devices before she hit upon anything at once so useful and so pleasing to the human eye.

It was—so he will tell us—a mere hundred million or so years ago that the very first flower opened its petals to the sun. And though that was a long time ago as we measure time, though ninety-nine million of those years were to pass before the first member of our own species was there to see a flower and to begin, no one knows how soon, his long love affair with it, still it was not long ago in the history of living things. Primitive green plants had already been thriving in the water for perhaps a billion years or even more. They had come out upon dry land many millions of years later, and the great forests that laid down the coal beds flourished at a time which antedates the first flowers by a longer stretch than that which separates the first flowers from us. Then, quite suddenly as such things go (so suddenly indeed that evolutionists are still puzzled by the phenomenon), the earth burst into bloom. Moreover, some of the earliest blossoms of which a record has been preserved in stone were already quite spectacular, and the late dinosaurs may have looked with dull eyes on the dogwood and the magnolia that their sluggish brains were no doubt incapable of admiring.

Having granted that much and instructed us thus far, the scientist will go on to say that the poets have, as usual, preferred their own silly fantasies to the truth and preferred them so persistently that it was not until about the time of the American Revolution, when mankind was already half a million years old at the very least, that he cared enough about facts to discover that the flower, like everything else in nature, is merely part of the struggle for survival. Thomas Gray could just possibly be forgiven for babbling about the flower that "wastes its fragrance on the desert air," because most of his contemporaries did not know that this fragrance was not wasted if it enticed the insects it was secreted to attract. But Wordsworth was only deceiving himself when he found in the meanest flower that blows "a thought too deep for tears," and as for Tennyson, who lived in one of the great ages of science, he ought to have been ashamed of himself to write anything so foolish as his apostrophe to the "Flower in the Crannied Wall":

> . . . if I could understand
> What you are, root and all, and all and all,
> I should know what God and man is.

The flower, the scientist will go on, was not invented (or rather did not mechanically invent itself) to please us. It flaunted its petals and spread its perfumes because the pollen wasted when distributed at random by the winds could be conserved if an insect could be tricked into carrying it directly from flower to flower. What we call a flower's beauty is merely, so he would conclude, a by-product and a human invention. The perfume isn't there to please us; it pleases us because it is there and we have been conditioned to it. A few flowers pollinated by flesh-eating flies have the odor of rotten meat. If that were usual, rather than unusual, we would by now love the stink.

In some of these contentions the scientist is right, or at least partly right, if you grant him his premise that man is a mere accident in nature, a freak to whose desires and needs nature is serenely indifferent. But there are other ways of looking at the matter. Nature did create man and did create his unique qualities, among which is the ability to believe that beauty, even if useful, is also its own excuse for being. That conviction is, therefore, as natural as anything else—as natural, for instance, as the struggle for survival. Man is quite properly proud of the fact that he sometimes succeeds in transforming the sex impulse into something beautiful, and he finds some of what the anatomists call "secondary sex characteristics" very appealing in themselves. But the plants were millions of years ahead of him, and if flowers are merely the organs of reproduction, they are the most attractive of such in all animate nature.

In fact, it was in this light that the eighteenth century tended to see its new realization that plants also could "love." Aristotle, the master of those who knew, had proved by logic absolute and to his own satisfaction that the vegetable kingdom was sexless; in spite of the fact that the people of the Near East had known since Babylonian times that their female date palms would bear no fruit unless they were married to the male blossoms from another tree. But even Linnaeus, the prince of botanists, saw this as a reason for, not an argument against, the poetic interpretation of the flowers he so much loved. And he described them in quaintly rapturous terms: "The petals of the flower contribute nothing to generation but serve only as bridal beds, gloriously arranged by the great Creator, who has adorned with such noble bed curtains and perfumed them with so many sweet perfumes that the bridegroom may celebrate his nuptials with all the greater solemnity." The grandfather of Charles Darwin wrote an enormously popular poem called "The Loves of the Flowers" in which he included such lines as these (which, incidentally, seemed very embarrassing to his famous descendant):

> With honey'd lips the enamoured woodbines meet,
> Clasped with fond arms, and mix their kisses sweet.

If that is extravagant, it is hardly more so than the sternly scientific view which sees nothing but mechanics in the evolution of the flower.

Is it wholly fantastic to admit the possibility that nature herself strove toward what we call beauty? Face to face with any one of the elaborate flowers which man's cultivation has had nothing to do with, it does not seem fantastic to me. We put survival first. But when we have a margin of safety left over, we expend it in the search for the beautiful. Who can say that nature does not do the same?

To that botanist who said that "the purpose of a flower is to produce seeds" John Ruskin replied in high indignation that it was the other way around. The purpose of the seed is to produce a flower. To be able to see the way in which Ruskin was as right as the botanist is itself one of the flowers of human sensibility and perhaps man's greatest creative act. If nature once interested herself in nothing but survival (and who knows that she did not care for anything else?) she at least created in time a creature who cared for many other things. There may still be something to learn from one of the first English naturalists who defended his science by insisting on man's duty to admire what he called The Works of God because "no creature in this sublunary world is capable of doing so, save man." Even if nature was blind until man made his appearance, it is surely his duty not to blind himself in the interests of what he calls "sober fact." It will be a great pity if science in its search for one kind of knowledge should forget to exercise a peculiarly human capacity. Gardeners who believe the purpose of seed is to produce the flower should keep that capacity alive.

1964

The Individual and the Species

A few mornings ago I rescued a bat from a swimming pool. The man who owned the pool—but did not own the bat—asked me why. That question I do not expect ever to be able to answer, but it involves a good deal. If even I myself could understand it, I would know what it is that seems to distinguish man from the rest of nature, and why, despite all she has to teach him, there is also something he would like to teach her if he could.

Nature books always explain—for the benefit of utilitarians—that bats are economically important because they destroy many insects. For the benefit of those more interested in the marvelous than in the profitable, they also usually say something about the bat's wonderful invention of a kind of sonar by the aid of which he can fly in the blackest night without colliding with even so artificial an obstruction as a piano wire strung across his path. But before lifting my particular bat out of the swimming pool, I did not calculate his economic importance and I did not rapidly review in my mind the question whether or not his scientific achievement entitled him to life.

Still less could I pretend that he was a rare specimen or that one bat more or less would have any perceptible effect on the balance of nature. There were plenty of others just like him, right here where I live and throughout this whole area. Almost every night I have seen several of his fellows swooping down to the swimming pool for a drink before starting off for an evening of economically useful activity. A few weeks before I had, as a matter of fact, seen near Carlsbad, New Mexico, several hundred thousand of this very species in a single flight. That had seemed like enough bats to satisfy one for a normal lifetime. Yet here I was, not only fishing a single individual from the water, but tending him anxiously to see whether or not he could recover from an ordeal which had obviously been almost too much for him.

Probably he had fallen in because he had miscalculated in the course of the difficult maneuver involved in getting a drink on the wing. Probably, therefore, he had been in the water a good many hours and would not have lasted much longer. But he looked as though he wanted to live and I, inexplicably, also hoped that he would. And that would seem to imply some sort of kindliness more detached, more irrational, and more completely gratuitous than any nature herself is capable of. "So careful of the type she seems, so careless of the single life."

At Carlsbad, so it seemed to me, I had seen bats as nature sees them. Here by the swimming pool, I had seen an individual bat as only man can see him. It was a neat coincidence which arranged the two experiences so close together, and I shall always think of them in that way.

Even I find it difficult to love, in my special human way, as many bats as I saw at Carlsbad. Nature is content to love them in her way and makes no attempt here to love them in the way that even I would fail at. She loves bats in general and as a species. For that reason she can never get enough of them. But as long as there are plenty in the world, she is unconcerned with any particular bat. She gives him his chance (or sometimes his lack of it) and if he does not, or cannot, take it, others will. A margin of failure is to be expected. The greatest good of the greatest number is a ruling principle so absolute that it is not even tempered with regret over those who happen not to be included within the greatest number.

Thus nature discovered, long before the sociologists did, the statistical criterion. Bureaucratic states which accept averages and curves of distribution as realities against which there is no appeal represent a sort of "return to nature" very different from what that phrase is ordinarily taken to imply. Insofar as the great dictators can be assumed to be in any sense sincere when they profess a concern with the welfare of their people or even with that of mankind, their concern is like nature's—indifferent to everything except the statistically measurable result. If they really love men, then they love them only as nature loves bats. She never devised anything so prompt and effective as the gas chamber, but her methods are sometimes almost equally unscrupulous. For she also has her methods—not always pretty ones—of getting rid of what she considers the superfluous. She seems to agree, in principle, with those who maintain that any decisive concern with a mere individual is unscientific, sentimental, and ultimately incompatible with the greatest good of the greatest number.

But one bat in a swimming pool is not the same thing as two or three hundred thousand at Carlsbad. Because there is only one of him and only one of me, some sort of relationship, impossible in the presence of myriads, springs up between us. I no longer take toward him the attitude of nature or the dictator. I become a man again, aware of feelings which are commonly called humane but for which I prefer the stronger word, human.

It was the barking of two young police dogs taking a natural, unsentimental interest in an individual in distress which first called my attention to what I still think of as "my" bat, though I am sure nothing in nature prepared him to believe that I would assume any responsibility for his welfare. At first, I did not know what he was because a fish out of water looks no less inexplicable than a bat in it. The enormous wings attached to this tiny mouse body had helped, no doubt, to keep him afloat, but they were preposterously unmanageable in a dense, resistant medium. The little hooks on his arms by means of which he climbs clumsily on a rough surface were useless on the vertical, tiled sides of the pool. When I lifted him out with a flat wire net, he lay inertly sprawled, his strange body so disorganized as to have lost all functional significance, like a wrecked airplane on a mountainside which does not look as though it had ever been able to take to the air.

A slight shiver which shook his body when I leaned over him was the only sign of life. The situation did not look promising, for I knew that a live bat is very much alive, with a heart which sometimes beats more than seven times as fast as mine. Since he obviously needed—if he was not too far gone to need anything—to be dry and to be warm I spread him on top of a wall in the full sun to which he had never, perhaps, been exposed before. Every now and then the tremor recurred; and as his fur dried, I began to be aware of a heart beating furiously. Possibly, I began to say, he may survive.

When I bent closer, he raised his head and hissed in my face, exposing a gleaming set of little white teeth before he collapsed exhausted again.

By now his leathery wings were dry and his fur hardly more than damp. But he still seemed incapable of any except the feeblest movements. I thought that at best it would be hours before he would be able to fly. I put a stone beside him to cast a semishadow and was turning away when I caught sight of something out of the corner of my eye. I looked, just in time to see him raise himself suddenly onto his bony elbows and take off. He half-circled the pool to get his bearings and, flying strongly now, he disappeared from my sight over the desert, not permanently the worse, I hope, for a near escape from the death which would not have been very important so far as the total welfare of the bat community is concerned. Inevitably, I have wondered whether he has since been among the bats I see drinking at the pool at evening. Or has he, perhaps, found some body of water with less unpleasant associations?

But why had I done more than, like the dogs, peer at him with curiosity? Why had I felt sad when I thought he would never recover, really joyful when I saw him fly away? He is not economically important, however much his tribe may be. If he had drowned, there would have been others left to catch insects as well as to demonstrate for the benefit of science the bat's sonar. Who am I that I should exhibit a concern which, apparently, the Great Mother of bats (and of men) does not share. What did I accomplish for bats, for myself, or for humanity at large when I fished my bat from the water?

These are not rhetorical questions. They probably have several answers, but there is one of which I am especially aware. What I had done was to keep alive an attitude, an emotion, or better yet a strong passion, of which only the faint beginnings are observable in any creature except man and which, moreover, appear in danger of extinction because of two powerful enemies. This sort of concern with a mere individual is scorned alike by the frank apostles of violent unreason and by those proponents of the greatest good for the greatest number who insist upon being what they call scientific rather than what they call sentimental.

It was nature which loved the race, and it was man who

added to that a love for the individual as such. Perhaps those two things, though not really incompatible under all circumstances, become so when one accepts also nature's passion for mere numbers. Perhaps, in other words, there really is something incompatible between the value which we put on the individual and nature's insatiable appetite for more and more of every kind of creature, at no matter what cost either to other species or to the individuals of any one species. Perhaps we have retained too much of her immoderate desire for multiplication while developing our own concern for the individual, whom we think of as rare or irreplaceable. Perhaps, in other words, it is easiest to love both man and men when there are not too many (or even not too obviously enough) of the last. Perhaps men should not be too common if they are to have value.

One thing is certain. However many of us there may be or come to be, no man and no group of men should have too much power over too many of us. It makes such men or such groups feel too much as though they were nature herself. So careful of the type they are—or claim to be; so careless of the single life they so indubitably become.

1952

The Colloid and the Crystal

Over the radio the weatherman talked lengthily about cold masses and warm masses, about what was moving out to sea and what wasn't. Did Benjamin Franklin, I wondered, know what he was starting when it first occurred to him to trace by correspondence the course of storms? From my stationary position the most reasonable explanation seemed to be simply that winter had not quite liked the looks of the landscape as she first made it up. She was changing her sheets.

Another forty-eight hours brought one of those nights ideal for frosting the panes. When I came down to breakfast, two of the windows were almost opaque and the others were etched with graceful, fernlike sprays of ice which looked rather like the impressions left in rocks by some of the antediluvian plants, and they were almost as beautiful as anything which the living can achieve. Nothing else which has never lived looks so much as though it were actually informed with life.

I resisted, I am proud to say, the almost universal impulse to scratch my initials into one of the surfaces. The effect, I knew, would not be an improvement. But so, of course, do those less virtuous than I. That indeed is precisely why they scratch. The impulse to mar and to destroy is as ancient and almost as nearly universal as the impulse to create. The one is an easier way than the other of demonstrating power. Why else should anyone not hungry prefer a dead rabbit to a live one? Not even those horrible Dutch painters of bloody still —or shall we say stilled?—lifes can have really believed that their subjects were more beautiful dead.

Indoors it so happened that a Christmas cactus had chosen this moment to bloom. Its lush blossoms, fuchsia-shaped but pure red rather than magenta, hung at the drooping ends of strange, thick stems and outlined themselves in blood against the glistening background of the frosty pane—jungle flower against frostflower; the warm beauty that breathes and lives and dies competing with the cold beauty that burgeons, not because it wants to, but merely because it is obeying the laws of physics which require that crystals shall take the shape they have always taken since the world began. The effect of red flower against white tracery was almost too theatrical, not quite in good taste perhaps. My eye recoiled in shock and sought through a clear area of the glass the more normal out-of-doors.

On the snow-capped summit of my bird-feeder a chickadee pecked at the new-fallen snow and swallowed a few of the flakes which serve him in lieu of the water he sometimes sadly lacks when there is nothing except ice too solid to be picked at. A downy woodpecker was hammering at a lump of suet and at the coconut full of peanut butter. One nuthatch was dining while the mate waited his—or was it her?—turn. The woodpecker announces the fact that he is a male by the bright red spot on the back of his neck, but to me, at least, the sexes of the nuthatch are indistinguishable. I shall never know whether it is the male or the female who eats first. And that is a pity. If I knew, I could say, like the Ugly Duchess, "and the moral of that is . . ."

But I soon realized that at the moment the frosted windows were what interested me most—especially the fact that there is no other natural phenomenon in which the lifeless mocks so closely the living. One might almost think that the frostflower had got the idea from the leaf and the branch if one did not know how inconceivably more ancient the first is. No wonder that enthusiastic biologists in the nineteenth century, anxious to conclude that there was no qualitative difference between life and chemical processes, tried to believe that the crystal furnished the link, that its growth was actually the same as the growth of a living organism. But excusable though the fancy was, no one, I think, believes anything of the sort today. Protoplasm is a colloid and the colloids are fundamentally different from the crystalline substances. Instead of crystallizing they jell, and life in its simplest known form is a shapeless blob of rebellious jelly rather than a crystal eternally obeying the most ancient law.

No man ever saw a dinosaur. The last of these giant reptiles was dead eons before the most dubious half-man surveyed the world about him. Not even the dinosaurs ever cast their dim eyes upon many of the still earlier creatures which preceded them. Life changes so rapidly that its later phases know nothing of those which preceded them. But the frostflower is older than the dinosaur, older than the protozoan, older no doubt than the enzyme or the ferment. Yet it is precisely what it has always been. Millions of years before there were any eyes to see it, millions of years before any life existed, it grew in its own special way, crystallized along its preordained lines of cleavage, stretched out its pseudo-branches and pseudo-leaves. It was beautiful before beauty itself existed.

We find it difficult to conceive a world except in terms of

purpose, of will, or of intention. At the thought of the some-thing without beginning and presumably without end, of something which is, nevertheless, regular though blind, and organized without any end in view, the mind reels. Consti-tuted as we are, it is easier to conceive how the slime floating upon the waters might become in time Homo sapiens than it is to imagine how so complex a thing as a crystal could have always been and can always remain just what it is—compli-cated and perfect but without any meaning, even for itself. How can the lifeless even obey a law?

To a mathematical physicist I once confessed somewhat shamefacedly that I had never been able to understand how inanimate nature managed to follow so invariably and so promptly her own laws. If I flip a coin across a table, it will come to rest at a certain point. But before it stops at just that point, many factors must be taken into consideration. There is the question of the strength of the initial impulse, of the exact amount of resistance offered by the friction of that particular table top, and of the density of the air at the moment. It would take a physicist a long time to work out the problem and he could achieve only an approximation at that. Yet presumably the coin will stop exactly where it should. Some very rapid calculations have to be made before it can do so, and they are, presumably, always accurate.

And then, just as I was blushing at what I supposed he must regard as my folly, the mathematician came to my rescue by informing me that Laplace had been puzzled by exactly the same fact. "Nature laughs at the difficulties of integration," he remarked—and by "integration" he meant, of course, the mathematician's word for the process involved when a man solves one of the differential equations to which he has reduced the laws of motion.

When my Christmas cactus blooms so theatrically a few inches in front of the frost-covered pane, it also is obeying laws but obeying them much less rigidly and in a different way. It blooms at about Christmastime because it has got into the habit of doing so, because, one is tempted to say, it wants to. As a matter of fact, it was, this year, not a Christmas cactus but a New Year's cactus, and because of this unpre-dictability I would like to call it "he," not "it." His flowers assume their accustomed shape and take on their accustomed color. But not as the frostflowers follow their predestined pattern. Like me, the cactus has a history which stretches back over a long past full of changes and developments. He has resisted and rebelled; he has attempted novelties, passed through many phases. Like all living things he has had a will of his own. He has made laws, not merely obeyed them.

"Life," so the platitudinarian is fond of saying, "is strange." But from our standpoint it is not really so strange as those things which have no life and yet nevertheless move in their predestined orbits and "act" though they do not "behave." At the very least one ought to say that if life is strange there is nothing about it more strange than the fact that it has its being in a universe so astonishingly shared on the one hand by "things" and on the other by "creatures," that man himself is both a "thing" which obeys the laws of chemistry or physics and a "creature" who to some extent defies them. No other contrast, certainly not the contrast between the human being and the animal, or the animal and the plant, or even the spirit and the body, is so tremendous as this contrast between what lives and what does not.

To think of the lifeless as merely inert, to make the contrast merely in terms of a negative, is to miss the real strangeness. Not the shapeless stone which seems to be merely waiting to be acted upon but the snowflake or the frostflower is the true representative of the lifeless universe as opposed to ours. They represent plainly, as the stone does not, the fixed and perfect system of organization which includes the sun and its planets, includes therefore this earth itself, but against which life has set up its seemingly puny opposition. Order and obedience are the primary characteristics of that which is not alive. The snowflake eternally obeys its one and only law: "Be thou six pointed"; the planets their one and only: "Travel thou in an ellipse." The astronomer can tell where the North Star will be ten thousand years hence; the botanist cannot tell where the dandelion will bloom tomorrow.

Life is rebellious and anarchial, always testing the supposed immutability of the rules which the nonliving changelessly accepts. Because the snowflake goes on doing as it was told, its story up to the end of time was finished when it first assumed the form which it has kept ever since. But the story of every living thing is still in the telling. It may hope and it may try. Moreover, though it may succeed or fail, it will certainly change. No form of frostflower ever became extinct.

Such, if you like, is its glory. But such also is the fact which makes it alien. It may melt but it cannot die.

If I wanted to contemplate what is to me the deepest of all mysteries, I should choose as my object lesson a snowflake under a lens and an amoeba under the microscope. To a detached observer—if one can possibly imagine any observer who *could* be detached when faced with such an ultimate choice—the snowflake would certainly seem the "higher" of the two. Against its intricate glistening perfection one would have to place a shapeless, slightly turbid glob, perpetually oozing out in this direction or that but not suggesting so strongly as the snowflake does, intelligence and plan. Crystal and colloid, the chemist would call them, but what an inconceivable contrast those neutral terms imply! Like the star, the snowflake seems to declare the glory of God, while the promise of the amoeba, given only perhaps to itself, seems only contemptible. But its jelly holds, nevertheless, not only its promise but ours also, while the snowflake represents some achievement which we cannot possibly share. After the passage of billions of years, one can see and be aware of the other, but the relationship can never be reciprocal. Even after these billions of years no aggregate of colloids can be as beautiful as the crystal always was, but it can know, as the crystal cannot, what beauty is.

Even to admire too much or too exclusively the alien kind of beauty is dangerous. Much as I love and am moved by the grand, inanimate forms of nature, I am always shocked and a little frightened by those of her professed lovers to whom landscape is the most important thing, and to whom landscape is merely a matter of forms and colors. If they see or are moved by an animal or flower, it is to them merely a matter of a picturesque completion and their fellow creatures are no more than decorative details. But without some continuous awareness of the two great realms of the inanimate and the animate there can be no love of nature as I understand it, and what is worse, there must be a sort of disloyalty to our cause, to us who are colloid, not crystal. The pantheist who feels the oneness of all living things, I can understand; perhaps indeed he and I are in essential agreement. But the ultimate All is not one thing, but two. And because the alien half is in its way as proud and confident and successful as our half, its fundamental difference may not be disregarded with impunity. Of us and all we stand for, the enemy is not so much death as the not-living, or rather that great system which succeeds without ever having had the need to be alive. The frostflower is not merely a wonder; it is also a threat and a warning. How admirable, it seems to say, not living can be! What triumphs mere immutable law can achieve!

Some of Charles Pierce's strange speculations about the possibility that "natural law" is not law at all but merely a set of habits fixed more firmly than any habits we know anything about in ourselves or in the animals suggest the possibility that the snowflake was not, after all, always inanimate, that it merely surrendered at some time impossibly remote the life which once achieved its perfect organization. Yet even if we can imagine such a thing to be true, it serves only to warn us all the more strongly against the possibility that what we call the living might in the end succumb also to the seduction of the immutably fixed.

No student of the anthill has ever failed to be astonished either into admiration or horror by what is sometimes called the perfection of its society. Though even the anthill can change its ways, though even ant individuals—ridiculous as the conjunction of the two words may seem—can sometimes make choices, the perfection of the techniques, the regularity of the habits almost suggest the possibility that the insect is on its way back to inanition, that, vast as the difference still is, an anthill crystallizes somewhat as a snowflake does. But not even the anthill, nothing else indeed in the whole known universe, is so perfectly planned as one of these same snowflakes. Would, then, the ultimately planned society be, like the anthill, one in which no one makes plans, any more than a snowflake does? From the cradle in which it is not really born to the grave where it is only a little deader than it always was, the ant-citizen follows a plan to the making of which he no longer contributes anything.

Perhaps we men represent the ultimate to which the rebellion, begun so long ago in some amoeba-like jelly, can go. And perhaps the inanimate is beginning the slow process of subduing us again. Certainly the psychologist and the philosopher are tending more and more to think of us as creatures who obey laws rather than as creatures of will and responsibility. We are, they say, "conditioned" by this or by that. Even the greatest heroes are studied on the assumption that they can be "accounted for" by something outside themselves. They are, it is explained, "the product of forces." All the emphasis is placed, not upon that power to resist and rebel which we were once supposed to have, but upon the "influences" which "formed us." Men are made by society, not society by men. History as well as character "obeys laws." In their view, we crystallize in obedience to some dictate from without instead of moving in conformity with something within.

And so my eye goes questioningly back to the frosted pane. While I slept the graceful pseudo-fronds crept across the glass, assuming, as life itself does, an intricate organization. "Why live," they seem to say, "when we can be beautiful, complicated, and orderly without the uncertainty and effort required of a living thing? Once we were all that was. Perhaps some day we shall be all that is. Why not join us?"

Last summer no clod or no stone would have been heard if it had asked such a question. The hundreds of things which walked and sang, the millions which crawled and twined were all having their day. What was dead seemed to exist only in order that the living might live upon it. The plants were busy turning the inorganic into green life and the animals were busy turning that green into red. When we moved, we walked mostly upon grass. Our pre-eminence was unchallenged.

On this winter day nothing seems so successful as the frostflower. It thrives on the very thing which has driven some of us indoors or underground and which has been fatal to many. It is having now its hour of triumph, as we before had ours. Like the cactus flower itself, I am a hothouse plant. Even my cats gaze dreamily out of the window at a universe which is no longer theirs.

How are we to resist, if resist we can? This house into which I have withdrawn is merely an expedient and it serves only my mere physical existence. What mental or spiritual convictions, what will to maintain to my own kind of existence can I assert? For me it is not enough merely to say, as I do say, that I shall resist the invitation to submerge myself into a crystalline society and to stop planning in order that I may be planned for. Neither is it enough to go further, as

I do go, and to insist that the most important thing about a man is not that part of him which is "the product of forces" but that part, however small it may be, which enables him to become something other than what the most accomplished sociologist, working in conjunction with the most accomplished psychologist, could predict that he would be.

I need, so I am told, a faith, something outside myself to which I can be loyal. And with that I agree, in my own way. I am on what I call "our side," and I know, though vaguely, what I think that is. Wordsworth's God had His dwelling in the light of setting suns. But the God who dwells there seems to me most probably the God of the atom, the star, and the crystal. Mine, if I have one, reveals Himself in another class of phenomena. He makes the grass green and the blood red.

1953

V. THE MEANING
OF CONSERVATION

The outstanding scientific discovery of the twentieth century is not television, or radio, but the complexity of the land organism. The last word in ignorance is the man who says of an animal or a plant: "What good is it?"

ALDO LEOPOLD

Dam Grand Canyon?

"In Grand Canyon Arizona has a natural wonder which, so far as I know, is in kind absolutely unparalleled throughout the rest of the world. . . . Leave it as it is. You cannot improve upon it. The ages have been at work on it, and man can only mar it. What you can do is to keep it for your children, your children's children, and for all those who come after you as one of the great sights which every American, if he can travel at all, should see."

Grand Canyon's Magna Carta should be those words, which Theodore Roosevelt pronounced when he first visited the region in 1903.

For more than sixty years his wisdom has been tacitly recognized. True, certain roads have been built and certain other facilities provided, without which it would not have been possible to accommodate the millions who have come for the legitimate purpose of admiring Grand Canyon's beauty and learning the lessons it teaches.

But, so far, nothing has ever been done for any purpose other than making accessible the Canyon's grandeur and its messages. There has been no talk of even that specious doctrine "multiple use" which, however seductive it may seem, blindly refuses to recognize the fact that some uses are incompatible with others.

Grand Canyon, so everyone seems to have agreed, is so stupendous and so nearly unique a natural wonder that it should not be "used" for anything except the purposes it has served since Theodore Roosevelt so clearly saw and defined them.

In none of the other most-visited national parks have the problems involved in providing for millions of visitors—

without destroying the natural character of the region—been so well solved. All the restaurants, overnight lodges, shops, and so forth have been concentrated in one spot instead of being spread, as they are in some parks, throughout the accessible areas. In accord with the wise policy of unique use rather than multiple use, even the one mining concession granted before Grand Canyon became a national park has been bought out and will cease to operate after a certain number of years.

Because this policy has been consistently followed, Grand Canyon National Park is a demonstration model of how a national park should be managed, just as Yellowstone is an awful warning of what happens when tourist facilities take over the whole area.

The Grand Canyon is, after all, one of the most visited spots on the face of the earth. Yet solitude—and almost completely untouched nature—can be found by those who desire it. Those who are merely checking another three-star sight off the list gather around the hotels and the terrace. They form there the crowd that many of us come to such places as the Canyon to escape. But it is very easy to evade them and have the whole landscape to one's self.

Roads along the rim stop only a few miles west of the tourist center. A few primitive roads, not thrust upon the visitor's attention, and just rough enough to discourage those who fear to leave the asphalt, lead to other points on the rim where one may sit in absolute solitude. There is no sign that man has ever been there before. An experience of that kind is one not easily come by and is uniquely valuable.

I am not happy in opposing the position taken by my friend Representative Morris Udall. Like his brother, the Secretary of the Interior, he has been, and still is, one of the best friends the move to preserve natural beauty has ever had. Nevertheless, he has, in this instance, taken what I am bound to consider the wrong side in the present controversy concerning the proposal to build one, and probably two, dams on the Colorado River, neither of which could possibly contribute to natural beauty. Ardent dam advocates, when pushed into a corner, can say no more than that the dams wouldn't, after all, do the Canyon serious damage.

The dam proposal, and the arguments which have been used to support it, are already familiar. (See "Ruin for the

Grand Canyon?" by Richard C. Bradley, *Audubon,* January-February, 1966.) I shall recapitulate them only briefly before stating what seems to me to be the strongest and the least emphasized argument against it.

The plan is to build two power dams, one in Marble Canyon just upstream from the main gorge and the other in Lower Granite Gorge; the latter would be the highest dam in the Western Hemisphere. This proposal is made as part of the Central Arizona Project, intended to supply Colorado River water to Arizona farmers. But when pressed, its proponents admit that the main purpose of the dams is not to further this project directly, but to generate power which, so it is claimed, could be sold for enough money to defray the expense of the water project and thus make a "package" more acceptable to Congress.

To the objection that either of these dams would destroy the natural scenic, geologic, and biological character of the area—one of whose chief values is undisturbed nature—it was at first stated that the dams would do nothing of the kind. When it was pointed out that the dams would destroy the whole river ecology and create a reservoir one hundred miles long, flooding the entire length of Grand Canyon National Monument and some thirteen miles of the national park itself, the reply came that the changes would be regarded as improvements because they would increase the "recreational" facilities.

As one propaganda publication exultantly proclaimed, "A blue lake at Bridge Canyon Dam would make this spectacular canyon easy of access for those who love to boat, fish, and swim." And whatever may be said of such activities—for which there are many opportunities elsewhere—it can hardly be said that they do not turn Grand Canyon into something quite different from that natural wonder which, as Theodore Roosevelt said, *man can only mar.*

These facts seem to me to constitute a conclusive argument. But it is even more important to point out that the proponents of the dams make a general assumption which could lead to the violation not only of Grand Canyon, but of the whole national park and monument system and the wilderness system. The most fundamental question they implicitly raise is simply this: Is the preservation of natural beauty a major or merely a minor objective? Does utility, economy even, always take precedence over every other consideration?

The arguments to which dam proponents always return as fundamental and unanswerable are these: Farmers need the water and this is the cheapest way of providing it. Alternate proposals, notably that of an atomic generating plant, are dismissed as more costly. The dams would make the whole project self-liquidating, the alternative proposals would not.

I will not go into the question of whether a further development of agriculture in the desert is actually in the interests of the country at large as distinguished from the interests of a group of Arizona farmers. But assuming, as I do not, that these water needs are real for the nation as a whole, the dangerous part of the argument is the assumption that the *cheapest* way to supply that need is obviously the one that must be adopted; adopted even though it involves what is treated as a very minor disadvantage—namely, the modification of, the tampering with, what is widely regarded as the most thoroughly unique of all the American natural beauties and wonders.

Are we really so poor that economy must always be the *first* consideration, cost what it may in terms other than the material? If that principle is accepted, then there is no limit to where it may lead.

Of how many existing parks can it be said that they could be used to meet some real or fancied need more *cheaply* than it could be met in any other way?

A recent editorial in a Phoenix newspaper ridiculed the "outsiders" who presume to teach Arizonans the value of Grand Canyon, and went on to assure readers that the state would not permit any damage to what is its most spectacular scenic feature and one of which it is very proud.

As a matter of actual fact, such confidence would be seriously misplaced. Arizona's attitude toward its unique characteristics has been, if anything, more careless than that of most states. Arizona tends to define the progress to which it is devoted, exclusively in terms of population growth and wealth, and it boasts of natural beauty only in the advertisements that are directed at the tourists who are expected to spend money there.

Arizona has been conspicuous in its preference for billboards over scenery. In fact, I cannot think of a single instance in which the tendency has not been to assume that beauty, comfort, or even health are mere frills which only impractical sentimentalists put first.

In Tucson, where I live, the problem of smog grows. But a recent editorial in one of the two local newspapers dismissed it with the remark that to control gases discharged from smelters would be (like the alternate proposals to the Grand Canyon dams) "too expensive," while the exhausts from automobiles would necessarily become heavier as the city continues its growth.

I am not suggesting that Arizona is very different from many other areas in this respect. But the real question is simply, What is *too expensive* when health and natural beauty are at stake? Our government does not demand that schools be built in the cheapest possible way, or that a health program must be self-liquidating. We can afford untold billions to get to the moon. Is that so much more important than clean air and the grandeur of this earth that we must dismiss as *too expensive* their effective preservation?

Does anyone seriously believe that a technology that can solve the innumerable problems of space exploration could not quickly find a practical method of controlling automobile exhaust—if one-twentieth of the funds available for the space program were allotted to a crash program for solving the smog problem?

Does anyone seriously believe that a nation that can afford the space program must consider nothing except cheapness when it comes to supplying the supposed needs of agriculture? Is the moon that much more important than our own earth and its disappearing beauty?

Do not forget that, whatever the proponents of the dams say, the minimum possible effect upon the Grand Canyon region will be to make artificial what is now one of the few remaining examples of what nature herself can do.

Is there nothing that man will keep his hands off of? Is he determined that he will "conquer" nature completely and leave not even a few examples of what she can do without his help or hindrance?

It is again the words of Theodore Roosevelt which say so succinctly what we should not allow anyone to forget: "Leave it as it is. You cannot improve on it. The ages have been at work on it, and man can only mar it."

A few dozen years ago English naturalist James Fisher toured the West with Roger Tory Peterson. In the last chapter of *Wild America,* the book they wrote together, Fisher summed up his impressions:

> [Americans] show us too little of their earthly paradise and publicize too little their determination to share it with wild nature. . . . Never have I seen such wonders or met landlords so worthy of their land. They have had, and still have, the power to ravage it, and instead have made it a garden.

Both of these statements were true then and, all things considered, they still are true. But national parks and the extent to which they should continue inviolate have recently become increasingly "controversial"— which means that while more people are actively alarmed for their safety, those who advocate encroachment of one sort or another are also more active.

The proposal to alter the character of Grand Canyon is one of the most serious threats, not only because of the extraordinary character of the Canyon itself, but because the arguments used to justify the dams might, if accepted, open the way to similar invasions elsewhere.

If the question is not whether some "use" of the park is necessary to supply a real or supposed need, but simply whether such an invasion is the *cheapest* way to satisfy it, then it is hard to see how any natural area, even a city park, can be considered safe.

Surely we can afford to say that Grand Canyon, at least, is not the place to save money. What is all our boasted affluence worth if we cannot afford to recognize the value of that beauty which is its own excuse for being?

1966

What Men? What Needs?

Many beautiful areas in many parts of the Southwest are far less accessible and far less frequented than Grand Canyon. Some of them I have visited again and again during the course of twenty years but never without seeing some evidence of human activity which had diminished or destroyed things I had come to enjoy. Something precious had disappeared because it could not coexist with energetic exploitation.

"Oh, well," I have sometimes said to myself, "most of it will probably outlast my time." But I have never been completely comforted by the thought. All concern for posterity aside, I do not like to think that something I have loved may cease to be, even when I am no longer here to take my joy of it.

Perhaps no radical and permanent solution of the problem is possible. The world grows more crowded year by year and at an ever increasing rate. Men push farther and farther in their search for "resources" to be exploited, even for more mere space to occupy. Increasingly they tend to think of the terrestrial globe as *their* earth. They never doubt their right to deal with it as they think fit—and what they think fit usually involves the destruction of what nature has thought fit during many millions of years.

Only the United States among highly developed nations can still offer its citizens the opportunity to visit large regions where nature still dominates the scene. And that is because only the United States began at a sufficiently early stage of its development to set aside as public land some of the most attractive of such regions. We had national parks before England had established so much as one small nature reserve. Insofar as this is true it suggests hope. We have not been entirely blind to what we have, nor to the danger of losing it.

257

"Never have I seen such wonders or met landlords so worthy of their land. They have, and still have, the power to ravage it; and instead they have made it a garden." Thus wrote the visiting English naturalist, James Fisher, in the book called *Wild America* upon which he and Roger Tory Peterson collaborated. Nor is the tribute wholly undeserved. But Mr. Fisher politely refrained from stressing either the unearned blessing we received when we inherited the continent from a red man too little advanced technologically to have defaced it, or the fact that the "power to ravage" which the National Parks Act was intended to hold forever in check still ominously exists. How much longer the check will hold is uncertain; and there are signs that the American people— or at least its leaders—are less concerned than was the generation of Theodore Roosevelt to preserve for posterity some of the wild portions of our heritage.

No one opposes "conservation" as such. But many insist upon defining it in their own way. There are always rival claims to every unexploited area, and even the parks cannot stand up against such claims unless the strength of their own claim is recognized. Unless we think of intangible values as no less important than material resources, unless we are willing to say that man's need of and right to what the parks and wildernesses provide are as fundamental as any of his material needs, they are lost.

Those who would cut the timber, slaughter the animals as game, turn cattle loose to graze, flood the area with dams, or even open them up to real estate subdivision are fond of saying, "After all, human needs come first." But of what needs and of what human beings are we thinking? Of the material needs (or rather profits) of a few ranchers and lumbermen, or of the mental and physical health, the education and spiritual experiences, of a whole population? We do not tear down a high school because the building industry can prove that it could profitably erect an apartment house on the site and that tenants would be glad to occupy it. We say, instead, that education pays off in a different way and that the space occupied by schools is not wasted. Much the same thing we say also of the space taken up by the green of a city square. But if parks and other public lands are to be held only until someone can show that a "use" has been found for them, they will not last very much longer. If we recognize that there is more than one kind of utility and that the parks are, at the present moment, being put to the best use to be found for them, then they may last a long time—until, perhaps, overpopulation has reached the point where the struggle for mere animal survival is so brutal that no school or theater, no concert hall or church, can be permitted to "waste" the land on which it stands.

No other recent threat is quite so fantastic as that recently raised in Arizona where a small group of farmers cultivating the irrigated desert have persuaded a small group of ranchers to adopt with them the highly unorthodox notion that the forests clothing the watersheds are "wasting" water which might be used for cotton or other crops.

Both ancient and modern history provide many examples of countrysides, even of whole nations, destroyed by the destruction of their forests. So far as I am aware, there is no known case where the stripping of mountains had any beneficial effect. Yet a picked group of experts was employed to report on the proposal; it issued a rather careful report— sponsored jointly by the Salt River Valley Water Users Association and the University of Arizona—which boils down to the statement that the deforestation of certain mountain ranges in northeastern Arizona *might* provide more water behind the dams. Then the interested groups distributed a so-called summary of the report in which the "mights" and other qualifications are largely removed and they enlisted the support of the governor of the state as well as of at least one of the largest banks.

Here are some of the highlights from one of the principal speakers at a meeting called by the proponents of the scheme: "Outside of agriculture, there's more confusion, more ignorance and more self-interest concerning the conservation movement than there is about almost any other important movement in the country. . . . We should forget about soil erosion as the banner of conservation. . . . I have just written off the forests of the Southwest and a large part of those located elsewhere in the United States. . . . No longer will millions of trees keep a large percentage of rain and snowfall from reaching the ground. . . . We need chemical sprays that will destroy trees and brush at low cost. . . . As this [public] land's productiveness is increased, I believe it should pass into the hands of private owners. . . . Private ownership of land is the basis of our democratic society. . . . Conservation is an economic problem. If we could amputate sentimentalism, romanticism and hobbyism from the body of conservation, progress would be faster and more certain than it is."

The official summary of the original report gives a more detailed picture both of what the plan proposes and of the kind of earth it envisages. "The program . . . includes drastic thinning of ponderosa pine stands. . . . The pulp industry will not develop fast enough to provide wholesale cleanup of all forested areas. . . . As an adjunct to a treatment program, a speed-up in the harvesting of timber on the watershed is indicated. . . . It is not beyond reasonable expectation that the cities of central Arizona will someday have to cover with plastic or other impervious material an area that will furnish those cities the highest quality of soft water."

Yet the forests this group proposes to destroy are not private property or even state property. They belong to the national government and therefore to all the people. But only, so it was assumed, this particular group has any real right to them because only its members propose to make a monetary profit. One of the most important newspapers in the state supports their claim in an editorial relying upon the premise that "human needs come first" without asking, as we have insisted upon asking, "What needs?" and "What human beings?"

The assumed answer is obviously "Only the 'needs' of a small group of men producing surplus commodities." Because these men hope to make a quick profit by disregarding, among so many other things, "soil conservation" and by destroying a national forest, they think they have the right, not only to seize public lands for a very dangerous and unpromising experiment, but also to deprive everybody else, including generations yet to come, of the benefits their government had assured them. Who needs surplus cotton as much as thousands of today (and millions of tomorrow) need space, fresh air, and a chance to see what a forest looks like?

Perhaps this monstrous proposal to adopt deforestation as a technique of "conservation" will be defeated by its inherent preposterousness rather than by a proper answer to the questions "What men?" and "What needs?" Yet in the end they will still be the crucial questions, and the answers we give will determine, not only the fate of all of our "resources," but also what such parks as we may be able to save will themselves become.

Just what needs of just what men should these parks and other natural areas serve? How natural should a "natural" area be kept? How much should it be "developed" when every development or "improvement" makes it just that much less natural and unspoiled?

Consider, for example, the question of "accessibility." An area that cannot be reached is obviously not being put to use. On the other hand, one reached too easily becomes a mere "resort" to which people flock for purposes just as well served by golf courses, swimming pools, and summer hotels. Parks are often described as "recreation areas" and so they are. But the term "recreation" as ordinarily used does not imply much stress upon the kind of experience which Grand Canyon, despite the flood of visitors that comes to it, still does provide—namely, the experience of being in the presence of nature's ways and nature's work.

Proponents of the recently defeated proposal to flood the Dinosaur Canyon by building a great water-storage dam answered defenders of the national monument within which it lies by saying that the "recreational value" would be increased rather than diminished. They were so sure of their case that they showed pictures of the gaunt canyon with the bones of prehistoric monsters exposed *in situ* and contrasted them with other pictures of artificial lakes behind other dams where bathing girls reclined on sand beaches and speedboats cut across the waters. From their own point of view they were right. But however delightful bathing girls and speedboats may be, they are at least different from, rather than merely better than, what Grand or Dinosaur Canyon provides. Moreover, the places where one may find bathing girls and speedboats are multiplying, while those where one may find solitude, quiet, and the grand spectacles of nature become fewer and fewer.

What is called progress is too often the exchange of one thing (good or bad) for something else, good or bad. Even education means too often learning something at the cost of forgetting something else. But both are pursued so uncritically that we seldom stop to ask whether what we get and learn is worth what we are losing and forgetting.

A majority, increasing perhaps, is ready to settle for "recreation" in this most recent sense, and many may by now actually prefer it. This is so much the age of technology and the machine that machines come to be loved for their own sake rather than used for other ends. Instead, for instance, of valuing the automobile because it may take one to a national park, the park comes to be valued because it is a place the automobile may be used to reach. A considerable number of automobilists would like when they get there to do what they do at home or at the country club. An even greater number prefers to drive straight through so that they can use their machine to get somewhere else. They feel that to stop is simply to waste time, because time spent without the employment of some gadget is time wasted—though it may to some extent be salvaged by turning on the radio. But is it for such as these that the parks should be maintained?

We, reply the proponents of developing further "the recreational facilities" of the national parks, live in a democracy, and the majority should rule. It is purely a question of the greatest good for the greatest number. But they forget to ask what if "the greatest good" and "for the greatest number" do not coincide? Suppose that the greatest number does want the kind of recreation to be had in so many other places and that only a smaller number wants something increasingly hard to find. Would the greater good of the smaller number justify the reservation of certain areas for them?

Granted that the greatness of a good is, unlike the greatness of a number, susceptible of only subjective estimation, we still do recognize to some slight extent the justice of reserving a limited number of airwave channels for the "educational" and "cultural" programs which the greatest number most certainly does not prefer to comedians and jazz. Of certain other "minority rights" we hear a great deal. But are all such rights exclusively political, religious, and racial? Are not the intellectual, aesthetic, and emotional rights of a minority just as sacred? Does democracy demand that they be disregarded?

The best possible compromise in the case of parks and other public lands is to recognize that they are competed for by both the exploiters to whom an absolute "No" must be said and by the seekers after "recreation" who have certain legitimate but not exclusive claims. To those with different "needs" should be allotted a reasonable share. That does not mean a share in each individual area, because to attempt to give that would inevitably be to destroy completely the share of the minority. It can only mean a distinction between some nationally administered areas which are primarily for "recreation" and others which preserve in a recognizable state something of nature herself.

The wilderness area, the protected nature reserve, and the recreation resort are different things: The first is for the smallest minority—that which is physically and psychologically up to the strenuousness of really primitive living. The second is for the larger minority which is interested in wild animals, in plant life, and in natural scenery, even though unprepared for life in a real wilderness. The third, of course, is for the majority whose tastes are not essentially different from those who frequent commercial resorts.

The increasing size and increasing mobility of our population makes it inevitable that the more sedate "nature lover" should favor whatever will facilitate his pushing into the wilderness area, and the seeker after mere recreation whatever would make the nature reserve more attractive to him. If the desires of either are too eagerly met, the ultimate result will be that only "resorts" can continue long to exist. But if the desirability of the distinctions is recognized, it is not difficult to maintain them. It is, indeed, largely a matter of easy accessibility and "modern facilities."

We have come to assume that "good roads" are, anywhere and everywhere, an absolute good and an unmixed blessing. Few if any other expenditures of public money are so generally approved as those for road building. Congress (and the public which elects it) can always be expected to hesitate longer over an appropriation to acquire or protect a national park than over one to build a highway into it. Yet there is nothing which so rapidly turns a wilderness into a reserve and a reserve into a resort. An astonishing number of those for whom a national park (or any other region commonly regarded as "worth seeing") is primarily an excuse for exercising their automobile will turn aside from even ten miles of a good unpaved road and take instead a four-lane highway, no matter where it leads. It is not unreasonable to protect both wilderness areas and nature reserves by keeping them for those who are willing to take a certain amount of trouble to get there.

Those who favor better roads and various other enticements are no doubt honest in their professed desire to promote what they call "fuller use" of the wildernesses and the parks. But what they are encouraging is not a fuller but a different use—incompatible with the original one. It would hardly be practicable to examine every visitor to wilderness or reserve and to make him prove that he has come for a legitimate purpose. But it is perfectly possible to make the test automatically by having the road ask the question: "Are you willing to take a little trouble to get there?" Though the proposal to prepare deliberately for such automatic questioning will seem fantastic to many, that is only because ours is an age—the very first, perhaps—which has come to assume that "the most accessible" is always "the best"—in education, art, and entertainment as well as in recreation.

Up until now the original purpose of the national parks and monuments has been fairly well preserved—partly as the result of a more or less conscious policy, more perhaps because limitations of money and time have slowed down the tendency to pervert them. Now that the integrity of the parks is being increasingly threatened by would-be exploiters as well as by the simple pressure of an increasing population looking for "recreation," a definite policy of protection from both ought to be formulated. Along with the question of "good roads," especially within the parks themselves, it would have to judge all the other "improvements" and "facilities" proposed and sometimes provided.

Grand Canyon is still what it should be: one of the most accessible of the nature reserves. Merely as a spectacle it is popularly recognized as one of the "wonders of the world" and could not reasonably be denied even to those who desire no more than to look at it and go away, satisfied that another item on the list has been checked off. Yet despite the tremendous number of visitors, the inaccessibility of all but a very limited part has prevented it from being spoiled as Yellowstone has been—to the extent that at Yellowstone one is reminded of man and his works at least as often as of nature's.

At the Canyon most of the visitors willingly confine themselves to a very restricted area, and if that area is by now almost a mere resort, there is a great deal left that is not. Diminishing accessibility acts as a very effective filter. Some (but not too many) make the little effort necessary to seek out the still lonely nearby portions of the rim where one may be alone with nature and one's thoughts. Fewer make the journey to the bottom. Fewer still—probably not so many as visit even the remoter of our wilderness areas—risk the considerable adventure any departure from the established trails involves. Plainly visible from the most frequented section of the rim are canyons and buttes which, so far as we know, no human foot has ever trod. There must be few other easily accessible places on earth where it is possible to look into areas never actually explored by man.

That all of this should still be true is due in part to the simple fact that the scale and ruggedness of the Canyon has made it very difficult to assimilate it into the routines of modern man. But it is due in part also to deliberate intention. First-class roads lead into the park and for a few miles along the south rim beyond the hotels and village. They stop there, and all the "facilities" have been confined to an even smaller area. Those who insist upon driving cars, listening to their radios, or writing post cards and are loath to get too far from conventional beds or restaurant food do not need any prohibition to keep them where they should be. Their own tastes are sufficiently eloquent persuaders. Thus the Grand Canyon National Park as it now stands and is now administered represents what is probably the best possible compromise between the desires and needs of the different classes of people who visit it and the limitations which have to be imposed if it is not to degenerate into a resort differing from other resorts only in being provided with a different backdrop. Even the fact that the north rim is less accessible to the most densely populated parts of the nation has made it less visited and, for that reaon, it is even more conspicuously still a "natural" area.

Most of our wildernesses not exploited out of existence are no doubt destined to become parks in time. Are the parks in turn doomed to become mere resorts? Ultimately perhaps. How rapidly will depend largely upon the philosophy which the Park Service formulates and the support it can win for it.

How much difference will it make whether it does or doesn't? How many people care or should care?

To all such questions the answer depends upon what one believes about the nature of man, about his desires and his needs, above all about the permanence and unique importance of certain among them.

If desire for contact with nature and some sense of unity and sympathy with her are merely vestigial hankerings surviving from the time when man lived in a more primitive culture; if these vestiges can, and should, fade gradually away as he becomes more and more completely adapted to a civilization founded upon technology rather than the natural processes—then obviously there is not much point in trying to preserve opportunities for gratifying the hankering. If what wildernesses and national parks supply is merely a kind of "recreation" for which more easily supplied kinds are equally useful and pleasant, then they are indeed merely extravagantly inefficient methods of providing it. If, in other words, interest and delight in nature are mere anachronisms, perhaps they should be discouraged rather than gratified, and the effort spent upon them devoted to weaning mankind away.

Many practical planners and many social philosophers— also, perhaps, the majority of unthinking men—go upon the more or less unqualified assumption that such is indeed the case. Robert Moses, who has done so much to mitigate the gauntness of concrete and steel in the New York area, has sometimes been accused of accepting too readily the parkway and the city park as substitutes for anything remotely suggesting the natural. And his reply is: "A lot of people . . . hate the country and love congestion. It's all very well to say, 'Who wants to live in Brooklyn?'—but the answer is, three million people do, and just try to move any of them."

So far as the facts go, Mr. Moses is undoubtedly right. Many people—whether you call them adjusted to or corrupted by the conditions under which they lived—prefer "God's concrete," which actually is more characteristic of the God they worship. Even if, dutifully rather than gladly, they "go away for a vacation," they prefer it to be at some highly artificial resort. Even at Grand Canyon they would complain that there isn't anything to *do* and nothing to be seen that you can't see in ten minutes.

Some of the more philosophically inclined, including some critics of literature and the arts, say something like this: "Ours is the age of man, machines, and useful knowledge. We are no longer part of nature either physically or emotionally. To the relatively slight degree that we are still dependent upon natural products, we have learned how to manage their production with maximum efficiency and there is no reason why we should let nature take her course about anything. Animals, other than domestic and game, are good for nothing except for what we can learn by dissecting or by experimenting upon them. All this fuss about saving the parks is merely a sentimental plea for wasting ground that could be grazed and lumber that could be cut. Millions today rarely see anything except concrete and steel and don't know what to make of anything else if they do happen to see it. Their proportionate numbers are bound to increase. Cities are healthier and more convenient anyway, and any regret over man's increasing self-sufficiency is merely what a certain well-known Columbia University professor used to call 'nostalgia for a lower form of civilization.' "

If you prefer to put it even more abstractly and in the grotesque new terms which abstraction calls upon, consider the remarks of the ecologist, I. Vernadsky, who proposed in the technical journal, *American Science* (1945), the new word "noosphere" to contrast with the term "biosphere" which ecologists—regrettably perhaps—are already accustomed to use. The biosphere is simply the earth as the processes, balances, and conflicts of nature make it; the noosphere is those portions of the earth where whatever conditions exist do so because man has imposed his will rather than nature's upon them. Civilization, according to this notion, is the process by which the noosphere destroys and replaces the biosphere, and it will be complete when no biosphere any longer exists. That, in philosophical language (or jargon), would represent the final achievement of that "conquest of nature" of which we boast so much.

As population grows, the biosphere inevitably shrinks, and for even the few who would like to live in a world where nature is very conspicuously present, it becomes harder and harder to do so—as even the suburbanite realizes while his suburb grows and "prospers." The Texan, J. Frank Dobie, once wrote: "Many times I have thought that the greatest happiness possible to a man—probably not to a woman—is to become civilized, to know the pageant of the past, to love the beautiful, to have just ideas of values and proportions, and then, retaining his animal spirits and appetites, to live in a wilderness where nature is congenial, with a few barbarisms to afford picturesqueness and human relations. . . . According to this ideal civilization is necessary to give man a perspective; but is otherwise either a mere substitute for primitiveness or else a background to flee from." And then he adds: "Such [an ideal] was never practicable except to a few individuals who in retreating from society substituted camp fires for ivory towers. In this shrinking world it becomes less and less practicable. It precludes the idea of a civilized democracy—though any democracy will be tolerant of nonconformists who draw off to one side as well as of those who march with the ranks."

The concession made in that last clause is a large one. Ivory towers (including those centered around a campfire) have often been more than things to shut oneself up in—they have been also towers to look out from, and places to think new thoughts or to remember old ones. The few who choose them are usually those who, granted their temperaments, could not have served society in any better way. And as Mr. Dobie says, a true democracy would recognize that fact. Even most of those who know that, for themselves, some contact with a biosphere means greater health, happiness, and content would not deny that what they desire is not to renounce civilization but to enjoy its intellectual and emotional developments without becoming completely a prisoner of its machinery. Even Thoreau who had, or thought he had, so much sympathy with aboriginal wildness often realized that it was not really the life he wanted to lead. "Decayed literature," he wrote, "makes the richest of all soils."

Considered as absolute goods, solitude and freedom from the shrieks and clatters of a mechanized civilization raise the same kind of questions as are raised by "Life in nature."

Few men want to be most of the time alone and this is surely their good fortune since most are probably destined to be so less and less often. The only question still worth asking in a civilization like ours which has committed itself to artificial living in a crowded environment is the question of whether or not solitude and quietness are important *as elements;* whether or not at least the opportunity to experience them occasionally as part of a vacation or, in the literal sense of the word, a re-creation, is important. Does to experience them even occasionally provoke thoughts and suggest values not only significant in themselves but likely to provide critical insights into civilization which may influence favorably the course it takes?

How such questions are answered will depend in part upon what one believes about the nature of man as well as upon what satisfaction one, as an individual, happens to take in solitude, quietness, or the spectacle of nature. How fundamental, how nearly unchangeable, is that desire for all these things? Have those who no longer seem to desire them advanced farther along the road to the future than those who do? Are they merely "better adjusted"? Or are they, by just that much less, whole men? Even on the rash assumption that someday mankind will have no contact with anything outside the noosphere, it may still be true that human nature cannot be remade as quickly as his environment can and that he will still, for a long time, suffer a sort of nostalgia for the universe he so long inhabited.

Albert Einstein once told the students at the California Institute of Technology that he doubted whether present-day Americans were any happier than the Indians who were inhabiting the continent when the white man first came. Not many are likely to agree with so extreme a statement, but quite a few, I think, would admit that, leaving the Indians out of it, we are not *as much* happier than our grandfathers as it would seem our gains in health, security, comfort, convenience, as well as our release from physical pain ought to make us. Does this failure to pay off have something to do with a misjudgment concerning what man really wants most or, at least, a failure to take into account certain of the things he wants besides comfort, wealth, and the rest?

Only more of the same is promised him by even the most optimistic utopians. The more intellectual among them talk in general terms of greater per capita wealth, of less poverty and less manual work, and of faster means of communication. Those who write the popular articles published over and over again in those periodicals which exist chiefly to make readers dissatisfied with their current refrigerator or automobile usually go into more detail. By 1980, they say, you will be broiling steaks in electronic stoves, owning a two-helicopter garage and, of course, looking at television in full color. These assurances are supposed to make it easier for the housewife to put up with mere electric ovens, ninety-mile-an-hour automobiles, and soap operas in black and white. From such makeshifts they are supposed to lift sparkling eyes toward a happier future. And perhaps that is precisely what they do do. But will they be as much happier as they now think they inevitably must be? Is it really what they want? Is the lack of these things soon to come chiefly responsible for the irritations, frustrations, and discontents they now feel?

Suppose they were promised instead that by 1980 the world in which they live will be less crowded, less noisy, less hurried and, even, less complicated. Suppose they were told that they will have more opportunities to see the beauties and to taste the pleasures of sea and mountain and stream, to have more contact with the wonders of trees and flowers, the abounding life of animal creatures other than human. Would the prospect look even brighter? Perhaps not. But that does not convince me that such a world would not, in actual fact, make for more happiness than the one they are promised.

A true democracy will, as Mr. Dobie said, have some consideration for the minority which wants what contact with nature it can get. Perhaps it will consider also the possibility that a larger minority would be the better for the opportunities it wants without always knowing that it wants them—as thousands are discovering every year on a first visit to one of the national parks.

The decision whether they and the wilderness areas are worth having is one that must be made anew. It was made once a generation ago when the Park System was established with the explicit statement that the areas set aside were to be *permanently* reserved for specific purposes—not just preserved until some other use could be found for them. The Dinosaur Canyon project was a deliberate challenge and (as some of its proponents explicitly stated) an attempt to establish a precedent. The attempt was frustrated; but similar attempts directed elsewhere will be made again. If the original intention is now reaffirmed, the parks, monuments, and wilderness areas may remain to refresh, educate, and inspire for an indefinite number of generations to come.

The discovery of America meant different things to different people. To some it meant only gold and the possibility of other plunder. To others less mean-spirited it meant a wilderness which might in time become another Europe. But there were also not a few whose imaginations were most profoundly stirred by what it *was* rather than by what it might become.

The wilderness and the idea of the wilderness is one of the permanent homes of the human spirit. Here, as many realized, had been miraculously preserved until the time when civilization could appreciate it the richness and variety of a natural world which had disappeared unnoticed and little by little from Europe. America was a dream of something long past which had suddenly become a reality. It was what Thoreau called the great "poem" before many of its fairest pages had been ripped out and thrown away. The desire to experience that reality rather than to destroy it drew to our shores some of the best who have ever come to them.

That most of it is no longer a wilderness is no cause for regret. But it is a cause for congratulation that the four centuries and more which have passed since Columbus set sail have not been long enough to permit men to take over the whole continent as completely as they long ago took over Europe. And that fact is responsible for an important part of the difference which still exists, spiritually as well as physically, between the Old World and the New. The frontier, so long an important influence on the temper of the American, no longer exists. But as James Fisher realized with surprised delight, the continent can still boast a spaciousness, a grandeur, a richness, and a variety which a European can hardly imagine until he has seen it.

These are things which other nations can never recover. Should we lose them, we could not recover them either. The generation now living may very well be that which will make the irrevocable decision whether or not America will continue to be for centuries to come the one great nation which had the foresight to preserve an important part of its heritage. If we do not preserve it, then we shall have diminished by just that much the unique privilege of being an American.

1958

The Most Dangerous Predator

In the United States the slaughter of wild animals for fun is subject to certain restrictions fairly well enforced. In Mexico the laws are less strict and in many regions there is little or no machinery for enforcement. Hence an automobile club in southern California distributes to its members an outline map of Baja purporting to indicate in detail just where various large animals not yet quite extinct may be found by those eager to do their bit toward eliminating them completely. This map gives the impression that pronghorn antelopes, mountain sheep, and various other "game animals" abound.

In actual fact, the country can never have supported very many such and today the traveler accustomed to the open country of our own Southwest would be struck by the fact that, except for sea birds, sea mammals and fish, wildlife of any kind is far scarcer than at home. This is no doubt due in part to American hunters but also in part to the fact that native inhabitants who once could not afford the cartridges to shoot anything they did not intend to eat now get relatively cheap ammunition from the United States and can indulge in what seems to be the almost universal human tendency to kill anything that moves.

Someday—probably a little too late—the promoters of Baja as a resort area will wake up to the fact that wildlife is a tourist attraction and that though any bird or beast can be observed or photographed an unlimited number of times it can be shot only once. The Mexican government is cooperating with the government of the United States in a successful effort to save the gray whale and the sea elephant but to date does not seem much interested in initiating its own measures of protection. As long ago as 1947, Lewis Wayne Walker (who guided me on our innocent hunt for the boojum trees he had previously photographed) wrote for *Natural History*

Magazine a survey of the situation, particularly as it concerns the pronghorn and the mountain sheep. A quarter of a century before, herds of antelope were to be found within thirty or forty miles of the United States border. But by 1933 they had all, so a rancher told him, been killed after a party of quail hunters had discovered them. In the roadless areas some bands of mountain sheep still existed (and doubtless do even today) but the water holes near traversable areas were already deserted by the mid forties. All the large animals of a given region must come to drink at the only pool or spring for many miles around, hence a single party need only wait beside it to exterminate the entire population inhabiting that area. Though Walker had driven more than ten thousand miles on the Baja trails during the two years preceding the writing of his letter, he saw only one deer, no sheep, and no antelope. Despite the publicity given it, "Baja is," he wrote, "the poorest game area I have ever visited."

The depredations of the hunter are not always the result of any fundamental blood lust. Perhaps he is only, more often than not, merely lacking in imagination. The exterminator of the noble animals likes the out-of-doors and thrills at the sight of something which suggests the world as it once was. But contemplation is not widely recognized as an end in itself. Having seen the antelope or the sheep, he must "do something about it." And the obvious thing to do is to shoot.

In the *Sea of Cortez* John Steinbeck describes how a Mexican rancher invited his party to a sheep hunt. They were reluctant to accept until they realized that the rancher himself didn't really want to kill the animals—he merely didn't know what other excuse to give for seeking them out. When his Indians returned empty-handed he said with only mild regret: "If they had killed one we could have had our pictures taken with it." Then Steinbeck adds: "They had taught us the best of all ways to go hunting and we shall never use any other. We have, however, made one slight improvement on their method; we shall not take a gun, thereby obviating the last remote possibility of having the hunt cluttered up with game. We have never understood why men mount the heads of animals and hang them up to look down on their conquerors. Possibly it feels good to these men to be superior to animals but it does seem that if they were sure of it they would not have to prove it." Later, when one of the Indians brought back some droppings which he seemed to treasure and presented a portion of them to the white men, Steinbeck adds: "Where another man can say, 'there was an animal but because I am greater than he, he is dead and I am alive and there is his head to prove it' we can say, 'there was an animal, and for all we know there still is and here is proof of it. He was very healthy when we last heard of him.'"

"Very pretty," so the tough-minded will say, "but hardly realistic. Man is a predator, to be sure, but he isn't the only one. The mountain lion killed sheep long before even the Indian came to Baja. The law of life is also a law of death. Nature is red in tooth and claw. You can't get away from that simple fact and there is no use in trying. Whatever else he may be, man is an animal; and like the other animals he is the enemy of all other living things. You talk of 'the balance of nature' but we are an element in it. As we increase, the mountain sheep disappear. The fittest, you know, survive."

Until quite recent times this reply would have been at least a tenable one. Primitive man seems to have been a rather unsuccessful animal, few in numbers and near the ragged edge of extinction. But gradually the balance shifted. He held his own; then he increased in numbers; then he developed techniques of aggression as well as of protection incomparably more effective than any which nature herself had ever been able to devise before the human mind intervened. Up until then, animals had always been a match, one for another. But they were no match for him. The balance no longer worked. Though for another 500,000 years "coexistence" still seemed to be a *modus vivendi* the time came, only a short while ago, when man's strength, his numbers, and his skill made him master and tyrant. He now dominated the natural world of which he had once been only a part. Now for the first time he could exterminate, if he wished to do so, any other living creature—perhaps even (as we learned just yesterday) his fellow man. What this means in a specific case; what the difference is between nature, however red she may be in tooth and claw, and the terrifying predator who is no longer subject to the limitations she once imposed, can readily be illustrated on the Baja peninsula. In neither case is the story a pretty one. Both involve a ruthless predator and the slaughter of innocents. But nature's far from simple plan does depend upon a coexistence. Man is, on the other hand, the only animal who habitually exhausts or exterminates what he has learned to exploit.

Let us, then, take first a typical dog-eat-dog story as nature tells it, year after year, on Rasa Island, where confinement to a small area keeps it startlingly simple without any of these sub-plots which make nature's usual stories so endlessly complicated.

This tiny island—less than a mile square in area and barely one hundred feet above sea level at its highest point—lies in the Gulf fifteen or twenty miles away from the settlement at Los Angeles Bay. It is rarely visited because even in fair weather the waters round about it are treacherous. Currents up to eight knots create whirlpools between it and other small islands and there is a tide drop of twelve to thirty feet, depending upon the season. It is almost bare of vegetation except for a little of the salt weed or Salicornia which is found in so many of the saline sands in almost every climate. But it is the nesting place of thousands of Heermann gulls who, after the young are able to fend for themselves, migrate elsewhere—a few southward as far as Central America but most of them north to various points on the Pacific coast. A few of the latter take the shortest route across the Baja peninsula but most take what seems an absurd detour by going first some 450 miles south to the tip of Baja and then the eight hundred or a thousand miles up its west coast to the United States—perhaps, as seems to be the case in various other paradoxes of migration—because they are following some ancestral habit acquired when the climate or the lay of the land was quite different.

My travels in Baja are, I hope, not finished, and I intend someday to set foot on Rasa to see what goes on there for myself. So far, however, I have observed the huge concentration of birds only from a low-flying plane and what I have to describe is what Walker has told me and what he wrote some ten years ago in an illustrated account for the *National Geographic Magazine*.

In late April, when the breeding season is at its height, the ground is crowded with innumerable nests—in some places no more than a yard apart, nowhere with more than twenty feet between them. Because man has so seldom disturbed the gulls here they show little fear of him though once they have reached the northern shore they rise and fly out to sea at the first sight of a human being.

If this were all there was to tell, Rasa might seem to realize that idyllic state of nature of which man, far from idyllic though he has made his own society, often loves to dream. Though on occasion gulls are predators as well as scavengers they repect one another's eggs and offspring on Rasa and live together in peace. But like most animals (and like most men) they are ruthless in their attitude toward other species though too utterly nature's children to rationalize as man does that ruthlessness. They know in their nerves and muscles without even thinking about it that the world was made for the exclusive use and convenience of gulls.

In the present case the victims of that egomania of the species are the two kinds of tern which share the island with them and have chosen to lay their eggs in a depression surrounded by gulls.

Here Walker had best tell his own story: "In the early morning of the second day a few eggs were seen under the terns but even as we watched, several were stolen by gulls. By late afternoon not an egg remained. Nightfall brought on an influx of layers, and morning found twice as many eggs dotting the ground. By dusk only a fraction of the number in the exact center of the plot had escaped the inroads of the egg-eating enemy.

"The new colony had now gained a permanent foothold. Accordion-like it expanded during the night, contracted by evening. Each twenty-four hour period showed a gain for the terns and a corresponding retreat in the waiting ranks of the killing gulls.

"By the end of a week the colony had expanded from nothing to approximately four hundred square feet of egg-spotted ground and it continued to spread. The gulls seemed to be losing their appetites. Like children sated with ice cream, they had found that a single diet can be over-done."

What an absurd—some would say what a horrid—story that is. How decisively it gives the lie to what the earliest idealizers of nature called her "social union." How difficult it makes it to believe that some all-good, omnipotent, conscious, and transcendental power consciously chose to set up a general plan of which this is a typical detail. How much more probable it makes it seem that any purpose that may exist in the universe is one emerging from a chaos rather than one which had deliberately created that chaos.

But a fact remains: one must recognize that the scheme works—for the terns as well as for the gulls. If it is no more than the mechanism which so many call it, then it is at least (to use the newly current terminology) a cybernetic or self-regulating mechanism. If the gulls destroyed so many eggs that the tern population began to decline, then the gulls, deprived of their usual food supply, would also decline in numbers and the terns would again increase until the balance had been reached. "How careful of the type she seems; how careless of the single life"—as Tennyson observed some years before Darwin made the same humanly disturbing fact a cornerstone of his theories.

Absurd as the situation on Rasa may seem, it has probably existed for thousands of years and may well continue for thousands more—if left to itself, undisturbed by the only predator who almost invariably renders the "cybernetic" system inoperable.

Consider now the case of the elephant seal, a great sea beast fourteen to sixteen feet long and nearly three tons in weight. Hardly more than a century ago it bred in enormous numbers on the rocky coast and on the islands from Point Reyes, just north of San Francisco, almost to the Magdalena Bay on the Pacific coast of Baja. Like the gray whale it was preyed upon by the ferocious killer whale which is, perhaps, the most formidable of all the predators of the sea. But a balance had been reached and the two coexisted in much the same fashion as the gulls and the terns of Rasa.

Unfortunately (at least for them) human enterprise presently discovered that sea elephants could become a source of oil second in importance to the whale alone. And against this new predator nature afforded no protection. The elephant seals had learned to be wary of the killer whale but they had known no enemy on land and they feared none. Because instinct is slow while the scheming human brain works fast, those who must depend upon instinct are lost before it can protect them against any new threat. Captain Scammon, always clear, vivid, and businesslike, describes how easy and how profitable it was to bring the seals as near to extinction as the gray whales were brought at approximately the same time:

"The mode of capturing them is thus; the sailors get between the herd and the water; then raising all possible noise by shouting, and at the same time flourishing clubs, guns, and lances, the party advances slowly towards the rookery, when the animals will retreat, appearing in a state of great alarm. Occasionally, an overgrown male will give battle, or attempt to escape; but a musket ball through the brain dispatches it; or someone checks its progress by thrusting a lance into the roof of its mouth, which causes it to settle on its haunches, when two men with heavy oaken clubs give the creature repeated blows about the head, until it is stunned or killed. After securing those that are disposed to showing resistance, the party rush on the main body. The onslaught creates such a panic among these peculiar creatures, that, losing all control of their actions, they climb, roll, and tumble over each other, when prevented from further retreat by the projecting cliffs. We recollect in one instance, where sixty-five were captured, that several were found showing no signs of having been either clubbed or lanced but were smothered by numbers of their kind heaped upon them. The whole flock, when attacked, manifested alarm by their peculiar roar, the sound of which, among the largest males, is nearly as loud as the lowing of an ox, but more prolonged in one strain, accompanied by a rattling noise in the throat. The quantity of blood in this species of the seal tribe is supposed to be double that contained in an ox, in proportion to its size.

"After the capture, the flay begins. First, with a large knife, the skin is ripped along the upper side of the body its whole length, and then cut down as far as practicable, without rolling it over; then the coating of fat that lies between the skin and flesh—which may be from one to seven inches in thickness, according to the size and condition of the animal—is cut into 'horse pieces,' about eight inches wide and twelve to fifteen long, and a puncture is made in each piece sufficiently large to pass a rope through. After flensing the upper portion of the body, it is rolled over, and cut all around as above described. Then the 'horse pieces' are strung on a raft rope (a rope three fathoms long, with an eye splice in one end) and taken to the edge of the surf; a long line is made fast to it, the end of which is thrown to a boat lying just outside of the breakers; they are then hauled through the rollers and towed to the vessel, where the oil is tried out by boiling the blubber, or fat, in large pots set in a brick furnace. . . . The oil produced is superior to whale oil for lubricating purposes. Owing to the continual pursuit of the animals, they have become nearly if not quite extinct on the California coast, or the few remaining have fled to some unknown point for security."

Captain Scammon's account was first published in the *Overland Monthly* in 1870. A few members of the herds he had helped to slaughter must have survived because in 1884 the zoologist Charles Haskins Townsend accompanied a party of sealers who hunted for two months and succeeded in killing sixty. Then, eight years later, he found eight elephant seals on Guadalupe, the lonely lava-capped island twenty-two by seven miles in extent which lies 230 miles southwest of Ensenada in Baja and is the most westerly of Mexican possessions.

It seems to be a biological law that if a given species diminishes in numbers, no matter how slowly, it presently reaches a point of no return from which even the most careful fostering cannot bring it back. Eight elephant seals would probably have been far too few to preserve the species; but there must have been others somewhere because when Townsend visited the islands again in 1911 he found 125, and in 1922 scientists from the Scripps Institution and the California Academy of Sciences counted 264 males at a time of year when the females had already left the breeding grounds.

Had Guadalupe not happened to be one of the most remote and inaccessible islands in our part of the world, the few refugees could hardly have survived. By the time it became known that on Guadalupe they had not only survived but multiplied into the hundreds, sealers would almost certainly have sought them out again to finish the job of extermination had not the Mexican government agreed to make Guadalupe a closed area. Because the elephant seal has again no enemy except the killer whale it now occupies all the beaches of the island to which it fled and has established new colonies on various other small islands in the same Pacific area, especially on the San Benitos group nearly two hundred miles to the east. By 1950 the total population was estimated at one thousand.

The earliest voyagers described Guadalupe, rising majestically from the sea to its four-thousand-foot summit, as a true island paradise and also, like other isolated islands, so rich in the unique forms of life which had been slowly evolved in isolation that half the birds and half the plants were unknown anywhere else. So far, I know it only by reputation and have not even seen it, as I have seen Rasa, from the air; but it is said to be very far from a paradise today. Though inhabited only by a few officers of the Mexican Navy who operate a meteorological station, whalers had begun to visit it as early as 1700 and disastrously upset the balance of nature by intentionally introducing goats to provide food for subsequent visits and unintentionally allowing cats and rats to escape from their ships. Several thousand wild goats as well as innumerable cats and rats now manage to exist there, but it is said that almost nothing of the original flora and fauna remains. Most of the unique birds are extinct; the goats have nibbled the trees as high as they are able to reach, and have almost completely destroyed all other plant life. In the absence of the natural predators necessary to establish a tolerable balance, many of the goats are said to die of starvation every year for the simple reason that any animal population will ultimately destroy its own food supply unless multiplication is regulated by either natural or artificial means. Guadalupe is, in short, a perfect demonstration of three truths: (1) That nature left to herself establishes a *modus vivendi* which may be based upon tooth and claw but which nevertheless does permit a varied flora and fauna to live and flourish; (2) that man easily upsets the natural balance so quickly and drastically that nature herself cannot reestablish it in any fashion so generally satisfactory as that which prevailed before the balance was destroyed; (3) that man, if he wishes, can mitigate to some extent the destructive effects of his intervention by intervening again to save some individual species as he seems now to have saved the gray whale and the elephant seal.

How important is it that he should come to an adequate realization of these three truths? Of the second he must take some account if he is not, like the goats of Guadalupe, to come up against the fact that any species may become so "successful" that starvation is inevitable as the ultimate check upon its proliferation and that from this fate not even his technology can save him ultimately, because even those cakes of sewage-grown algae with which he is already experimenting could do no more than postpone a little longer the final day of reckoning. He has proved himself so much cleverer than nature that, once he has intervened, she can no longer protect him just as she could not protect either the life indigenous to Guadalupe or the goats man had introduced there. Having decided to go it alone, he needs for his survival to become more clever still and, especially, more farseeing.

On the other hand, and if he so wishes, he can, perhaps, disregard the other two laws that prevent the gradual disappearance of every area which illustrates the profusion and variety which nature achieves by her own methods and he may see no reason why he should preserve from extinction the elephant seal, which will probably never again be commercially valuable, or for that matter any other of the plants and animals which supply none of his physical needs. None of them may be necessary to his survival, all of them merely "beautiful" or "curious," rather than "useful."

Many arguments have been advanced by those who would persuade him to take some thought before it is too late. But the result may depend less upon arguments than upon the attitudes which are essentially emotional and aesthetic.

Thoreau—perhaps the most eloquent exponent we have ever had of the practical, the aesthetic, and the mystical goods which man can receive from the contemplation of the natural as opposed to the man-made or man-managed—once wrote as follows:

"When I consider that the nobler animals have been exterminated here—the cougar, the panther, lynx, wolverine, wolf, bear, moose, deer, the beaver, the turkey and so forth and so forth, I cannot but feel as if I lived in a tamed and, as it were, emasculated country . . . Is it not a maimed and imperfect nature that I am conversing with? As if I were to study a tribe of Indians that had lost all its warriors . . . I take infinite pains to know all the phenomena of the spring, for instance, thinking that I have here the entire poem, and then, to my chagrin, I hear that it is but an imperfect copy that I possess and have read, that my ancestors had torn out many of the first leaves and grandest passages, and mutilated it in many places. I should not like to think that some demigod had come before me and picked out some of the best of the stars. I wish to know an entire heaven and an entire earth."

To what proportion of the human race such a statement is, or could be made, meaningful I do not know. But upon the answer that time is already beginning to give will depend how much, if any, of the "poem" will be legible even a few generations hence.

Many of us now talk as if, until recently, there was no need to talk about "conservation." Probably there are today more men than ever before who could answer in the affirmative Emerson's question:

"Hast thou named all the birds without a gun?
Loved the wild rose, and left it on its stalk?"

But in absolute rather than relative numbers there are vastly more men today equipped with vastly more efficient instruments of destruction than there ever were before and many of them respect neither the bird nor the wild rose. As of this moment it is they who are winning against everything those of us who would like to preserve the poem are able to say or do.

1961

Baja California and Progress

Being no Rousseauist, I have never had any illusions about the noble savage or any desire to lead the simplest possible life above the savage level. But is there no choice except that between overdevelopment and underdevelopment, between desperate scarcity and almost suffocating abundance, between a lack of tools and the tyranny of machines, between deprivation and surfeit? Is there no such thing as an optimum degree of mechanization complexity, perhaps even of abundance? Is it simply a matter of how far we can go in the direction of a good which never pays diminishing returns or generates positive evils?

Supposing even that the answer to this question is that we are about to pass (if we have not already passed) beyond a definable optimum point. Is there then anything we can do about the situations? Are those right who say: "You must continually progress or regression is sure. There is no halfway house between the primitive and the complex. Ultimately the choice must be between that economy of still more desperate scarcity into which Baja would decline if she were not as progressive as she finds it possible to be and that almost inconceivable wealth, complexity, and mechanization which our own tomorrow will bring." Are we caught in a trap? Is it true that, while industrialization makes a large population possible, it is also true that, once this large population has been achieved, we must keep on growing if industry is not to collapse and bury us under the wreckage?

Being but little versed in political science or sociology, I asked several specialists whether they knew of any attempt even to raise the question how populous, how mechanized, how complicated, and how abundant a society should be if what we want most is not numbers, mechanization, complexity, and abundance for their own sakes but the best life possible for a creature who has the needs, the preferences, and the potentialities of the human being. I drew blanks in every instance except one when I was advised to consult Aristotle's *Politics* as perhaps the most recent work to concern itself with such a question even to the extent of seeming to assume that it might be a legitimate one. But I have not found even Aristotle so very enlightening. True, he does remark in passing: "Most persons think it is necessary for a city to be large, to be happy." And since most people today seem to believe the same thing or are at least convinced that their village, or town, or city would be happier if they could make it bigger, I conclude that more than two thousand years has been too short a time for Aristotle's exposure of the fallacy to produce conviction.

Most of the citizens of the United States and the other advanced nations seem to assume that just as every community should grow as fast and as much as its Chamber of Commerce can succeed in making it grow, so civilization should itself strive to accelerate if possible its already prodigious progress in the directions it has taken. But what of the sizable minority of critics who find much to dislike today and are afraid that tomorrow will be worse? Why does it confine itself to terrifying pictures of that tomorrow with only the warning that it will be dreadful? Why does it make no attempt to suggest where progress should stop; or, even if I dare say it, where progress should have stopped?

Perhaps the answer is that even the enemies of endless progress in the same straight line doubt that we could, even if we would, change its direction. Perhaps they are convinced that even though the "dialectic of matter," "the logic of evolving technology," and the other formulae of Marxism do not completely account for what happens to man in his civilizations these forces are, nevertheless, so powerful that we cannot effectively oppose the general course which they determine for us, whether we like it or not. Such at least is what I deduce from many current books about "world conditions" such as Robert Heilbroner's recent and interesting *The Future as History* where the fundamental premise is that the main outlines of the future actually are already "history" in the sense that we can write it by a process of extrapolation from that part of history which is already written. Much of his future history already formed in the womb of time the

author does not look forward to with satisfaction. Tec}
nology will continue to advance, thereby creating of nece
sity a more and more elaborate bureaucratic state. Abunda1
production will create a situation in which making a living
so easy that economic pressure will not be sufficient to for
anyone into the less attractive occupations and the state w
therefore have to assign some persons willy-nilly to then
Communism will not ultimately rule the world, but for mar
years to come it will be adopted in one after another of th
"underdeveloped" countries simply because they will wan
above everything else, a rapid industrialization and exper
ence has shown that communism is the system which ca
industrialize most rapidly. Mr. Heilbroner does not say th:
we cannot have any effect upon this future whose outlines a1
fixed. But he does imply that we cannot change it radicall
no matter how much we may wish that we could.

But surely—and no matter how minor a factor our desire
intentions, and efforts may be—we still need to know in wh:
direction we want their influence to be exerted and it is sti
worthwhile to ask the direct question when (if ever) h:
society achieved, or threatened to pass, the optimum point i
size, complexity, and mechanization? Sociology is very fon
of "proposing criteria" for this and that. But if any have ev
been proposed for any of these optimum points, I have n
come across them in my limited reading. The "problem
created" by great size, enormous complexity, and overpr
duction are recognized and methods for extenuating the1
are discussed. But the assumption seems always to be eith
that we should not or could not call a halt.

Yet criteria no more precise and no less difficult to measu1
are thought worth proposing in connection with other soci
problems. If we can satisfy ourselves that the largest possib
number of children per family is not the best number an
even suggest that the number be intentionally limited, wh
should we refuse to accept Aristotle's premise that cities ca
be too populous even though changed conditions would r
quire a modification of his criteria?

Is it not obvious that mechanization has passed its optimu1
point when it has ceased to make life more leisurely, le
tense, and more comfortable and become instead a burden 1
maintain—as is proved by the very fact that we are now mo1

hurried than we were when we could not travel so fast and are nervously if not also physically more overburdened than before we had so many labor-saving devices? Does that not suggest that we have already reached the point where things are in the saddle and ride mankind? If, for example, people are urged to go into worrisome debt to buy a new automobile, not because they have a need for it but because automobile workers will be out of a job and lead the way to economic collapse if the unneeded automobiles are not bought, does that not suggest that we have reached a point where men exist for the sake of the industry rather than industry for the sake of the men? And is not this only a single example of the way in which we have come, in general, to consider first "the needs of industry," the "needs of our economy," and even the "needs of science," rather than the needs of the human being? Has the optimum point not been passed when we refuse to ask whether industry and science exist for man or whether, as seems often the case, man exists for them? Isn't the high standard of living actually too high when men are driven to exhaustion and harassed into a nervous frenzy by the supposed necessity of maintaining and even elevating it? Has not production become too great if consumption becomes a problem?

Aristotle was at least on the right track when he asked what the *raison d'être* of a city is and when he replied, "to make a good life possible." Neither economics nor politics need be a dismal science if that aim is kept in mind. But though most citizens of a modern city would not, perhaps, reject it explicitly, they act as though they had done so. In Tucson where I now live and where the civic leaders are almost frantically (and successfully) engaged in doing everything possible to transform it into a typical industrial center, an "inquiring reporter" asked at random a dozen "men on the street" whether or not they approved and all replied that they did. "Do you think," he then asked, "that it will make this a pleasanter place to live?" And in every case he got the answer "No." "Then why do you approve?" "Well," was the usual reply, "one must be in favor of Progress." Could there be a better example of what is meant by an acquiescence in the assumption that things not only are, but should be, in the saddle and ride mankind?

Baja is not a park or a museum and it has not been set asid
as a "wilderness area." The good of its own population come
first. But what future would be most desirable for those t
whom it is home? Perhaps that is their business, not ours. Bu
without having asked the question we have resolved to mak
it our business, there and everywhere else in the world.

When today we undertake to bring the supposed blessin
of our civilization to the lesser tribes we are more likely to ca
ourselves technicians than missionaries. We do not call ther
"savage" or even "pagan"; we call them only "under
developed." We bring them sanitation and machinery an
are less concerned with their souls than with what we ca
their standard of living. But our zeal is great and our faith i
what we bring is no less uncritical than the faith which per
suaded the padres to pursue a course which ended in th
extermination of the whole population of Baja California. W
believe that if baptism will not save them, machinery wil
and when we have taught one of our converts to drive a truc
we are as sure that we have conferred a boon as ever th
Jesuits were when they had persuaded a native of Baja t
recite the Creed. We are also equally unlikely to ask eithe
whether our new religion is really sound or whether, suppos
ing that it is, it can be understood and successfully practice
by those who are snatched from one long familiar way of lif
and plunged into another. Who knows but that some futur
historian of the twentieth-century missionary effort may b
compelled to fall back upon the only incontestable defens
which can be made of those who Christianized and depopu
lated Baja: "They meant well."

No doubt our motives are not entirely unself-regarding bu
there is, nevertheless, an element of genuine missionary zea
And when I say that, I am reminded of the results achieve
two centuries ago by missionary zeal at least equally pure. T
those who now propose that the United States should "de
velop" the whole globe the presuppositions of the Spanis
padres are wholly incomprehensible. They cannot regar
them as anything other than an aberration near insanit
though it was to these padres a simple and obvious truth
namely, that extermination was a small price to pay for th
salvation which it assured the victims.

Can we safely take it for granted that aberrations whic
will ultimately seem as incomprehensible cannot possibl

lourish in the enlightened twentieth century? Is it possible that "economic development," imposed from above on every clime and race, will sometime seem as uncritically proposed as Christianity, and that, under some circumstances, giving primitive man a motor scooter is only a form of baptism no more effective than the other kind in assuring him salvation.

Even if we are surer than we have any right to be that our own way of life is so admirable that the whole world should adopt it, are we sure that all the "backward peoples" are any better prepared to imitate us than the Indians of Baja California were prepared to become Spanish Christians? The Indians could live in their own way; they could only die when another was imposed upon them. Is Americanism obviously a success in Japan? Just how "democratic" are the liberated Africans likely to remain? If this sounds somewhat cynical, it is partly because I happen to be just old enough to remember, very dimly, when the touchstone of liberalism was sympathy for the brave Boers in their struggle against English tyranny. Who would then have supposed that within one lifetime these same Boers would have become the best current example of all that is reactionary and reprehensible?

"If history repeats itself and the unexpected always happens, then man must be incapable of learning from experience." Who first said this I do not remember. The catch is, I suppose, that sly history modulates the repetitions just enough to make them unrecognizable at first sight. Hence, we seldom learn her lessons until it is too late—but we might at least try.

What desirable future could Baja have? Is there some optimum degree of development which it could achieve? Or must it, like the rest of the world, emerge from something like destitution only to find itself all too soon immersed in all the problems, pressures, and perplexities of modern civilization? Perhaps there is no answer to that question unless there is also an answer to the same question as it applies to the whole of the world where we still do not know how we may have something to ride without discovering, soon after, that it is riding us.

"Men have," wrote Thoreau, "an indistinct notion that if they keep up this activity of joint stocks and spades long enough all will at length ride somewhere, in next to no time

and for nothing; but though the crowd rushes to the depot
and the conductor shouts 'all aboard!' when the smoke is
blown away and the vapor condensed, it will be perceived
that a few are riding, but the rest are run over . . . and it will
be called, and it will be, a melancholy accident."

To date there has been in Baja very little activity of either
spades or joint stock companies.

196.

Conservation Is Not Enough

Suppose I began by saying that the more thickly populated an area is, the fewer animals other than man will be found to be living there. No doubt I should be told not to waste my reader's time by telling him that. But the truth of the matter is that the statement would be false or questionable at best.

Consider for example a few square blocks in one of the most densely populated sections of New York City. There are, to be sure, probably fewer insects and worms below the surface of the soil than in the country. But if you count the rats, the mice, the cockroaches, the flies, the fleas, the bed-bugs, and the whatnots, the chances are that the nonhuman population above ground would be much greater than it is in most wild areas of equal extent. Even in the streets and in the air above there might well be more English sparrows than there are of all kinds of birds put together in a woodland-bordered meadow.

What we will have to say if we want to be truthful is something more like this: As man moves in, the larger, more conspicuous and, usually, the most attractive animals begin to disappear. Either they "take to the hills," go into hiding, or are exterminated in one way or another. What remain, and often prodigiously increase, are the creatures which either escape attention or find in the filth which crowds of men bring with them a rich pasture.

Even in a region as thinly populated by man as the Sonoran Desert, this law began long ago to operate. There are still a good many of the larger animals to be found if one looks for them in the right places. But they are both fewer and more wary than they were not so long ago. For them the problem of how to live in the desert was complicated by a new factor when man put in an appearance, and the technique which often becomes most completely indispensable reduces itself to one general principle: Keep out of his way. Moreover, the cover of darkness becomes more and more important and some, like the deer, which were once not nocturnal at all tend to become largely so. To find even the larger remaining animals the naturalist with the most benign intentions is compelled to act like a hunter and stalk his game.

A human community thus becomes a sort of sieve with the fineness of the mesh depending upon the thickness of the population. Just where I live, ten or twelve miles from Tucson, you might call the mesh "medium coarse." Jack rabbits as well as cottontails often come almost to my door and are pretty certain to spring up whenever one walks a few hundred yards toward the mountains. There are ground-squirrel burrows all about, pack rats here and there, and an occasional rock squirrel—a pepper-and-salt-colored creature about the size of an eastern gray squirrel but with a bushy tail which he always carries behind him instead of in orthodox squirrel fashion. Infrequently I hear at night the yipping of a coyote and on at least one occasion I have had to get porcupine quills out of the nose of a neighbor's dog. But all the larger, more spectacular mammals have been screened out, probably within the last decade. Double the distance from town and you may see deer crossing the road. Go twenty-five miles away to a forest ranger's cabin and the ring-tailed cats as well as the foxes sneak up for table scraps. There are even more surprising animals in the rugged area of recent volcanic mountains just west of town. But they have to be looked for.

Though I have never seen a mountain lion in the wild they are quite common in some of the more mountainous regions of Arizona and one was shot not long ago thirty or forty miles away from here. Bobcats roam wild, if very wary, even closer at hand. A week or two ago I sat for a few hours in a photographer's blind beside a small man-made water hole about fifteen miles from town. First came a buck and a doe who stood on guard while their fawn took a long drink, then the curious little spotted skunk and, finally, two of the wild pigs or peccaries locally known as javelinas. At such a moment one feels that even this close to a city there is some wilderness left. But if the city continues to grow it will probably not be left much longer. Deer and javelinas adapted themselves quite happily to the saguaro forest, nibbling the smaller cacti and browsing on the fruit and leaves of desert shrubs. Mountain lions and bobcats kept the population within reasonable limits without exterminating it. But for the larger mammals the question of how to live in the desert tends to become unanswerable when the desert is inhabited by man.

Some of us might be better reconciled to this fact if the war to the death between man and the creatures whom he is dispossessing really was necessary to man's own success. But much of the war is not and sometimes it actually militates against him. To protect his sheep and cattle, the rancher tries to destroy all the mountain lions and bobcats. He comes so near succeeding that the coyote population grows larger. He then enlists government aid to poison the coyotes and when the coyotes are almost eliminated the ground squirrels and the gophers, on which the coyotes fed, begin to get out of hand.

Somewhat belatedly, certain ranchers are beginning to talk about protecting the coyote. If they ever get around to it they will probably, in time, have to begin protecting the mountain lion also. But by that time it probably will be too late. If they had only been content to be a little less thorough in the first place, we might all, including the wild creatures, be better off. And a natural balance is pleasanter than an artificial one, even when the artificial can be made to work.

That this is no mere sentimentalist's fancy is attested by the fact that at least one ranchers' association representing more than 200,000 acres in Colorado has recently posted its land to forbid the killing of coyotes and taken as strong a stand on the whole matter. "We ranchers in the vicinity of Toponas, Colorado . . . are also opposed to the widespread destruction of weasels, hawks, eagles, skunks, foxes and other predatory animals. . . . The reason for this attitude is that for ten years or so we have watched the steady increase of mice, gophers, moles, rabbits and other rodents. Now we are at a point where these animals take up one-third of our hay crop. . . . What with government hunters and government poison . . . the coyote is nearly extinct in our part of the state. Foxes and bobcats have succumbed to the chain-killing poisons, etc. . . . This spring rodents have even killed sagebrush and quaking aspen trees . . . serious erosion is taking place."

Yet at last report the government was still setting cyanide gas guns and developing the "chain-poisoning" technique which involves killing animals with a poison that renders their carcasses deadly to the scavengers which eat them. And in Arizona the bounty on mountain lions continues.

Moralists often blame races and nations because they have never learned how to live and let live. In our time we seem to have been increasingly aware how persistently and brutally groups of men undertake to eliminate one another. But it is not only the members of his own kind that man seems to want to push off the earth. When he moves in, nearly everything else suffers from his intrusion—sometimes because he wants the space they occupy and the food they eat, but often simply because when he sees a creature not of his kind or a man not of his race his first impulse is "kill it."

Hence it is that even in the desert, where space is cheaper than in most places, the wildlife grows scarcer and more secretive as the human population grows. The coyote howls farther and farther off. The deer seek closer and closer cover. To almost everything except man the smell of humanity is the most repulsive of all odors, the sight of man the most terrifying of all sights. Biologists call some animals "cryptozoic," that is to say "leading hidden lives." But as the human population increases most animals develop, as the deer has been developing, cryptozoic habits. Even now there are more of them around than we realize. They see us when we do not see them—because they have seen us first. Albert Schweitzer remarks somewhere that we owe kindness even to an insect when we can afford to show it, just because we ought to do something to make up for all the cruelties, necessary as well as unnecessary, which we have inflicted upon almost the whole of animate creation.

Probably not one man in ten is capable of understanding such moral and aesthetic considerations, much less of permitting his conduct to be guided by them. But perhaps twice as many, though still far from a majority, are beginning to realize that the reckless laying waste of the earth has practical consequences. They are at least beginning to hear about "conservation," though they are not even dimly aware of any connection between it and a large morality and are very unlikely to suppose that "conservation" does or could mean anything more than looking after their own welfare.

Hardly more than two generations ago Americans first woke up to the fact that their land was not inexhaustible. Every year since then more and more has been said, and at least a little more has been done about "conserving resources," about "rational use," and about such reconstruction as seemed possible. Scientists have studied the problem, public works have been undertaken, laws passed. Yet everybody knows that the using up still goes on, perhaps not so fast nor so recklessly as once it did, but unmistakably nevertheless. And there is nowhere that it goes on more nakedly, more persistently, or with a fuller realization of what is happening than in the desert regions where the margin to be used up is narrower.

First, more and more cattle were set to grazing and overgrazing the land from which the scanty rainfall now ran off even more rapidly than before. More outrageously still, large areas of desert shrub were rooted up to make way for cotton and other crops watered by wells tapping underground pools of water which are demonstrably shrinking fast. These pools represent years of accumulation not now being replenished and are exhaustible exactly as an oil well is exhaustible. Everyone knows that they will give out before long, very soon, in fact, if the number of wells continues to increase as it has been increasing. Soon dust bowls will be where was once a sparse but healthy desert, and man, having uprooted, slaughtered, or driven away everything which lived healthily and normally there, will himself either abandon the country or die. There are places where the creosote bush is a more useful plant than cotton.

To the question why men will do or are permitted to do such things there are many answers. Some speak of population pressures, some more brutally of unconquerable human greed. Some despair; some hope that more education and more public works will, in the long run, prove effective. But is there, perhaps, something more, something different, which is indispensable? Is there some missing link in the chain of education, law, and public works? Is there not something lacking without which none of these is sufficient?

After a lifetime spent in forestry, wildlife management,

and conservation of one kind or another, after such a lifetime during which he nevertheless saw his country slip two steps backward for every one it took forward, the late Aldo Leopold pondered the question and came up with an unusual answer which many people would dismiss as "sentimental" and be surprised to hear from a "practical" scientific man. He published his article originally in the *Journal of Forestry* and it was reprinted in the posthumous volume, *A Sand County Almanac,* where it was given the seemingly neutral but actually very significant title "The Land Ethic."

This is a subtle and original essay full of ideas never so clearly expressed before and seminal in the sense that each might easily grow into a separate treatise. Yet the conclusion reached can be simply stated. Something *is* lacking and because of that lack education, law, and public works fail to accomplish what they hope to accomplish. Without that something, the high-minded impulse to educate, to legislate, and to manage becomes as sounding brass and tinkling cymbals. And the thing which is missing is love, some feeling for, as well as some understanding of, the inclusive community of rocks and soils, plants and animals, of which we are a part.

It is not, to put Mr. Leopold's thoughts in different words, enough to be enlightenedly selfish in our dealings with the land. That means, of course, that it is not enough for the farmer to want to get the most out of his farm and the lumberer to get the most out of his forest without considering agriculture and wood production as a whole both now and in the future. But it also means more than that. In the first place, enlightened selfishness cannot be enough because enlightened selfishness cannot possibly be extended to include remote posterity. It may include the children, perhaps, and grandchildren, possibly, but it cannot be extended much beyond that because the very idea of "self" cannot be stretched much further. Some purely ethical considerations must operate, if anything does. Yet even that is not all. The wisest, the most enlightened, the most remotely long-seeing exploitation of resources is not enough, for the simple reason that the whole concept of exploitation is so false and so limited that in the end it will defeat itself and the earth will have been plundered no matter how scientifically and farseeingly the plundering has been done.

To live healthily and successfully on the land we must also

live with it. We must be part not only of the human community, but of the whole community; we must acknowledge some sort of oneness not only with our neighbors, our countrymen, and our civilization, but also some respect for the natural as well as for the man-made community. Ours is not only "one world" in the sense usually implied by that term. It is also "one earth." Without some acknowledgement of that fact, men can no more live successfully than they can if they refuse to admit the political and economic interdependency of the various sections of the civilized world. It is not a sentimental but a grimly literal fact that unless we share this terrestrial globe with creatures other than ourselves, we shall not be able to live on it for long.

You may, if you like, think of this as a moral law. But if you are skeptical about moral laws, you cannot escape the fact that it has its factual, scientific aspect. Every day the science of ecology is making clearer the factual aspect as it demonstrates those more and more remote interdependencies which, no matter how remote they are, are crucial even for us.

Before even the most obvious aspects of the balance of nature had been recognized, a greedy, self-centered mankind naïvely divided plants into the useful and the useless. In the same way it divided animals into those which were either domestic on the one hand or "game" on the other, and the "vermin" which ought to be destroyed. That was the day when extermination of whole species was taken as a matter of course and random introductions which usually proved to be either complete failures or all too successful were everywhere being made. Soon, however, it became evident enough that to rid the world of vermin and to stock it with nothing but useful organisms was at least not a simple task—if you assume that "useful" means simply "immediately useful to man."

Yet even to this day the *ideal* remains the same for most people. They may know, or at least they may have been told, that what looks like the useless is often remotely but demonstrably essential. Out in this desert country they may see the land being rendered useless by overuse. They may even have heard how, when the mountain lion is killed off, the deer multiply; how, when the deer multiply, the new growth of trees and shrubs is eaten away; and how, when the hills are denuded, a farm or a section of grazing land many miles away is washed into gulleys and made incapable of supporting either man or any other of the large animals. They may even have heard how the wonderful new insecticides proved so effective that fish and birds died of starvation; how on at least one Pacific island insects had to be reintroduced to pollinate the crops; how when you kill off almost completely a destructive pest, you run the risk of starving out everything which preys upon it and thus run the risk that the pest itself will stage an overwhelming comeback because its natural enemies are no more. Yet, knowing all this and much more, their dream is still the dream that an earth for man's use only can be created if only we learn more and scheme more effectively. They still hope that nature's scheme of checks and balances which provides for a varied population, which stubbornly refuses to scheme only from man's point of view and cherishes the weeds and "vermin" as persistently as she cherishes him, can be replaced by a scheme of his own devising. Ultimately they hope they can beat the game. But the more the ecologist learns, the less likely it seems that man can in the long run do anything of the sort.

"Nature's social union" is by no means the purely gentle thing which Burns imagined. In fact it is a balance, with all the stress and conflict which the word implies. In this sense it is not a "social union" at all. But it is, nevertheless, a workable, seesawing balance. And when it ceases to seesaw, there is trouble ahead for whatever is on the end that stays up, as well as for those on the end which went down.

Thus, for every creature there is a paradox at the heart of the necessary "struggle for existence" and the paradox is simply this: Neither man nor any other animal can afford to triumph in that struggle too completely. Unconditional surrender is a self-defeating formula—even in the war against insect pests. To the victor belong the spoils in nature also, but for a time only. When there are no more spoils to be consumed, the victor dies. That is believed by some to be what happened to the dominant carnivorous dinosaurs many millions of years ago. They became too dominant and presently there was nothing left to dominate—or to eat. It

is certainly what happens to other creatures like the too-pro-
tected deer in a national forest who multiply so successfully
that their herds can no longer be fed, or, more spectacularly,
like the lemmings who head desperately toward a new area to
be exploited and end in the cold waters of the North Sea
because that area does not exist.

Curiously, the too tender-minded dreamed a dream more
attractive than that of the ruthless exploiters but no less
unrealizable. They dreamed of "refuges" and "sanctuaries"
where the "innocent" creatures might live in a perpetually
peaceful paradise untroubled by such "evil" creatures as the
fox and the hawk. But it required few experiments with such
utopias to demonstrate that they will not work. A partridge
covey or a deer herd which is not thinned by predators soon
eats itself into starvation and suffers also from less obvious
maladjustments. The overaged and the weaklings, who would
have fallen first victims to their carnivorous enemies, survive
to weaken the stock, and as overpopulation increases, the
whole community becomes affected by some sort of nervous
tension—"shock" the ecologists call it—analogous to that
which afflicts human beings crowded into congested areas.

No more striking evidence of this fact can be found than
what happened when it was decided to "protect" the deer on
the Kaibab Plateau in the Grand Canyon region. At the
beginning of this century there was a population of about
4000 occupying some 127,000 acres. Over a period of years
the mountain lions, wolves, and coyotes which lived at its
expense were pretty well exterminated. By 1924 the 4000 had
become 100,000 and then calamity struck. In one year, 1924,
60,000 victims of starvation and disease disappeared and then,
year by year, though at a decreasing rate, the population
dwindled.

Wild creatures need their enemies as well as their friends.
The red tooth and red claw are not the whole story but they
are part of it, and the park superintendent with his gun
"scientifically" redressing the balance is a poor but necessary
substitute for the balance which the ages have established.
We may find nature's plan cruel but we cannot get away from
it entirely. The lion and the lamb will not—they simply cannot—lie down together, but they are essential to one another
nonetheless. And the lesson to be learned is applicable far

outside the field of conservation. It is that though the laws of nature may be mitigated, although their mitigation constitutes civilization, they cannot be abolished altogether.

So far as the problem is only that of the Kaibab deer, one common solution is the "open season" when man himself is encouraged to turn predator and hunters are permitted, as some conservationists put it, to "harvest the crop." To some this seems a repellent procedure and even as a practical solution it is far from ideal. Other beasts of prey destroy first the senile and the weaklings; man, if he selects at all, selects the mature and the vigorous for slaughter. The objection to this method is much the same as it would be to a proposal that we should attack the problem of human population by declaring an annual open season on all between the ages of eighteen and thirty-five. That is, of course, precisely what we do when a war is declared, and there are those who believe that the ultimate cause of wars is actually, though we are not aware of the fact, the overgrazing of our own range and the competition for what remains.

What is commonly called "conservation" will not work in the long run because it is not really conservation at all but rather, disguised by its elaborate scheming, only a more knowledgeable variation of the old idea of a world for man's use only. That idea is unrealizable. But how can man be persuaded to cherish any other ideal unless he can learn to take some interest and some delight in the beauty and variety of the world for its own sake, unless he can see a "value" in a flower blooming or an animal at play, unless he can see some "use" in things not useful?

In our society we pride ourselves upon having reached a point where we condemn an individual whose whole aim in life is to acquire material wealth for himself. But his vulgarity is only one step removed from that of a society which takes no thought for anything except increasing the material wealth of the community itself. In his usual extravagant way Thoreau once said: "This curious world which we inhabit is more wonderful than it is convenient; more beautiful than it is useful; it is more to be admired than it is to be used." Perhaps that "more" is beyond what most people could or perhaps ought to be convinced of. But without some realization that "this curious world" is at least beautiful as well as useful, "conservation" is doomed. We must live for something besides making a living. If we do not permit the earth to produce beauty and joy, it will in the end not produce food either.

Here practical considerations and those which are commonly called "moral," "aesthetic," and even "sentimental" join hands. Yet even the enlightened Department of Agriculture is so far from being fully enlightened that it encourages the farmer to forget that his land can ever produce anything except crops and is fanatical to the point of advising him how to build fences so that a field may be plowed to the last inch without leaving even that narrow margin in which one of the wild flowers—many of which agriculture has nearly rendered extinct—may continue to remind him that the world is beautiful as well as useful. And that brings us around to another of Aldo Leopold's seminal ideas:

> Conservation still proceeds at a snail's pace; . . . the usual answer . . . is "more conservation." . . . But is it certain that only the *volume* of education needs stepping up? Is something lacking in *content* as well? . . . It is inconceivable to me that an ethical relation to land can exist without love, respect and admiration for land, and a high regard for its value. By value, I of course mean something far broader than mere economic value; I mean value in the philosophical sense.

Here in the West, as in the country at large, a war more or less concealed under the guise of a "conflict of interests" rages between the "practical" conservationist and the defenders of national parks and other public lands; between cattlemen and lumberers on the one hand, and "sentimentalists" on the other. The pressure to allow the hunter, the rancher, or the woodcutter to invade the public domain is constant and the plea is always that we should "use" what is assumed to be useless unless it is adding to material welfare. But unless somebody teaches love, there can be no ultimate protection to what is lusted after. Without some "love of nature" for itself there is no possibility of solving "the problem of conservation."

Any fully matured science of ecology will have to grapple

with the fact that from the ecological point of view, man i
one of those animals which is in danger from its too success
ful participation in the struggle for existence. He has upse
the balance of nature to a point where he has exterminate
hundreds of other animals and exhausted soils. Part of thi
he calls a demonstration of his intelligence and of the succes
which results from his use of it. But because of that intelli
gence he has learned how to exploit resources very thorough!
and he is even beginning to learn how to redress the balanc
in certain minor ways. But he cannot keep indefinitely jus
one step ahead of overcrowding and starvation. From th
standpoint of nature as a whole, he is both a threat to ever
other living thing and, therefore, a threat to himself also. I
he were not so extravagantly successful it would be better fo
nearly everything except man and, possibly therefore, better
in the longest run, for him also. He has become the tyran
of the earth, the waster of its resources, the creator of th
most prodigious imbalance in the natural order which ha
ever existed.

From a purely homocentric point of view this may seer
entirely proper. To most people it undoubtedly does. Is it nc
our proudest boast that we have learned how to "contro
nature"? Does not our dream of the future include a fina
emancipation from any dependence upon a natural balanc
and the substitution for it of some balance established b
ourselves and in our exclusive interest? Is not that, in fac
what most people have in mind when they think of the fin
triumph of humanity?

But what every "practical" ecologist is trying to do is mair
tain the balance of nature without facing the fact that m
himself is part of it, that you cannot hope to keep the balanc
unless you admit that to some extent the immediate interes
of the human species may sometimes have to be disregarded
No other single fact is so important as man himself in crea
ing the often disastrous imbalances which continually develop
It is not possible to reestablish them for long without under
taking to control the organism which has most obviousl
entered upon a runaway phase. Must we not recognize th
fact that any real "management of resources" is impossibl
unless we are willing to sacrifice to some extent the immediat
interests not only of certain individual men but also those o

the human species itself? Most of us have reached the point where we recognize that the immediate interests of the lumberman or the rancher must sometimes be sacrificed to "the general good." Ultimately we may have to recognize that there is also a conflict between what is called the general good and a good still more general—the good, that is to say, of the whole biological community.

The more completely we bring nature "under control," the more complicated our methods must become, the more disastrous the chain reaction which is set up by any failure of wisdom, or watchfulness, or technique. We are required to know more and more and we are always threatened by the impossibility of achieving adequate knowledge, much less of adequate wisdom and virtue.

Every increase in the complexity of organization has made the situation more precarious at the same time that it has increased our comfort and our wealth. Until we learned to support a population far larger than would have been believed possible a century ago, there was no danger of general starvation, however disastrous and common local famines may have been, and though Malthus was obviously wrong in his estimates, it is by no means certain that he was wrong in his general principle. Until we increased the wealth of nations by linking them one with another we were not exposed to the danger of world-wide economic collapse. Until we learned how to "control" the atom there was no danger that atomic phenomena would get out of control and hence it is still not clear whether we are running machines or machines are running us. We have three tigers—the economic, the physical, and the biological—by the tail and three tigers are more than three times as dangerous as one. We cannot let any of them go. But it is also not certain that we can hold all of them indefinitely.

If one is prepared to admit that there is a limit to the extent to which we can exercise a biological control exclusively in our own interest, then it is certainly worthwhile to ask how we might know when we are approaching that limit.

It will hardly do to say simply that the limit has been passed when a society is obviously sick. Too many different reasons have been given to explain that sickness, and several of them can be made to seem more or less convincing—

indeed, several of them may be partially correct. But there is a criterion which it seems to me not wholly fanciful to apply.

Might it not have something to do with nature's own great principle, live and let live? Might it not be that man's success as an organism is genuinely a success so long, but only so long, as it does not threaten the extinction of everything not useful to and absolutely controlled by him; so long as that success is not incompatible with the success of nature as the varied and free thing which she is; so long as, to some extent, man is prepared to share the earth with others?

If by any chance that criterion is valid, then either one of two things is likely to happen. Perhaps outraged nature will violently reassert herself and some catastrophe, perhaps the catastrophe brought about when more men are trying to live in our limited space than even their most advanced technology can make possible, will demonstrate the hollowness of his supposed success. Perhaps, on the other hand, man himself will learn in time to set a reasonable limit to his ambitions and accept the necessity of recognizing his position as the most highly evolved of living creatures but not, therefore, entitled to assume that no others have a right to live unless they contribute directly to his material welfare.

The now popular saying, "No man is an island," means more than it is commonly taken to mean. Not only men but all living things stand or fall together. Or rather man is of all such creatures one of those least able to stand alone. If we think only in terms of our own welfare we are likely to find that we are losing it.

But how can man learn to accept such a situation, to believe that it is right and proper when the whole tendency of his thought and his interest carries him in a contrary direction? How can he learn to value and delight in a natural order larger than his own order? How can he come to accept not sullenly but gladly, the necessity of sharing the earth?

As long ago as the seventeenth century, as long ago, that is, as the very time when the ambition to "control nature" in any large ambitious way was first coming to be formulated and embraced, a sort of answer to these questions was being given in theological terms. John Ray, one of the first great English biologists, formulated them in a book which was rea for a hundred years, and what Ray had to say cuts two ways because it was directed against the egotism of man as expressed both by the old-fashioned theologians who thought that everything had been *made* for man's use and by the Baconians who assumed that he could at least *turn it* to that use.

"It is," Ray wrote, "a general received opinion, that all this visible world was created for Man; that Man is the End of Creation; as if there were no other end of any creature, but some way or other to be serviceable to man. . . . But though this be vulgarly received, yet wise men now-a-days think otherwise. Dr. Moore affirms, that creatures are made to enjoy themselves as well as to serve us." The greatest profit which we can get from the observation and study of other living things is, Ray went on to say, often not that we learn how to use them but that we may contemplate through them the wonders and the beauties of God's creation. What Ray was saying is precisely what Thoreau was restating in secularized form when he insisted that "this curious world . . . is more to be admired and enjoyed than it is to be used."

Since our age is not inclined to be interested in theological arguments, it is not likely to find Ray's exposition a sufficient reason for accepting gladly the continued existence on this earth of "useless" plants and animals occupying space which man might turn to his own immediate profit. Our generation is more likely to make at least certain concessions in that direction as the result of absorbing what the ecologist has to say about the impossibility of maintaining a workable balance without a much more generous view of what is "useful" and what is not. But it is not certain that on that basis man will ever make quite enough concessions and it *is* entirely certain that he will not make them happily, will not find life pleasanter just because he makes them, unless he can learn to love and to delight in the variety of nature.

Perhaps, if we cannot send him as far back as the seventeenth century to be taught, we can at least send him back to the eighteenth. Pope, speaking half for metaphysics and half for science, could write:

Has God, thou fool! work'd solely for thy good,
Thy joy, thy pastime, thy attire, thy food?

. . . .

> Know, Nature's children all divide her care;
> The fur that warms a monarch, warm'd a bear.

This is precisely what most men even two centuries later do not really understand.

1955

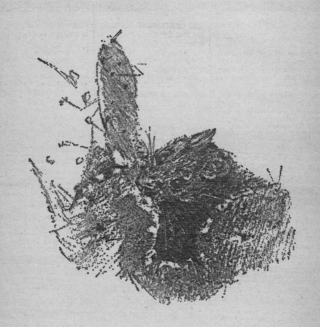

BOXED SETS

New and exciting—permanent additions to the reader's home library and ideal year-round gifts.

GREAT RELIGIONS OF MAN

Concise histories of the growth of the major faiths, with analyses of their ideas, beliefs, rituals, dogmas, and world role, as well as extensive selections from ancient and modern writings, introductions, and interpretations.

BUDDHISM—Richard A. Gard, ed.
CATHOLICISM—George E. Brantl, ed.
HINDUISM—Louis Renou, ed.
ISLAM—John Alden Williams, ed.
JUDAISM—Arthur Hertzberg, ed.
PROTESTANTISM—J. L. Dunstan, ed.

6 volumes   59353 $3.60

HELOISE

America's champion homemaker offers hundreds of hints and how-to's to make life in the kitchen and at home more enjoyable, more economical, and more efficient.

Heloise's HOUSEKEEPING HINTS
Heloise's KITCHEN HINTS
Heloise ALL AROUND THE HOUSE

3 volumes   59356 $1.75

THE DECLINE AND FALL OF THE ROMAN EMPIRE
by Edward Gibbon
Edited by D. M. Low

An edition abridged by the leading authority on Gibbon and the Roman Empire, presenting major chapters intact, and with an epilogue tracing Rome to the dawn of the Renaissance.

3 volumes   W 9701 $2.95

U. S. A.
by John Dos Passos

The turmoil of American life before, during, and after World War I as seen through a major work of modern American fiction.

THE 42nd PARALLEL
1919
THE BIG MONEY

3 volumes   59354 $1.80

THE CENTENNIAL HISTORY OF THE CIVIL WAR
by Bruce Catton

A stunning history of the Civil War.
THE COMING FURY
TERRIBLE SWIFT SWORD
NEVER CALL RETREAT

3 volumes   59361 $2.85

THE COMPLETE SHORT STORIES OF W. SOMERSET MAUGHAM

The stories of one of the most versatile and popular authors of the twentieth century, including the Ashenden stories, the model of the genre of espionage fiction.

Book I
RAIN and other stories
Book II
THE LETTER and other stories
Book III
THE BOOK BAG and other stories
Book IV
THE HUMAN ELEMENT and other stories

4 volumes   59355 $3.00

THE WORLD'S GREAT THINKERS
Edited by Saxe Cummins and Robert N. Linscott

Major works and selections by the most significant contributors to the history and development of world thought.

MAN AND THE UNIVERSE:
The Philosophers of Science
MAN AND SPIRIT:
The Speculative Philosophers
MAN AND THE STATE:
The Political Philosophers
MAN AND MAN:
The Social Philosophers

4 volumes   59352 $3.00

THE ALEXANDRIA QUARTET
by Lawrence Durrell

Major works of fiction focusing on the theme of love viewed from every aspect, explored on every level in the setting of modern Alexandria—a perfumed city of fleshly delights and moral decadence.

JUSTINE
BALTHAZAR
MOUNTOLIVE
CLEA

4 volumes   59362 $3.00

AMERICAN LITERATURE
Edited by Carl Bode, Leon Howard, and Louis B. Wright

An anthology of American writing—with critical comment — ranging from the early colonial period to the late nineteenth century.

Volume 1
THE 17th AND 18th CENTURIES
Volume 2
THE FIRST PART OF THE 19th CENTURY
Volume 3
THE LAST PART OF THE 19th CENTURY

3 volumes   59351 $2.70

POCKET HOUSEHOLD LIBRARY

Basic books for the well-run home.

Heloise's HOUSEKEEPING HINTS
Heloise's KITCHEN HINTS
THE HOUSEHOLD ENCYCLOPEDIA
FIRST AID FOR THE AILING HOUSE
California FAMILY
MEDICAL ENCYCLOPEDIA
THE LEGAL ENCYCLOPEDIA

6 volumes   98099 $3.95